Akhenaten

CYRIL ALDRED

Akhenaten
King of Egypt

With 107 illustrations

THAMES AND HUDSON

Frontispiece: The royal pair, Akhenaten and Nefertiti, at the palace balcony, or
Window of Appearance, with their three eldest daughters bestowing gifts on their
followers.

© 1988 Thames and Hudson Ltd, London·
First published in the United States in 1988 by Thames and Hudson Inc.,
500 Fifth Avenue, New York, New York 10110

Library of Congress Catalog Card Number 87–51153

Printed and bound in the German Democratic Republic

Contents

PART IV · THE AMARNA PERIOD

Preface

The character and deeds of King Akhenaten, who for seventeen years directed the fate of Egypt and the civilized world in the fourteenth century BC, continue to engross and mystify the historians. From being one whom his people did their best to forget, he has become, thirty centuries later, the celebrated subject of novels, operas and other works of the imagination. The present study does not claim such an appeal. Its aim has been to bring his story up to date, a delicate enough task in view of the incomplete evidence and disputed interpretations. In recent years he has lost the esteem he enjoyed in the late nineteenth century when his history was first uncovered. No longer regarded as a religious reformer, a witness to the truth, a forerunner of Moses; he has now been dismissed as a voluptuary, an intellectual lightweight, an atheist, ultimately a maniac.

In essence his doctrine rejected the universal concept of idolatry. He taught that the graven images in which Egyptian gods revealed themselves had been invented by man and made by the skill of artisans. He proclaimed a new god, unique, mysterious, whose forms could not be known and which were not fashioned by human hands.

The single-minded zealotry with which Akhenaten promoted the worship of a spirit, self-created daily, and transcendental, in place of a tangible repository of numinous power, reveals a self-assurance which has provoked modern critics to class him, and his chief queen Nefertiti, as religious fanatics; just as their subjects in their day recognized their exceptional charisma with backs bent low in adoration. Nevertheless, although the royal pair share in the divinity of their god, they recognize its supremacy and prostrate themselves abjectly in its presence.

This new-found deity was yet a very old one – the sky-god Horus that since prehistoric times had been incarnate in the king and carried the Aten, the disk of the daytime sun, Rē, across the heavens upon giant falcon wings. In the Rē-Herakhte of Akhenaten, however, the falcon was soon transformed from the bearer of the solar disk upon its vertex into the disk itself, shooting forth its rays, each ending in a human hand, thus manifesting itself as an active force, a heavenly king like Rē, reigning over the Horizon where lay the realms of light. Within a few months this solar symbol of deity had developed into an abstraction and a sole god. During the remainder of the reign it became increasingly regal, predominately abstract, and at the last brooked no rival.

Coincident with this novel concept of godhead, the king invented a new style of art in which to express his religious ideas. These centred particularly on the form of the pharaoh who was the offspring of the new god and its embodiment. The same perception was adopted for the queen, and for his followers who shared his beliefs, or who professed to do so. Those officials who were attached to the former regime ignored such innovations and adhered to the traditions of the past.

The king who espoused these revolutionary ideas in religion and art, was in other respects ostensibly orthodox, and did not alter the conceptual basis of Egyptian art. His entourage repeated his claim that he had been created by his god from the sunbeams. This belief, however, was almost as old as the pharaonate itself. Every king was an incarnation of the great sky-god Horus, and since early times had borne the title, 'Son of Rē', the active solar deity to whom he would be assimilated at death. In the world of the Late Bronze Age ruled by divine kings, only such potentates could alter belief without creating impiety. Akhenaten was worshipped by his followers as the true son of a supreme god, whose chief prophet and interpreter he became immediately on his accession. His courtiers boast of their obedience to his teaching but they are also scrupulous to enumerate the rewards that their loyalty will earn them.

Although Akhenaten has been censured because neither he nor his god seem to show much compassion for their subjects, the Chief Servitor of the Aten hails his king as 'the good ruler who loves mankind'. While the cynic may discount such praise as the flattery of a sycophant, the memorials that Akhenaten left behind him do reflect a generally benevolent disposition with an international outlook. That such a benign ruler should be erased so soon from the memory of his people has aroused the suspicion that his character and conduct did not win their attachment. But failure at home and abroad would suffice to condemn a divine king whose policies had proved ill-starred. His fate was to leave behind him no successor with the resolution and ability to perpetuate his ideas. When his creed was thought to have proved disastrous, all that was left to his heirs to do was to suppress it, together with the recollection of its author.

Cyril Aldred

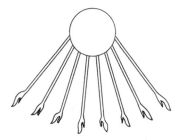

INTRODUCTION

The Chronological Context

About 1358 BC, when Akhenaten ascended the throne of his ancestors, the Egyptian kingdom had already been in existence for over eighteen centuries. The great pyramids at Giza had been standing in silence and decay for over 700 years; and another thirteen centuries were to pass before the last pharaoh Caesarion, the son of Cleopatra VII by Julius Caesar, was to be murdered on the orders of Augustus, and his realm annexed as the personal estate of the Roman emperors.

During this long epoch the civilization of Egypt had enjoyed periods of prosperity and progress; at other times it suffered interludes of decline and disorder. But because its rulers had been regarded as divine, incarnations of the great sky-god Horus whose falcon wings spanned the heavens, the chronicles of the kings were as carefully recorded as any religious phenomena. Already by the time of Akhenaten, lists of such kings certainly existed among temple archives, together with the length of each reign, although the only record that now survives is a heavily damaged and incomplete papyrus in Turin, which was compiled some sixty years after the death of Akhenaten. Similar data must have been available to Manetho, the High Priest of the sun-god in Heliopolis, when he was commissioned by Ptolemy I in the third century BC to write a history of Egypt. This work is now lost, though its king-list is preserved in copies quoted by early Christian chronographers and by the Jewish historian Josephus.

Manetho divided his list of kings into houses, or dynasties in chronological sequence, following ancient precedent which further indicated longer divisions of time, as in the Turin papyrus, by noting significant events, such as the accession of King Djoser at the beginning of the Third Dynasty, and the end of the Seventh Dynasty at the fall of the Old Kingdom 955 years after the advent of Menes, the first pharaoh.

Despite the lacunae and inaccuracies of the copyists of Manetho, modern historians make selective use of his system of numbering the dynasties of the kings, and rendering their names in Greek versions, where they exist (thus, *Amenophis* rather than *Amenhotep, Amenhetep, Amunhotpe*, etc.). They also

9

follow the ancient practice of grouping the dynasties into longer time-spans coinciding with periods when a distinct cultural pattern prevailed, separated by obscure intervals of upheaval and privation, when rival kings often ruled coevally from different residences.

DYNASTY	PERIOD	APPROXIMATE DATE BC
I–II	Archaic	3168–2705
III–VII	Old Kingdom	2705–2230
VIII–X	First Intermediate	2230–2035
XI–XIII	Middle Kingdom	2035–1668
XIV–XVII	Second Intermediate	1720–1540
XVIII–XX	New Kingdom	1540–1070
XXI–XXXI	Late	1070–332
Ptolemaic	Greek	332–30
Emperors	Roman	30–AD 395

The dates of the various periods, the less accurate as one penetrates further into the past, have been established largely by working forwards and backwards from one or two key points determined from chance recordings of astronomical phenomena.

The chronology with which we shall be almost exclusively concerned in the following pages is that of the New Kingdom, and in particular, the Eighteenth Dynasty, as follows:

PHARAOHS OF THE NEW KINGDOM

The Eighteenth Dynasty (Ahmosides)

NOMEN	PRENOMEN	DATE BC	CHIEF QUEEN
Amosis	Nebpehtirē	1540–1515	Ahmose-Nefertari
Amenophis I	Djeserkarē	1515–1494	Meritamun (?)
Tuthmosis I	Aakheperkarē	1494–1482	Ahmose
Tuthmosis II	Aakheperenrē	1482–1479	Hatshepsut
Hatshepsut	Maetkarē	1479–1457	
Tuthmosis III	Menkheperrē	1479–1425	Hatshepsut Meritrē
Amenophis II	Aakheperurē	1427–1393	Tia
Tuthmosis IV	Menkheperurē	1394–1384	Mutemwiya
Amenophis III	Nebmaetrē	1384–1346	Tiye

NOMEN	PRENOMEN	DATE BC	CHIEF QUEEN
Amenophis IV			Neferneferuaten-
Akhenaten	Neferkheperurē	1358–1340	Nefertiti
Neferneferuaten/			
Smenkhkarē-			
Djeserkheperu	Ankhkheperurē	1342–1340	Meritaten
Tutankhamun	Nebkheperurē	1340–1331	Ankhesenamun
Ay	Kheperkheperurē	1331–1326	Tey
Haremhab	Djeserkheperurē	1326–1299	Mutnodjme

The Nineteenth Dynasty (Ramessides)

Eight kings ruling from 1299 to 1185 BC

The Twentieth Dynasty (Ramessides)

Six kings ruling from 1185 to 1070 BC

The End of the New Kingdom

The Twenty-First Dynasty (Tanites)

Six kings ruling from Tanis from 1070 to 946 BC

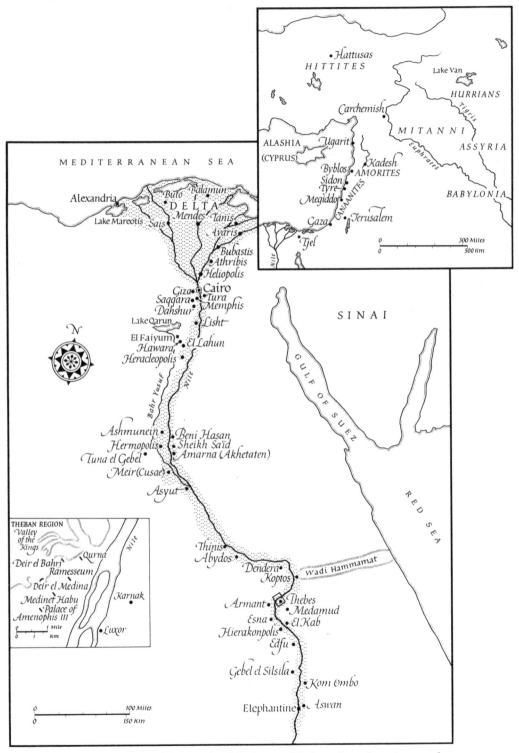

1 Ancient Egypt and the principal sites mentioned in the text. The inset shows the main area of the Levant important in this period of Egyptian history.

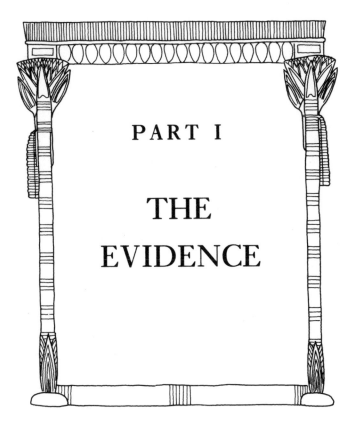

PART I

THE
EVIDENCE

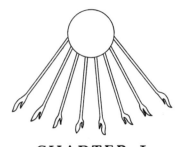

CHAPTER I

The Discovery of Akhenaten

Almost 300 kilometres south of Cairo about midway between ancient Memphis and Thebes, on the west bank of the Nile, lie the ruins of Hermopolis. This was the seat in pagan times of the moon-god Thoth, whom the Greeks equated with their Hermes, and the capital of a thriving district that extended to a depth of nearly 20 kilometres to meet the verges of the Libyan Desert on the west. By contrast with this still fertile and populous tract, the opposite bank presents an inhospitable face with sheer limestone cliffs plunging headlong into the Nile and scarcely affording space for a continuous highway at the water's edge. The vast escarpment extends further south for some 65 kilometres, when at Sheikh Sa'id the bluffs recede from the river in an abrupt curve for a distance of 12 kilometres and a maximum depth of 5, before resuming their southward course. This opening in the rocky wall forms the sandy plain of Amarna, a vast natural amphitheatre in which one of the great dramas of ancient Egypt was played out in little more than a decade in the fourteenth century BC when it became 'a chance bivouac in the march of history, filled for a moment with all the movement and colour of intense life, and then was abandoned to a deeper silence, as the camp was hurriedly struck and the course of Egyptian history relapsed again into more wonted highways'. For this was the site to which King Akhenaten, visionary and religious reformer, was directed by divine inspiration in his fifth regnal year as the place where his sole god, Rē-Herakhte, immanent in the sunlight that streamed from the Aten, or disk of the sun, had manifested himself at the creation of the world. It was here that the king founded a capital city on virgin ground, which was built for the Aten, extended during the remaining twelve years of his reign, and forsaken soon after his death.

All this, of course, was unknown to the European travellers who came to this spot in the early years of the nineteenth century. They found a desert tract covered with scrub and low mounds of pebble-strewn rubbish, sloping from the crescent of eastern hills to a narrow strip of cultivation bordering the river and scored by shallow wadis. This untamed place was not made any more inviting by the evil reputation of the inhabitants of the wretched villages strung out at intervals along the river bank from north to south at Et Til, El Hagg Qandil, El Amirya and El Hawata. These were occupied by the sullen and quarrelsome descendants of the Beni Amran, nomads who had left the Eastern Desert in the early eighteenth century and settled on the river banks giving their name to the whole region. The full description of their northernmost village, Et Til el Amarna, was mis-heard by early travellers as Tell el Amarna, and still persists, though it is a misnomer, since there is no single 'tell' or great mound marking the ancient site. Scholars have now generally agreed to call the place El Amarna, or more simply, Amarna.

Despite such deterrents, in 1824 the first of the notable modern explorers stopped at Et Til and visited some of the open tombs cut in a terrace that extended half-way up the cliffs at the northern edge of the site. This was John Gardner Wilkinson who had come to Egypt three years earlier in search of a more congenial climate in which to cosset his fragile health, and stayed for a further decade investigating the monuments, particularly those at Thebes. He returned to Amarna in 1826, this time in company with James Burton, an elder brother of the more famous architect Decimus, and a member of a team that had made a geological survey of Egypt for Mohammed Ali in 1822. Wilkinson and Burton copied scenes and made squeezes in the tombs of the High Steward of the Queen-Mother, Huya (No. 1); the King's Private Secretary, Ahmose (No. 3); the High Priest, Meryrē I (No. 4); the Chief Servitor, Pinhasy (No. 6); the Cupbearer, Parennefer (No. 9); the Chamberlain, Tutu (No. 8); and the Master of the Horse, Ay (No. 25).

Not that the two copyists were aware of the names and titles of the former owners of these tombs. At this time the knowledge of how to decipher hieroglyphs, following upon Champollion's initial discoveries of 1822, had hardly been sufficiently developed to enable Wilkinson and Burton to read the name of the ancient site, which they identified as the late Roman Alabastronopolis from a nearby alabaster quarry, one of several in the northern hills. It is under this name that Wilkinson published the source of his copies and extracts from the tomb scenes in his *Manners and Customs of the Ancient Egyptians* which in its various editions had such a profound influence on Victorian ideas of ancient Egypt. Apart from this, and a page in Burton's *Excerpta Hieroglyphica*, nothing was published from the site, although in subsequent years several expeditions and individuals examined the monuments at Amarna. The Scottish midshipman Robert Hay, later laird of Linplum, and his team of copyists worked there in 1830 and 1833, and not only examined all the tombs that were open, but cleared others from beneath extensive drifts of sand in the foothills on the southern limits of the site. In this way they added to the tally the tombs of the Overseer of the Royal Harim, another Meryrē (No. 2); and the Governor of the City, Neferkheperu-

Pl. 14

hersekheper (No. 13). The careful and often exquisite copies of scenes that they *Pl. 3* secured with the aid of the camera lucida have never been published, except in extracts. The original drawings and notes have survived in their portfolios among the manuscripts of the British Library.

A similar fate befell the copies made by the French draughtsman Nestor L'Hôte, who had accompanied Champollion on his expedition in 1828, and again on his own account ten years later. His manuscripts and drawings are in the Bibliothèque Nationale in Paris. So are those of the Breton archaeologist and artist Prisse d'Avennes who went to Egypt to work as an engineer for Mohammed Ali, and stayed on to excavate and explore. He came to Amarna in the early 1840s and copied in the northern tombs there.

The attraction that brought these men and the general tourist to the private tombs at Amarna, in spite of hardships, was the unique nature of the reliefs with which they were decorated. Unlike those of other tombs in Egypt they were large, unified compositions, the subject-matter of which was exclusively concerned with the activities of a royal family, consisting of a king and queen and several of their infant daughters. They were shown not in the formal attitudes of worship repeated so insistently on every temple wall, or as triumphant conquerors smiting the foreign foes, but in intimate and vivid detail as human beings engaged in everyday domestic affairs, embracing their

2 Parennefer receiving rewards beneath the palace balcony.

Fig. 10   children, riding in their chariots to attend worship in the local shrines, feasting
in the privacy of their palaces, or honouring their followers with valuable
Fig. 2   rewards taken from their treasure chests. In all these scenes there was an entire
absence of that funerary ambience which tinged the decoration of the painted
tombs of Thebes, and even the reliefs in the stone mastabas of the Old
Kingdom at Saqqara. Indeed, the scenes radiated a vibrancy in the pose of the
participants in the drama, with onlookers expressing excitement and even
ecstasy in the presence of their rulers, and joy and pride in the awards that were
bestowed upon them. There was also a fervency evident in the sacrifices which
the royal pair offered up before a heaped altar under a radiant sun. Everywhere
there was movement, in the cantering of the royal cavalcade, in the plucking of
strings by the expressive fingers of the musicians who were so much in
evidence, in the dances of jubilation by onlookers, and the waving of palm
fronds and olive branches in the hands of those welcoming the subjects whom
royalty had honoured.

Pl. 8   There was also, however, a certain prevailing mystery. The royal figures in
the scenes were drawn in a style that differed markedly from what was
generally accepted as the ancient Egyptian mode. The king, and to a lesser
extent the queen, was represented as though his head were deformed, with a
long nose, thick lips, a hanging chin and a long serpentine neck. His physique,
too, was distinctly feminine, with its heavy breasts, swelling hips and ample
thighs. The question arose of whether a king and his consort were in question
cf. Fig. 6   at Amarna, or two queens, one masquerading as a pharaoh. This enigma, so far
from discouraging visitors, only enhanced the appeal of the place.

Despite such attractions, the tombs lying open on the northern hill terraces
were in a sorry condition. Most of them were badly damaged and polluted by
the attentions of generations of squatters in early Christian times, and colonies
of bats ever since. The Christians had damaged the walls and built their rude
houses in the forecourts: some of the innermost chambers had been used as
burial places. The tomb of Pinhasy had even been extensively remodelled as a
Coptic church, with a deep font for total immersion before the apse. But apart
from such desecration, it was apparent to early visitors that the reliefs had also
suffered from the hammers of iconoclasts who had defaced the figures of the
king and queen and removed their names from the inscriptions. So thoroughly
had this destruction been wrought that it was not easy to find an intact
cartouche bearing the name of the king or queen, and still less was it possible to
come upon an undamaged portrait of the royal pair. Nevertheless there were
oversights, in places difficult of access or evidently inaccessible by the time that
the work of defacement began.

In this predicament it was customary for early visitors to Amarna to refer to
the people represented on the reliefs as the 'Disk-worshippers', from the image

3 (top) Early and (above) Late versions of the name of the Aten.

of the sun shooting forth a dozen or more rays, each ending in a hand, which dominated the upper part of nearly every scene and which was clearly a special symbol of veneration. It did not require particularly acute perception to see that this rayed disk with its protective uraeus, had a special connection with the royal pair. Its hands brought the *ankh* or sign of life to their nostrils, or clasped their limbs or persons as though to support them; but such privileges were denied to their subjects however exalted. It, too, was accompanied by two cartouches enclosing its names, like the two great names of a king, but they were larger than the cartouches of the pharaoh, and surrounded by a double border. The signs within these were difficult to interpret but were evidently the same as those which accompanied a representation of the sun-god, Rē-Herakhte, as a falcon-headed man, found on a few monuments elsewhere, *Pl. 27* though not at Amarna. Eventually, following the opinion of German scholars, the contents of the two great cartouches were recognized as a 'didactic' name of an age-old kingly god in his aspect of the entire day-time sun, 'Rē-Horus, who rejoices in the horizon in his name of the light which is in the sun-disk'.

19

Whatever this name meant, and new interpretations were to appear with each generation of scholars, the important element was ⟨☉⟩, Aten, the sun's disk, which was frequently used alone as though it were an abbreviated form of the longer name. It did not go unobserved either that a different version of the didactic name also existed.

Fig. 3

The excision of the names of the king and queen, and sporadically of the god himself, and of other members of the royal family, suggested that the 'Disk-worshippers' had incurred some kind of odium. Their names did not appear on the lists of pharaohs which about this time were coming to light at Saqqara, Karnak and elsewhere. The family at Amarna bore all the signs of being regarded by their successors, if not their contemporaries, as heretics, whose figures and faces and names were anathema. Such marks of execration only added to the mystery of the place.

In 1842, however, fresh light was admitted to dispel some of the obscurities when the Prussian Epigraphic Expedition under Richard Lepsius, a disciple of Champollion and the foremost Egyptologist of his day, arrived in Egypt to begin their immense survey. The team paid two visits to Amarna in 1843 and 1845, where in the course of a total of twelve phenomenally busy days they copied scenes and inscriptions and took paper squeezes of reliefs in the northern tombs and of those in the southern group which had been opened by Hay a dozen years earlier. These records, still happily housed in Berlin, are invaluable, since not infrequently they are now the only evidence we have of what existed on walls that have since been damaged or totally destroyed. Lepsius's explorations were mostly concerned with a more accurate and complete knowledge of monuments already brought to light, rather than with an increase in the sum-total of new excavations and discoveries. But his main contribution to the advance of the subject was the worthy publication of results in the twelve mighty volumes of the *Denkmaeler aus Aegypten und Aethiopen*, 1849–59, which were devoted solely to illustrations, and the five volumes of letter-press, 1897–1913, which appeared posthumously. It was this work that enabled scholars in subsequent years, with their increasing knowledge of ancient Egyptian archaeology and philology, to improve their understanding and elucidation of the Amarna monuments, and to begin a serious attempt to write the history of the site.

Notwithstanding the excised cartouches of the main actors in the drama, it soon became apparent that they were indeed a male pharaoh and his chief queen, whose names did not appear in the official king-lists. His name was read as Khuenaten, but by the end of the century this version had been corrected to Akhenaten. Further study revealed that the king had at some stage in his career changed his nomen from Amenophis (Amenhotep), a name which was the same as that of his predecessor, though accompanied by a slightly different epithet, 'Divine Ruler of Thebes', in place of 'Ruler of Thebes'. This revocation of the name of Amun seemed to have some connection with the excision of the name and figure of this god wherever they appeared, though they had generally been restored at a later date, apart from oversights. *Pl. 51*

The chief queen, whose figure appeared inseparably with her husband's in most of their representations, retained her name of Nefertiti without alteration; but after a time she added an epithet to it, Neferneferuaten ('Fair is the Beauty of the Aten') in an expanded version. The names of their six daughters were also recovered, as was that of the ancient township which had stood in the plain at Amarna and which was still visible as a straggle of dark sandy mounds dappled with white pebbles. This was found to be Akhetaten, 'the Horizon (or Seat) of the Aten', an appellation not encountered in the records except for chance scribbles on the rocks at Aswan. *Fig. 13*

More than a century of study and exploration has torn the veil from the mystery, without however plucking out its heart; and Akhenaten, so far from being execrated and forgotten, bids fair to become the most over-exposed of all the pharaohs; while the features of his wife, Nefertiti, thanks to the much publicized painted bust found at Amarna, are probably more familiar now than *Pl. 17* Cleopatra's, that *femme fatale* of the Hellenistic world.

Such a turn of Fortune's wheel would have appealed to the Egyptian of Roman days who frequently offered his prayers to the gryphon of Nemesis.

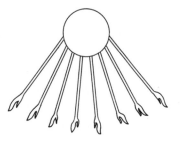

CHAPTER 2

The Private Tombs of Amarna

Following on from the hurried visit of the Prussian Expedition of 1845, the French sent their Mission Archéologique to Amarna in 1883, where they worked intermittently until 1902. During their campaign, they examined particularly the southern tombs which were not ranged high along a ridge in the cliffs like the northern tombs, but hewn low in the poor rock of the foothills of the Gebel Abu Hasah. Their site is subject to sanding-up in the eddying winds that blow in this quarter, a circumstance that has preserved them from being infested with bats and human squatters, not to mention tourists who are usually in too much of a hurry to spare the time required to reach them.

In the course of their work, the Mission uncovered a number of additional tombs left untouched by Hay, including those of the Chief-of-Police, Mahu (No. 9); the Steward, Ipy (No. 10); the General, Ramose (No. 11); and the Royal Secretary, Any (No. 23). Rubbish, and intrusive burials of a late date, were removed, and the work was completed in 1893 by fitting iron gates to all the inscribed tombs that were standing open, unfortunately not before deplorable damage had been done to some of the inscriptions and scenes. Even this protection failed to prevent subsequent vandalism by vindictive villagers with a grudge against the Antiquities Service.

Ill-health and administrative changes hampered the progress of the Mission and the full publication of their discoveries did not emerge until 1903. Two years earlier, however, another copyist had appeared at the northern tombs. This was Norman de Garis Davies, the surveyor of the Egypt Exploration Fund (later Society), a private organization which had been founded in Britain in 1882 to further the 'elucidation of the history and arts of ancient Egypt', among other aims. In 1890 it extended its scope to include an archaeological survey for recording and publishing the standing monuments before they suffered any more irreparable damage and dilapidation. For six seasons Davies worked at Amarna for the survey virtually single-handed, during which time he succeeded in copying all the decorated and inscribed private tombs, often under very trying conditions. The six volumes of *The Rock Tombs of El Amarna*, 1903–08, in which his descriptions and tracings of the reliefs, sketches and texts were rapidly and economically published, are among the most considerable and abiding of the Fund's enterprises. The scenes which Davies recovered in line and photogravure, together with his commentaries, are almost our only means of learning of events that happened at this critical and exciting moment in Egyptian history, although they have been rivalled by the recent retrieval of earlier reliefs ('talatat') at Karnak (see Chapter 7).   *Pls. 30, 31*

The private tombs at Amarna were, as we shall see, the gift of the king to his loyal followers, and evidently no expense was to be spared in their cutting and decoration. The rock in which they are hewn, however, is limestone of inferior quality, and deficiencies had to be made good by a liberal use of plaster; but this work is of a high order. In some instances, the plaster was modelled by the spatula while it was still wet, a technique of long tradition in Middle Egypt as at Meir. In the tomb of the king's physician, Pentu (No. 5), and to a lesser extent in that of Ahmose, the figures and their surrounds have been cut intaglio to be filled with plaster and delicately modelled, a unique practice probably suggested by the inlaying of glass and faience tesserae cast in moulds for insertion in walls of mudbrick or limestone. The tomb of Pentu, however, has suffered the loss of all its plaster inlays, apart from a few fragments, and its scenes are now reduced to silhouettes with sketchy outlines where the sculptor's chisel has bit deepest. For this reason, too, inscriptions are badly damaged.

The lavish intentions of the king evidently outran his resources. None of the tombs is complete: the decoration of walls is often left unfinished, and in some the main chamber is but partially hewn with its pillars still attached to their   *Pl. 3* matrix. Only two tombs show some signs of being made ready for the interment of their owners with completely hewn burial vaults. The shrine in the chapel of Any, who was a very old man when he came to Akhetaten, has been hastily finished with sketches in red paint of the deceased receiving the last rites. The shrine in the tomb of Huya was less hurriedly prepared with reliefs of a full set of funerary equipment, offerings, mourning men and women, and the last farewell at the tomb door. The funeral rites appear to follow orthodox practice and a *setem*-priest is present (see Chapter 25), but the prayer is the usual Atenist petition for food and water and the remembrance of the deceased's name after death.

These are the only funerary echoes among scenes which are exceptional for their exclusive concern with the vital activities of the royal family, at which the owner may occasionally assist as a mere servant or onlooker, or at best as a participant only when he is honoured by the king.

The subjects which occur most frequently are the royal family making offerings before heaped altars under the rayed disk of the Aten, accompanied   *Pl. 8* by one or more daughters shaking sistrums, and the bestowing of golden

collars, decorations, food and other gifts upon favoured courtiers from a palace
balcony before a concourse of foreign delegates and palace officials. Other
scenes show the royal pair followed by their daughters and their court driving
in chariots to a temple where they are received by the priesthood and the choir
assembled at the entrance pylon. The royal family at table, or drinking wine
together, is encountered in no fewer than seven tombs. Such pictures are of
general significance; but scenes of historical import appear to be two different
representations of the reception of foreign gifts in Year 12 of the reign, and the
induction of the Queen-Mother Tiye into her special sunshade temple late in
the reign.

In spite of their incomplete and damaged condition, the tombs are
architecturally impressive. They follow the pattern of the contemporary, or
near-contemporary, tombs at Thebes, which in turn are developments of the
classic tombs of the earlier Eighteenth Dynasty. The slope of the hillside was
cut back to release a platform before a vertical façade from which a passageway
was driven horizontally into the rock to terminate in a shrine containing a
statue of the deceased hewn out of the living rock. This is the essential design,
as in the tomb of Any. But in most examples, a cross-corridor was cut giving a
cruciform shape to the ground-plan. In the larger tombs, this cross-corridor
was expanded into a hall with its ceiling upheld by two or more columns. The
tomb of Meryrē I and Pinhasy had two such hypostyle halls, giving not only
more space for wall-reliefs but scope for cutting additional shrines for housing
statues carved *in situ*, as in the tombs of May (No. 14) and Tutu (see Chapter
8). The largest tomb at Amarna was that of Ay, which was designed to have a
first hall of twenty-four columns in three rows, but little more than half the
chamber was cut and partly decorated before all work on it ceased.

It seems clear that the necropolis workmen tackled several tombs at a time,
the quarrymen driving their tunnels into the hillside and hewing a part at least
of the internal chambers before moving on to the next site, to be followed in
turn by the rest of the team. As soon as a wall or column was released from the
mass of stone by the masons, it would be made plane and true by the plasterers,
thus providing a suitable surface on which the draughtsmen could draw their
designs ready for the chisels of the sculptors. All work was in sunk relief which
could be more rapidly carved than the classical low relief employed in some of
the near-contemporary tombs at Thebes. The final coat of paint in glue
tempera is frequently wanting, and where it has been applied is now almost
totally discoloured or has fallen away. The Amarna hypogea thus lack the
brilliance of the Theban private tombs, and have a generally dingy and
battered appearance, except in one or two of the southern group which have
escaped the dilapidation and discolouration that have blighted the rest.
Nevertheless, some of the larger tombs almost attain the status of rock temples

Frontispiece, Fig. 2

Fig. 10

Figs. 27, 29

Pl. 3

with their imposing façades and columned halls. They won the admiration of Davies who praised their architectural qualities as follows:

> The row of complex columns [namely, fasciculated papyrus columns with clustered bud capitals] finishing at the wall in pilasters with cavetto-cornice, and carrying either a simple or a corniced architrave, is an architectural element which, by its harmonious blending of straight lines with curves and of the plain with the broken surface, may bear comparison with features of classical architecture that have become imperishable models.

Although the tombs appear to have been cut almost by a mass-production method in the space of a few years, no two are exactly alike in design and decorative features. Even the popular icons of the royal family worshipping the sun-disk, or the rewarding of the tomb-owner, vary in their details and their expression, as though the draughtsman had made a conscious attempt to differentiate the design of one tomb from that of the next. In this they reveal the restless spirit of the artists, revelling in the opportunity to create novelties, for the new iconography had not yet become fixed by tradition.

The tombs can be dated from inscriptional evidence that will be mentioned later, from the earliest at the southern end of the row of such sepulchres to the most recent at the northern extremity, although as a result of the desultory way in which the cutting and decoration proceeded, there are anachronisms, and the generalization cannot be carried too far. Thus while the tomb of Ahmose, from its position in the sequence, and in conformity with some features of its decoration, should be late in date, the inscriptional evidence suggests that it was early, or at least it was started early. It may be objected that as a mere seven years may have separated the earliest from the latest tomb at Amarna, such discrimination is excessive.

Nevertheless the tombs seem to fall into two broad categories. The earlier group took as its exemplar the tomb of Ay, the penultimate at the southern terminal, which was designed as the largest and most important in the private necropolis, an indication no doubt of the standing of its owner at the court of Akhenaten. Such tombs show among their subjects the figure of Mutnodjme, *Fig. 20* sister of Queen Nefertiti, with her attendants in the royal retinue. They also have a relief of the royal family worshipping the Aten in the left-hand thickness of the entrance portal, as one enters it, and another of the owner kneeling to recite a hymn to the Aten in the opposite thickness. In the later tombs the figure of Mutnodjme is missing from the entourage of the princesses; and the icons of the royal family, and the kneeling owner worshipping the Aten at the entrance, are replaced by standing figures of the owner adoring the rising and setting sun. Other scenes are elaborated such as the details of the Great Temple

Pl. 66   with its many altars loaded with offerings, and the chariot drive to the temple. Events in the later years of the reign, such as the great durbar, or reception of gifts presented by foreign legates to the king and queen seated upon their thrones, their six daughters ranged beside them, are illustrated in two tombs. The visit of the king's mother, Queen Tiye, to Akhetaten, or her sojourn in it

Fig. 29   about the same time, is also represented in the tomb of her steward, Huya.

Besides such changes in subject matter, there are also some modifications in the style of the tomb reliefs. The heads of many of the figures in the later scenes are disproportionately large. The features of the royal family tend to be less gaunt and lined than in earlier reliefs, and the appearance of their figures less exaggerated. Conversely, however, the paunch of the king is more pendulous, perhaps indicating physiological changes with advancing years. But these alterations in stylistic details may be the innovations of new master-designers replacing older artists. The evidence on which a secure opinion can be based is entirely lacking.

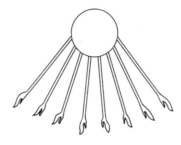

CHAPTER 3

The Tombs in the Royal Wadi

By the eighties of the last century, if any scholar was aware that Akhenaten had left a declaration that his tomb should be hewn in the eastern hills at Amarna, and his burial and that of Nefertiti and their eldest daughter Meritaten should be made in it, then he kept that information to himself. Moreover, if the final resting-place was sought among the private tombs by the various expeditions and individuals that came to Amarna in the first half of the century, they must have searched in vain. The truth is that, as so often occurs in archaeology, the discovery was made not by the expert, but by casual seekers after loot.

In the early eighties, it would appear that native rummagers must have stumbled upon the Royal Tomb. In 1882 items of gold jewellery, later reputed *Pl. 5* to come from the tomb, were sold by villagers of Hagg Qandil to the Revd W. J. Loftie, an English clergyman and amateur antiquarian, who spent some years wandering around Egypt acquiring antiquities. He sold these pieces of goldwork, with the exception of two finger-rings, to a London dealer, who in turn disposed of them to the Royal Museum of Scotland in Edinburgh. Here they were fated to repose unnoticed until 1917 when Professor A. M. Blackman discussed their significance, and drew attention to a heavy gold finger-ring of Nefertiti which was included in the hoard. By this time the location of the Royal Tomb was no longer a mystery but was well known to European travellers, though it had been incompletely published. The hoard comprised jewellery of two distinct periods, work of the late Eighteenth Dynasty, and a few pieces of Roman or Coptic date. It has therefore been conjectured that what Loftie bought from the villagers at Hagg Qandil was a number of pieces belonging to the original deposit, probably purloined and hidden in the vicinity at the time when the burials were being removed elsewhere during the abandonment of Akhetaten. As often happens in such cases, the thieves never returned to retrieve their loot. Mixed with the trinkets sold to Loftie was goldwork presumably rifled by the villagers from intrusive burials of the third century AD, which they must have found at the same time in the Royal Tomb or its environs.

In the early nineties, while the French Mission were operating at the southern tombs at Amarna, the site of the Royal Tomb was disclosed to them by local villagers who doubtless had satisfied themselves that nothing portable of value had been left in it. Alexandre Barsanti, the engineer of the Mission, fitted iron gates to the entrance early in 1892, though he claimed to have discovered it some weeks earlier. The reason why the tomb had escaped discovery for so long was because it was situated in the eastern hills, not among the private tombs but in a remote northern side-valley almost 6 kilometres up the Wadi Abu Hasah el Bahri (the Royal Wadi) which pierces the semicircle of cliffs and hills that encloses the plain of Amarna on the eastern bank of the Nile, and separates the northern from the southern group of private tombs.

The Royal Wadi is a savage place, gashed into a high and arid plateau, devoid of vegetation and shade, but of an awesome beauty in the morning and evening lights. Occasionally, sudden storms breaking over the area discharge torrents of water to scour the gullies, and wash detritus down the main wadi. In this way debris and fragments from the tomb have been carried far beyond its mouth, a circumstance well known to the local inhabitants who have combed the region many times in the hope of finding antiquities that others have

cf. Pls. 11, 12 overlooked.

The entrance to the Royal Tomb is at the level of the floor of the side-valley and faces east, the region where the Aten dawns each day. This event, the sunrise and awakening of the temple and its worshippers to life, is one of the unusual themes represented in the reliefs carved into the walls of the interior chambers. The design of the tomb, like its decoration, departs abruptly from that of the tombs of preceding kings of the dynasty (see Introduction). It is

Fig. 4 virtually a long wide corridor descending by means of two steep staircases, separated by a long sloping passageway, for a distance of 28 metres into the hillside, to debouch into an anteroom giving on to the burial hall. The anteroom is at the foot of the second staircase and leads through a doorway to the 'protective well' which had been excavated to a depth of 3.5 metres. Such wells or pits are a feature of most of the tombs of the pharaohs of the New Kingdom, and the presumption has been that they were not cut until after the burial had been deposited together with the funerary furniture. In this particular case, evidence has been found to suggest that the well was filled with dressed limestone blocks. The walls of the room that forms the upper part of the well were once plastered, decorated in relief and inscribed, but all that now remains shows that the entrance was flanked by two elaborate, carved reliefs of

cf. Pl. 75 floral bouquets, a feature also found in some of the private tombs at Amarna. Other scenes in the well-room included figures of the king and queen offering to the Aten, and of the elder princesses on the end walls. The egress from this room leads directly to the doorway of the burial hall, which had evidently been sealed after the burial by a wall of limestone blocks, similar in size to those found in the well. This suggests that at some time subsequent to the initial burial the blocking of this chamber was torn down and thrown into the well, to bridge the gap in the floor and facilitate removal of the deposit elsewhere. The lowermost course of stones is still in position above the sill at the threshold.

The burial hall is an impressive chamber about 10 metres square and 3.5 metres high, hewn with a platform on the left, 33 centimetres high, supporting the remains of two square piers. The masons had begun to cut a doorway to another chamber in the upper corner of the right-hand wall, but the operation did not get very far. The reliefs and inscriptions carved in the plastered walls of this hall were almost entirely obliterated not long after the death of the king. Traces of inscriptions, in a very fragile state near the line of the ceiling, give the titles and names of the Aten, Akhenaten and Nefertiti. The scenes that were once represented here can, with difficulty, be made out as the usual offering ceremonies to the Aten, at which the royal family officiated. Great quantities of food, drink and flowers were shown heaped upon the altars of the Aten. Items of funerary furniture and equipment for the dead were figured in a more elaborate version of the similar theme which is illustrated in the private tomb-

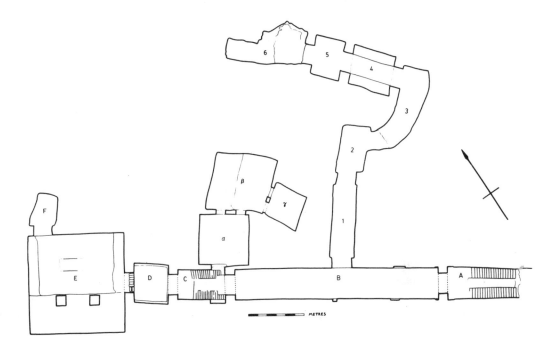

4 Plan of the Royal Tomb at Amarna.

chapel of Huya. Groups of officials and soldiers also appear, taking a last farewell of their king; and mourning women tear their hair and give vent to lamentations.

In addition to the main chambers of the tomb, two separate suites of rooms were hewn, one leading off the right-hand wall of the descending corridor half-way down, and the other at its foot, where it entered the antechamber. The upper group, consisting of three continuous passages admitting to three rooms in echelon, is in a rough unfinished state, but closely resembles in its lay-out a king's tomb, even to the sloping approach corridor. Opposite its entrance in the main corridor, on the left-hand wall, a doorway has been tentatively cut as the entrance, apparently, to another suite of rooms, but no further progress with the cutting has been made.

A similar feature is found at the lower end of the main corridor, where on the left a doorway has been indicated by preliminary cuts, while opposite it an entry has been hewn into a suite of three chambers leading into each other. Since their discovery by the French, they have been designated as chambers α, β and γ, of which beta, lying between the other two, is undecorated, whereas alpha and gamma have their walls carved with reliefs, albeit now extensively damaged.

Chamber alpha is about 5.5 metres square and nearly 3 metres high. All the walls have been finished and decorated with reliefs. These are carved rather crudely in the rock which is here very hard; but when they left the sculptor's hands they were covered with a layer of painted plaster more delicately cut and modelled. The plaster, however, has now fallen away, though traces of colour survive, mostly as a red stain where flesh tones had been applied. Two long scenes show the royal family, with five of their daughters, making offerings in a temple-court with the Aten dawning on the east wall, and setting on the opposite wall. The other walls are interrupted by doorways, but have reliefs of charioteers in attendance on the worshippers waiting outside the temple gates together with the military escort.

Fig. 5   Other scenes show the king and queen in a room mourning the death of a woman, queen or princess, on a bier. The Aten shines into the room: but in a duplicate scene immediately below, the rayed sun-disk is absent, perhaps indicating a night vigil. Outside the room, mourners wail and pour dust over their heads. A vizier is among the weepers, recognizable in his long bouffant robe. A nursemaid emerges from the death chamber bearing an infant whose high rank is indicated by the presence of a fan-bearer. The scene has been interpreted as the royal family mourning the death in childbirth of one of their number.

A peculiar feature of the reliefs is that some of the figures have been recarved to mitigate the unflattering style of art in fashion in the earlier years of the

5 Mourning over a dead princess.

reign, and well exemplified by a stela found lying loose on the debris in a room   *Pl. 8*
of the upper suite. The figures of certain princesses have also been plastered
over, giving rise to the surmise that they may have died in the interim; but as
their names have not been touched, this conclusion does not necessarily follow.

The identity of the dead person upon the bier is also uncertain. Her name
has been expunged, and as this was done before the French copied the scene,
the presumption is that the excisions were probably made in antiquity. From
closely similar scenes of mourning in chamber gamma, it has long been
assumed that the corpse on the bier is Meketaten, Akhenaten's second
daughter, and the entire suite of three rooms was reserved for her entombment.
But this assumption has recently been challenged, and it has been suggested
that in the absence of a specific name in the damaged inscription, the body on
the bier could well be another royal daughter, or even a minor queen of
Akhenaten. We shall have to return to this problem later.

It is in this chamber that four niches have been cut in the walls, after their decoration was complete, for the reception of 'magic bricks'. Such devices, made of unbaked clay and carrying different amulets, were inscribed with spells from Chapter 151 of *The Book of the Dead*, which at this period were supposed to protect the deceased from intruders. In royal tombs these 'bricks' were usually sealed in loculi cut in the walls; but no evidence exists of such special treatment in the very few cases in which they have been recovered from private tombs.

Chamber gamma is the smallest of the three in the lower suite. It is roughly 3.5 metres square, with one side prolonged to 4 metres, and 1.8 metres high; it was evidently designed as a burial chamber with the intercommunicating room beta serving as a storeroom, perhaps for both alpha and gamma. As a burial chamber one of the walls of gamma was decorated in relief with pictures of funerary furniture, but its main feature is another death-bed scene, similar to the one in room alpha, represented in the reliefs on another wall. The dead princess rests on a funerary couch in a bedroom, but her figure and name have been expunged. She is mourned by her weeping parents and two distraught attendants, while standing outside the death-chamber is a nurse suckling an infant held in her arms, followed by two fan-bearers. The inference seems inescapable that this princess also died in childbirth. A large concourse of courtiers, ladies-in-waiting and state officials, joins in the lamentations with grief-stricken gestures.

Fig. 28 A companion scene on the opposite wall shows the king and queen, followed by the four surviving princesses and a host of mourners, pouring dust over their heads. Before them is a flower-decked arbour in which an effigy of the dead princess, either as a statue or her mummy, garlanded and anointed, stands to receive the last farewells, as at a tomb door. In this scene the identity of the deceased is unambiguously revealed by the inscription which names her as Princess Meketaten. The text referring to the nurse and the infant she holds is unfortunately completely destroyed, probably anciently.

All the reliefs in the decorated chambers of the tomb were carved in walls that had been heavily plastered, according to the common practice at Amarna, a technique that has left them particularly vulnerable to the hammer of the iconoclast and the chisel of the antiquity hunter. The decoration of the walls has suffered grievously from their attentions. Even after iron gates were fitted to the entrance, the reliefs were further damaged by a series of depredations, the last onslaught as recently as 1972. When the French epigraphists began to copy the reliefs in rooms alpha and gamma in 1894, the scenes were practically complete, but now they are little more than ghostly sketches of the original designs, with the plastered surfaces gone, and only the deeper cuts of the masons' chisels visible on the limestone walls.

1 *Limestone relief, with official portraits of Akhenaten and Nefertiti in the style of the later years of their reign. It served as a model by a master-sculptor for the guidance of craftsmen engaged upon royal work, and was found at Amarna by villagers who sold it to the American Egyptologist Charles Edwin Wilbour during his visit to the site in 1881.*

2 *Aerial view of the central part of Amarna during excavations in 1932, looking north, the eastern cliffs on the skyline with the Nile on the left bordered by dark patches of modern cultivation and the broad highway of the 'royal road'. The Mansion of the Aten occupies the centre of the site, its sanctuary white with chips of destroyed stonework. The Great Palace on the left and the Great Temple in the distance still await investigation in this view.*

4 (above) Relief, originally part of
the tomb of Ay at Amarna but now
in the Cairo Museum, showing the
owner and his wife Tey in festal
attire standing before the palace
balcony to receive gifts tossed down to
them by the royal family (cf.
Frontispiece). Both recipients are
loaded with gold shebu collars, and
Ay is just receiving an imitation
floral collar composed of polychrome
faience elements.

3 (left) View of the interior of Tomb
No. 13 in the southern group at
Amarna, first opened by Robert Hay
in 1830. It is exceptional for its
spotless condition, but like nearly all
the tombs at Amarna is unfinished.
The cross-chamber is divided down
the centre-line by a row of graceful
clustered papyrus-bud columns which,
owing to the masons' manner of
working, are finished in their upper
parts while the lower portions are in
a rudimentary state. According to
Davies, the slim columns seem to be
emerging slowly and immaculately
from a subsiding bank of rock. The
tomb was planned for the Governor
of Akhetaten, a parvenu with a
name, Neferkheperuhersekheper,
based upon the king's prenomen and
meaning in effect that he has created
him.

5 (below) Goldwork from a group of jewels retrieved by the
villagers of Hagg Qandil from the Royal Tomb, or its environs, in
1882 and now in Edinburgh. Included in the find is a signet ring
(inverted), incised with the cartouche of Nefertiti, another with the
bezel in the form of a frog, the underside inscribed, 'Mut, mistress of
Heaven', and two ear-studs with the boss in the form of a flower-head.

6 (left, above) *Fragment of a parapet in hard white limestone from Carter's excavation of the dump on the southeast verges of the Great Temple during Petrie's explorations in 1891–2. Nefertiti is shown wearing the short Nubian wig with double uraei and offering a device symbolizing the Aten in festival.*

7 (left, below) *Torsos in hard limestone recovered from the same dump. The epicene anatomy of the king is well illustrated here, the one on the right being hardly distinguished from the other which is inscribed for the queen.*

8 *Limestone relief found in Room 4 of the Royal Tomb and probably intended as a model for workmen carving the chapel walls. The design shows the king and queen making floral offerings before altars heaped with flowers beneath the radiant disk of the sun-god who brings the symbols of life and power by means of his rays. The two eldest daughters are also in attendance shaking their sistrums. This characteristic icon of the royal family worshipping the Aten is in the more bizarre style of the earlier half of the reign.*

9, 10 *The decoration of public buildings at Amarna made great use of inlays of polychrome faience, the first appearance of the characteristic Near Eastern contribution to architectural ceramics. One fragmentary tile (above) has a design of black and white calves gamboling in the flowering rushes in russet and green, evidently inspired by earlier painted motives on walls in the Malkata Palace (cf. Pl. 49). Another incomplete example (right) has a design of a dumpalm in green, brown and yellow on a white ground, the foliage executed in fluid line with masterly verve.*

11, 12 *Upper parts of two fragmentary shawabti figures of Akhenaten holding* ankh-*signs. Alternatively, such figures may hold royal sceptres (cf. Fig. 23) in place of the more usual pick, hoe and basket of manual workers in the fields of the Osirian otherworld.*

13 *Tablet of sun-dried clay impressed with cuneiform signs, part of the despatches from Tushratta, king of the Mitanni, and found in the ruins of the records office at Amarna (see Pl. 23). Now in the British Museum, it is a letter to Amenophis III with an ink docket written on a blank area by an Egyptian filing-clerk saying that it was a copy received at Thebes during Year 36. Another tablet, also from Tushratta, but addressed to Akhenaten, found in the same cache, is now in Berlin and carries a similar docket on one edge to say that it had been delivered by messengers from Naharin in Year [1]2.*

14 *Pencil drawing by Robert Hay made in 1827 of one of his team in Turkish dress contemplating Boundary Stela A on the western cliffs south of Tuna el Gebel. The attendant groups of statuary hewn in the living rock show Akhenaten and Nefertiti upholding an offering tray and a stela bearing the names of the Aten. Their two eldest daughters are seen beside them and the name of the third, together with her figure, have been added in relief to the infill.*

The French also made a photographic record which, if complete, would be invaluable today but, alas, it is now lost. Their line-drawings which were published in 1903 are incomplete. They are not facsimiles copied from tracings, but schematic sketches lacking detail. Nevertheless, they provide at present the only indication of the style and iconography of the wall decorations. In addition, Barsanti in two clearances transferred from the tomb to the Cairo Museum various fragments of two granite sarcophagi and some parts of an alabaster Canopic chest. Other objects, recovered from the tomb and the wadi outside its mouth, included the panel or stela carved with a scene of the royal *Pl. 8* family worshipping the Aten, in the grotesque style of the earlier half of the reign. At the same time, Barsanti also retrieved a number of broken shawabti figures (see Chapter 21) of Akhenaten in various stones and in faience. Other *Pls. 11, 12* examples of such funerary adjuncts picked up by locals in the tomb and its environs, particularly in the wadi during illicit diggings in 1934, have long since entered the antiquities market and have been dispersed among the

6 (above) *Copy in line of the upper part of Stela S, made by N. de G. Davies eighty years after Hay had sketched Stela A (see Pl. 14). The lunette of Stela S is carved in sunk relief with confronted figures of the king and queen and their two eldest daughters worshipping the radiant symbol of the Aten. The stela is hewn with flanking groups of statuary at the foot of cliffs on the opposite bank of the Nile some 29 km southeast of Stela A. Both carry the later proclamation, and have a postscript dated to Year 8; but S excludes any mention of the third daughter, and was therefore probably carved before Stela A.*

world's collections. Some other fragments recovered by the Antiquities Service (now the Antiquities Organization of Egypt) while investigating this ransacking have entered the Cairo Museum.

In 1931 and 1935 the Egypt Exploration Society examined the Royal Tomb and the wadi very thoroughly, shifting dumps of spoil left by earlier excavators down to bedrock, and scraping and brushing the sides of the valley. They succeeded in recovering a mass of fragments, including parts of three stone bowls inscribed with the names of the earlier kings Tuthmosis III, Amenophis III and Khephren, evidently palace heirlooms deposited in the tomb with the burials. They also made a photographic record with tracings of what remained of the tomb reliefs and inscriptions. Their expectation of publishing these was thwarted, however, by the outbreak of war in 1939 and the dispersal of their team. In recent years, Professor Geoffrey T. Martin of University College, London, has resumed their task and already published, as Part VII of *The Rock Tombs of El'-Amarna*, a volume describing the operations both official and illicit, of which some report has been made, together with a catalogue raisonné of all objects which have been recovered from the Royal Tomb, or which can be traced back to it. A further volume containing a facsimile record in line-drawings of the tomb scenes is in the press. In the meantime, he has issued a brief interim report, to which this chapter owes much.

It is regrettable that virtually a century has elapsed before this ruined tomb has been fully published, so that much has been lost in the interval. But in the case of Amarna studies we shall find that it is futile to bewail the omissions and mistakes of the past. We must be content if eventually some honest account is rendered.

Professor Martin's researches have been instrumental in dispelling certain inaccuracies, conjectures and rumours that have always circulated around operations in the Royal Wadi. In particular, he has given good grounds for believing that Akhenaten was buried in the large pillared hall of the tomb. One set of pink granite fragments belongs to his sarcophagus, while another group in grey granite comes from its lid. There were also parts of another sarcophagus in red granite, with a grey granite cover, that belonged to a woman, presumably the Princess Meketaten whose death and funeral pomps are illustrated in chamber gamma. Both sarcophagi, however, have been viciously smashed into little pieces and scattered far and wide, losing so much in the process that it has proved impossible to reconstruct them completely. Nevertheless a good idea of the design of the king's sarcophagus can be recovered, showing that it had figures of Queen Nefertiti carved in high relief and extending protective arms at the corners like the guardian goddesses of the four quarters. The owner of the other sarcophagus is less clear. The presumption is that it was made for Meketaten; but the names of Akhenaten, Amenophis III, Nefertiti, Tiye and

Meritaten, besides Meketaten, appear on fragments from the coffer and lid.

Martin believes that chamber alpha, despite the similarity of its mourning scenes to those for Meketaten in chamber gamma, was used for another of the royal women, and he points to the presence of the niches, cut in the walls after the decoration was complete, for housing the four 'magic bricks'. In his opinion this indicates that the chamber was adapted to accommodate the burial of a sovereign or royal consort. We know so little of the exact circumstances in which such 'bricks' were installed, since they have rarely been found *in situ* and none refers to a queen or princess, that it would be unwise to dogmatise. It is noteworthy, however, that no provision for such niches was made in the burial hall of this tomb in which Akhenaten is presumed to have lain. We shall return later to the burial arrangements that may have been made for members of the royal family in this tomb.

The Royal Tomb is not the only hypogeum to have been quarried in this area of the Royal Wadi: several others have been found in the main wadi, the southern side-valley and the northern side-valley itself. All are incomplete, however, and for the most part mere preliminary cuttings in the rock. Four tombs only warrant attention as having reached some modest dimensions.

One with an impressive entrance, stairway, and sarcophagus-slide, penetrates the hillside of the main wadi to a depth of nearly 40 metres. It was evidently designed for a sovereign, perhaps the heir apparent, but it remains in an unfinished state beyond the first corridor, and is full of mud deposited by past torrents that have washed into it. Potsherds, some with dockets, have been found in the dumps outside two other tombs with precipitous entries in the southern side-valley. This may suggest that they were used during the Amarna period. One of them, smaller in extent, but more elaborate in its architecture, may have been designed for the Mnevis bull, the sacred animal of the sun-cult of Heliopolis, which Akhenaten promised burial in the eastern hills. The fourth tomb worthy of mention on account of its size is in the northern side-valley nearly opposite the Royal Tomb, but work on it had not progressed beyond the first sloping corridor.

In the dumps outside one of the larger unfinished tombs in the southern side-valley, a fragment of pottery was recovered in 1984 by Dr Aly el Kouly of the Antiquities Organization of Egypt. It bore an inscription referring to 'the robing-room of Neferneferurē', suggesting that the fifth daughter of Akhenaten was once buried there, but further details are awaited. If this discovery is confirmed, the fact that she was not buried in the Royal Tomb gives rise to the presumption that it was already sealed at the time of her death, and she therefore outlived her father, but probably by a few months only before Akhetaten was abandoned.

43

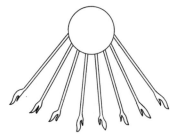

CHAPTER 4

The Boundary Stelae

The royal and the private tombs are not the only standing monuments to mark the site of the Horizon of the Aten. Its boundaries are more precisely delimited by a unique kind of antiquity not found elsewhere in Egypt. It was during the last century that scholars began to take particular note of a peculiar feature of the region – the existence of large immovable tablets or stelae hewn at different points in the surrounding cliffs, both on the east bank and on the west. The most accessible and best preserved of these was cut into the rocks 5 kilometres south of modern Tuna el Gebel, the ancient necropolis of Hermopolis on the west bank, facing the northern end of El Amarna on the opposite side of the *Pl. 14* river 18 kilometres to the east. This landmark was first notified to Europeans by the Jesuit scholar Claude Sicard who came upon it in 1714 during his travels in Egypt. It was rediscovered by Wilkinson some years before 1827 when it was drawn by Hay.

It is now the best surviving example of a class of monument of which fourteen have so far been identified and listed, each with a distinguishing letter, the last as recently as 1901. The cliff at this point on the west bank has been cut back to make a deep recess sheltering the stela which stands within, proud of the back wall. Now known as Stela A, it is 4.3 metres high and 2.3 metres broad, carved with figures of Akhenaten and Nefertiti and their two eldest daughters Meritaten and Meketaten worshipping the Aten, manifest as a radiant sun-disk. A hieroglyphic inscription incised into eight vertical columns and twenty-five horizontal lines contains a royal proclamation. The stela is flanked on its left side at the back by two groups of statuary also hewn out of the living rock, and each consisting of a pair-statue of the king and queen accompanied by a smaller dyad of the two daughters, Meritaten standing next to her mother with an arm extended to touch her robe. One of the life-size pair-statues of the king and queen holds tablets with arms outstretched at shoulder height; the other holds shorter tablets with arms extended from the elbows. The tablets bear the names of the Aten and those of the royal pair, who are thus seen to be literally 'upholding the name of the Aten', and so fulfilling one of the claims in the name of the king. The titles and names of the two eldest daughters appear on the spine of rock that connects the figure of Nefertiti to the cliff: but in this particular stela the third daughter, Ankhesenaten (*sic*), also appears with her sisters in sunk relief on the infill of the longer tablet that the king and queen are supporting. All the statuary and the figures in the reliefs are sculpted in the exaggerated epicene style of the early monuments at El Amarna, though the forms are exquisitely rendered with swelling hips, thighs, buttocks and breasts beneath the diaphonous garments where they are released from the cuboid infills that join the adult bodies to the tablets.

These rock-hewn stelae which marked the exact bounds of the city of Akhetaten are now in a sad state. The heads with their crowns were knocked off the statues soon after the abandonment of the city, and other mutilations have been inflicted on the reliefs and inscriptions. Most of the stelae were carved in areas of poor rock and have lost their plaster fillings and patches of finer limestone. Stela P was blown up with gunpowder by Copts in 1906 under the common delusion that it was a doorway in the rock leading to an Ali Baba cave full of treasure. Stela S was cut in a location where the limestone is as hard as *Fig. 6* alabaster, and at the beginning of this century had survived the hand of time and the despoiler substantially intact: but today it is a mere wreck of its former self.

Not all this dilapidation is man-made. Natural decay has worked its will on all such carvings exposed to searing sun by day and the desert frost by night. Rock-falls and weathering have almost totally demolished one stela and severely damaged others. In fact it is probable that some began to disintegrate soon after they were carved. In a later proclamation Akhenaten vows that if any stela is damaged or destroyed he will renew it in the place where it formerly stood. This is in fact what may have been done when Stela K was carved a few hundred yards south of Stela M, which is in a greatly eroded condition and may have partially collapsed even before its carving was completed.

Stela A, however, is still in fair condition and is easily reached by the Nile tourist: but the other thirteen are awkward of access and sometimes difficult to locate. Most students are content to study them in publications, particularly the pioneer work that Norman de Garis Davies produced in Part V of his *The Rock Tombs of El Amarna* (1908). This volume, produced almost single-handed, but with the editorial assistance of Francis Llewelyn Griffith, has held the field for the last eighty years. It will now, however, have to be supplemented by the study promised by William J. Murnane and Charles C. van Siclen of the Oriental Institute, Chicago, as the fruit of their survey of the stelae in 1984 and 1985. Using modern technical aids and profiting from improvements in epigraphical disciplines, they have succeeded in clearing up some long-standing ambiguities and obscurities in the texts, though unfortunately the complete recovery of the critical inscription on the heavily damaged earlier Stelae X, K, or M, will never be possible. This chapter takes into account their findings as announced in their preliminary reports.

The stelae are of different sizes ranging in height from 2 metres (R) to 8 metres (U). When they were complete they were designed with a semi-circular upper part in which the topmost border is an arched sky-sign above the dominant symbol of the Aten as a radiant sun-disk. The rest of the lunette beneath is occupied by figures in sunk relief of Akhenaten and Nefertiti extending their arms from the shoulders and raising their hands in an adjuration of the Aten. Except in the three early examples, they are followed by their eldest daughters Meritaten and Meketaten rattling sistrums. In Stelae X and M only Meritaten appears in the royal group. In Stela K the figure of Meketaten is interpolated in the margin as an afterthought. In Stelae A and B the third daughter is represented in relief only on the infill of the long tablets held by the royal pair, as already noted above; but on the floor of Stelae P, Q, and U, holes have been cut to take the under-base tang of a separate statue of her fixed beside the dyad of her sisters, again as a later addition.

Three of the stelae (X, M, and K) have no sculptures at their bases; but in the rest, the niche is extended, either on the left-hand side to include the two groups of statuary (A, J, and R), or on both sides to incorporate a single group of statuary on each flank (B, N, P, Q, S, and U). At the site of Stela K, however, rock-falls have so eroded the base that it is not certain whether it ever had niches for sculpture: the presumption is that it did not.

In some stelae (A, B, J, K, M, S, and U), the opening of the proclamation is incised in vertical columns within the lunette and continued in horizontal lines below it. In others (B, P, Q, R, and S), the lunette is occupied by confronted groups of the royal family on either side of a central altar. In addition, two *Fig. 6* stelae (B and S) have made space for the opening sentences of the vertical inscription by dispensing with the altar.

The habit worn by the king conforms to contemporary royal fashion. He wears a kilt tied around the waist by a broad sash from which depends a jewelled apron or codpiece in front, and an imitation bull's tail appendage behind. His upper body is bare, lacking any collar or armlets. His crown is almost invariably the Blue Crown, but in one example (P) it is the Red Crown of Lower Egypt on the northern half of the stela, and the White Crown of Upper Egypt on the southern half. A similar orientation appears to have been observed in the flanking statuary at the base of Stela R.

The dress of the queen comprises a long robe touching the ground, tied by a ribbed girdle, and a shawl covering one shoulder. She, too, wears no jewellery. Her headgear, however, is more varied. It is usually the characteristic blue cap (R and Q), sometimes surmounted by double plumes and disk (N), and with the addition of horizontal rams' horns (A). But occasionally she may wear a long curled wig with a coronet of uraei, topped by the double plumes and vertical cow horns (K), or a similar headgear with a modius in place of the coronet (P and S).

The daughters are shown in the reliefs as wearing long gowns reaching to the ground and their hair plaited into the side-lock of infancy, but not confined by a slide: nor do they wear other jewels. In the accompanying statuary, they are represented naked and hold each other by the hand, or place an adjacent arm around each other. Both parents and their children have sandals on their feet.

Such stylistic details are not examples of a cataloguer's pedantry. They have been the means by which it has been possible for the Chicago scholars to recover the history of the stelae and the sequence in which each was carved over a four-year period.

Three of the stelae (K, M, and X) bear a longer and more interesting text than the others, but unfortunately they are all badly damaged, particularly in their lower parts. Stela M is almost a total wreck, and serious gaps in the inscriptions on the other two begin to appear at about the same point and rapidly increase to produce total loss. Only one, K, bears a date that can be deciphered, and the recent survey has succeeded in establishing this as Year 5 'beyond doubt'. The other stelae bear a date which is a year later; and of these, eight (A, B, N, P, Q, R, S, and U) carry a postscript of Year 8. The text on the first group has been called by Davies, 'The Earlier Proclamation', and the text on the others, 'The Later Proclamation'.

The Earlier Proclamation, in so far as it can be recovered, begins with a sonorous recital of the names and titles of Rē-Herakhte-Aten, followed by those of the king and an encomium upon him:

Year 5, Month 8, Day 13.
May the Good God live who delights in Truth, Lord of Heaven and Lord of Earth, Aten, the Living, the Great, illuminating the Two Lands!
May the Father live, divine and royal, Rē-Herakhte, rejoicing in the Horizon in his aspect of the Light which is in the sun-disk, who lives for ever and ever, Aten, the Great, who is in jubilee within the temple of the Aten in Akhetaten!
And May the Horus live, *Strong Bull beloved of Aten*;
He of the Two Ladies, *Great of Kingship in Akhetaten*;
Horus of Gold, *Upholding the Name of the Aten*;
the King of Upper and Lower Egypt, Living in Truth, Lord of the Two Lands, Neferkheperurē, Wa'enrē (*Good like the Forms of Rē, the Only One of Rē*);
the Son of Rē, Living in Truth, Lord of Crowns, Akhenaten (*the Glorified Spirit of the Aten*), Great in his Duration, Living for Ever and Always.

The Good God, Unique one of Rē, whose beauty the Aten created, truly excellent in mind to his Maker, contenting Him with what his spirit desires, doing service to Him who begot him, administering the land for Him who put him upon his throne, provisioning his eternal home with very many things, upholding the Aten and magnifying His name, causing the Earth to belong to its Maker. . .

This is followed by a eulogy of the king's chief wife:

And the Heiress, Great in the Palace, Fair of Face, Adorned with the Double Plumes, Mistress of Happiness, Endowed with Favours, at hearing whose voice the King rejoices, the Chief Wife of the King, his beloved, the Lady of the Two Lands, Neferneferuaten-Nefertiti (*Good like the Beauty of the Aten: A Beautiful Woman Comes*), May she live for Ever and Always.

This long preamble introduces a description of the event which is being celebrated:

His Majesty mounted a great chariot of electrum, like the Aten when He rises on the horizon and fills the land with His love, and took a goodly road to Akhetaten, the place of origin which [the Aten] had created for Himself that he might be happy therein. It was His son Wa'enrē who founded it for Him as His monument when His Father commanded him to make it. Heaven was joyful, the earth was glad, every heart was filled with delight when they beheld him.

The declaration goes on to state that the king made a great oblation to the Aten, and this is the theme which is illustrated in the lunettes of the stelae where he stands with his queen and eldest daughter before an altar heaped with offerings under the Aten, while it shines upon him rejuvenating his body with its rays.

He then summoned his courtiers and the great men of the entire land. They abased themselves before him while he addressed them, pointing out the extent of Akhetaten which his god desired him to build as a monument to Him in the great name of his majesty for ever. It was solely the Aten who had directed him to this virgin site, and indeed his majesty found that it did not belong to any god or goddess, or to a prince or princess, and no one had any claim to act as its owner.

The onlookers responded with fulsome praise of the king and queen, assuring them that it was the Aten who communed with his majesty alone and exalted no other ruler elsewhere; but the Aten would send the people of all foreign lands to Akhetaten with gifts for the king whose god had enabled them to live and breathe.

Akhenaten then raised his hand to the Heavens to swear an oath 'unto Him who had formed him'; but he prefaced this with an apostrophe upon his god which, in view of the fact that the text purports to be the record of an actual event, must repeat the very words used by the king on this occasion. As such, it is practically the only testimony to survive of the king's view of the deity whom he had elevated to supreme power, and therefore merits quotation as *ipsissima verba*:

> The great and living Aten . . . ordaining life, vigorously alive, my Father . . . my wall of millions of cubits, my reminder of Eternity, my witness of what is eternal, who fashions Himself with His two hands, whom no craftsman has devised, who is established in rising and setting each day ceaselessly. Whether He is in heaven or earth, every eye beholds Him without [hindrance?] while He fills the land with His rays and makes everyone to live. With seeing whom my eyes are satisfied daily when He rises in this temple of the Aten at Akhetaten and fills it with His own self by means of His rays, beauteous with love, and embraces me with them in life and power for ever and ever.

The solemn oath that follows is couched in verbose quasi-legalistic terms as though to avoid any ambiguity. Akhenaten vows that he will make Akhetaten in that particular locality and nowhere else, namely in the place which the Aten enclosed (with hills) on the eastern bank for His own self. Nor would the queen nor anyone else in the entire land persuade him to make Akhetaten in a different place. For it was he who had found this Akhetaten for the Aten according to the latter's desire, and with it He is well pleased for ever.

The king then proceeds to list the buildings that he will erect upon the site, naming them in each case as being 'for his Father the Aten, in Akhetaten, in this place'. Thus he will make a 'House [or Estate] of the Aten', a 'Mansion [or Temple] of the Aten', a 'Sunshade temple for the Chief Wife of the King', a 'House of Rejoicing in the Island "Exalted in Jubilees"', and all other (works) which are to be undertaken for the Aten.

There were also to be built the 'Apartments of Pharaoh', and the 'Apartments of the Queen'. The tomb of the king was to be prepared in the eastern hills of Akhetaten and his burial was to be made there after the many years of jubilees which the Aten his Father had ordained for him. And the burials were also to be made in it of Nefertiti, his chief wife, and his daughter Meritaten, after their many years. He goes on to declare that if he were to die in any town in the north, south, east or west, after his many years, he would be brought back to Akhetaten for burial. A similar destiny was promised for Nefertiti and Meritaten, even if they were to die away from Akhetaten.

The tomb of the sacred Mnevis bull of the sun-god in Heliopolis was now to be hewn in the eastern mountains, and its burial to be made therein. The high priests and ordinary priests of the Aten, the palace officials and high officers of state were also to have their tombs in the eastern hills where their burials were to be made.

From this point onwards, the text becomes ever more fragmentary and only disjointed scraps of the proclamation remain. Thus there follows a declaration by the king that, as Father Aten lived, something had been said which was more evil than what the king had heard in his Year 4 . . . more evil than what he had heard in his Year 1 . . . more evil than what King (Amenophis III?) had heard . . . more evil than what King Tuthmosis IV had heard. . . . An earlier reading restored the missing evil as somehow connected with 'priests', an interpretation that has reinforced the view that Akhenaten had experienced some kind of organized opposition to his religious innovations from various priesthoods. More recent study, however, by removing all mention of illusory 'priests', has suggested that what Akhenaten was referring to in his ornamental language was a rumour or report to the effect that his followers were not to be buried in the necropolis near their king, and he declares in an emphatic way what a deplorable thing that would be.

The remainder of the broken text, consisting of isolated phrases, gives tantalizing references to the land of Kush, festivals of the Aten, the imposition of custom dues (?), the celebration of jubilees (?), and the demarcation of the site and its dedication to the Aten. Disjointed scraps mentioning 'gazelles and addaxes' and the 'headland of the Northern Stela', suggest that part of the missing inscription was concerned with the fixing of stelae as markers along the boundary line of the eastern cliffs; and a vow that if they suffered damage from the attention of desert antelopes in the rutting season, or from any other cause, the king would renew them.

These last matters are given fuller treatment in the Later Proclamation dated to Year 6, which is inscribed on the other eleven stelae. This is much more explicit, since there are enough examples in better condition to provide alternative readings for damaged passages or missing words. Unfortunately, the content is not so full or florid as in the earlier text and is concerned almost exclusively with the demarcation of the precise bounds of Akhetaten on both sides of the river. The stelae bear a date exactly one year later than the text of the Earlier Proclamation, and the preamble follows closely its same wording, except that the additional information is disclosed that the king is now reposing in a tent at Akhetaten, and it was from there that he set out to establish the main boundaries of the city.

This was done by confirming the position of the initial markers fixing the north, south, east and west extremities of the city on both banks, and indicating the sites where corresponding stelae were to be hewn.

Once more Akhenaten mounted his great state chariot and drove southwards, evidently following the Nile on the east bank, to the southern extremity of Akhetaten near to Stela M. Here he halted and swore an oath by his Father the Aten, and by his hope that Nefertiti and her two eldest daughters would enjoy a long life, that the southern stela on the east bank was to be definitely at that point, and that he would never pass beyond it. The corresponding stela (F) on the west bank should be hewn opposite it. This too he would not pass beyond.

He then retraced his route and observed the same ceremony in turn at the site of the middle stela (V), and at the northern stela (X). 'And Akhetaten shall be established from the south stela (J) to the north stela (X), measured from tablet to tablet on the eastern bank, [a distance of] 6 *iteru* 1 *khe*, and 4 cubits [amounting to approximately 15 kilometres].' The same measurement is also to be made on the west bank between the respective stelae (Stela F to Stela A).

The area enclosed by these landmarks was Akhetaten in its proper self, and all within it, either then or in the future, should belong to the Father, the Aten. The king further declared that he would not neglect this oath: indeed, it should be carved on the stelae at the southern and northern extremities, and if they were damaged in any way he would renew them.

A postscript was added to certain of the stelae dated to Year 8, Month 5, Day 8, in which it is stated that the oath was repeated when royalty was again in Akhetaten, and the king mounted 'a great chariot of electrum' in order to inspect the stelae on the southeastern boundary (see Chapter 12). Apparently he had visited the west bank eight days earlier for the same purpose, for a codicil appended to Stelae A and B is dated to Year 8, Month 4, Day 30. In this he affirms that the six stelae (namely, X, V, S and A, B, F) determine the extent of Akhetaten in its length and breadth, and it should be for the Father, the Aten . . . all its hills, deserts, inhabitants, animals and produce, eternally, 'and his rays are glorious when they receive them'.

We shall examine later (Chapter 23) the wider significance of these Boundary Stelae as they relate to the progress of the king's opinions and events in his reign.

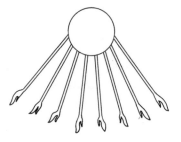

CHAPTER 5

The Buried Evidence: the Early Finds

While the attention of travellers and students was directed to the visible monuments at Amarna, the evidence below ground was generally neglected. The site obviously lacked any vestiges of those massive stone constructions that it was the ambition of excavators in the nineteenth century to free from engulfing sands. It was left to the local villagers by their occasional grubbings among the mounds of decayed mudbrick and wind-blown sand to bring chance finds to light. In this way stray antiquities were hawked to visitors such as Perring and Wilbour when they came to Amarna, at their different times, and acquired objects that aroused the polite interest of their more scholarly friends.

Pl. 1

But in 1887 a discovery was made which was to bring Amarna universal fame and an attention which was to persist for the next century. A peasant woman digging among the mounds of debris for *sebakh*, the nitrous compost into which ancient brickwork in Egypt so often decays, unearthed a cache of over 300 clay tablets impressed with cuneiform signs in what we now know were the ruins of the 'House of the Correspondence of Pharaoh'. By the time these tablets were recognized for what they really were, the diplomatic despatches of Asiatic envoys to Egypt during the reign of Akhenaten, and not the forgeries that local dealers had pronounced them to be, they had been bought up by discerning specialists and deposited among the museums of Berlin, Cairo, London and Paris. Amarna awoke to a wider renown with the informed public, and a more intense interest among archaeologists anxious to scour the place and find more 'Amarna Letters', as they came to be known.

Pl. 23

Pl. 13

The first upon the scene was Flinders Petrie, who three years later received permission from the Egyptian Antiquities Service to excavate the town mounds. Although his explorations would now rank as little more than a sondage, with his usual flair, in the course of a brief season, he succeeded in investigating the remains of the Great Temple ('House of the Aten'), the Smaller Temple ('Mansion of the Aten'), the Great Official Palace (sometimes referred to as the Great Palace), the King's House, the Records Office ('House of the Correspondence of Pharaoh') and several private houses in the central and southern parts of the city. All the stonework of the buildings had been

Fig. 7

robbed in antiquity and only chips and splinters remained to show its presence, but enough evidence was recovered by Petrie to reveal that the Great Official Palace was built in a very opulent fashion. Inlays of coloured stone, faience and glass had been employed on what in earlier times would have been mere painted mudbrick. The palm-leaf capitals of columns had their details made of red and blue glazed chevrons set between ribs of gilded stone, the whole effect being similar to cloisonné jewellery on a huge scale; although in places where the light was dim, paint was resorted to in the interests of speed and economy. Hieroglyphs, cut from red quartzite and limestone, black granite and obsidian, white calcite and coloured glass, were inlaid in stones of contrasting colour. Apart from inscriptions and decorative features set into white limestone walls, glazed tiles were also used, painted with plants and flowers, fish swimming in *Pls. 9, 10* tanks of water, and other translations into ceramics of designs that are known from painted walls and pavements of the time. Indeed, painted plaster floors, sealed with clear varnish, were found in the harim quarter of the palace; and much time was spent by Petrie in preserving them. Some twenty years later they were hacked up in a village feud and only fragments of them are now displayed in the Cairo Museum.

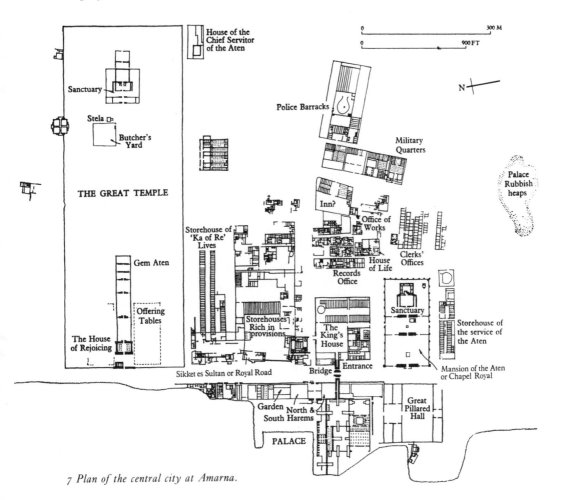

7 Plan of the central city at Amarna.

He had more success with a mural decoration in the room of a large house (his No. 13) now known as the King's House, built of mudbrick on the opposite side of the road flanking the east wall of the palace to which it was connected by a bridge. He was able with great dexterity to twitch from a crumbling mud wall a fragment of a remarkable conversation piece of the entire royal family,

Fig. 26   painted in glue tempera on a thin plaster ground. The rescued portion, which shows two of the younger princesses seated on cushions at their mother's feet and fondling each other, is now one of the treasures of the Ashmolean Museum in Oxford. Adjacent to this large house, on the south side, lay the ruins of a temple, now identified as the Mansion of the Aten, mentioned in the Boundary Stelae among the buildings that the king proposed to erect at Akhetaten. Its main features can still be traced without much difficulty at Amarna, the mudbrick entrance pylon with vertical channels for the reception of the four great cedar flag-poles being substantially intact; but the interior stonework is missing apart from a few disjointed fragments.

Another temple to the north of the King's House and separated from it by extensive magazines, proved to be the House of the Aten, like the Great Palace, an enormous structure, $\frac{3}{4}$ kilometre long by over $\frac{1}{4}$ kilometre wide. Within this walled compound, the most brutal destruction had been wrought in antiquity, yet Petrie was able to make out the main features of a novel temple-complex, with its great entrance pylon, forest of brick altars, central raised avenue, and the sanctuary at its east end.

For three months in 1892 Petrie was joined by a young artist, Howard Carter, who had been commissioned by Lord Amherst to excavate certain parts of the town site. Thirty years later, Carter was to make the most spectacular contribution to Amarna studies by finding the almost intact tomb of Tutankhamun, the successor of Akhenaten. In 1892, however, Carter confined himself to exploring the site of the sanctuary of the Great Temple, without finding much more than two or three blocks of the great quartzite stela which seems to have been the focus of the cult. But greater success attended his efforts in sifting a mound of rubbish outside the boundary wall on the south. Here he unearthed portions of at least seventeen hard limestone statues of the king and queen. It was doubtless from this region that the fragmentary head, earlier acquired by Perring, had been retrieved. The finds, which included about a ton

Pls. 6, 7   of debris, remained unrecorded in the Amherst Collection and were dispersed at its sale in 1921. Apart from three or four torsos and other large fragments sold individually, the bulk of the material was disposed of in four lots, most of which found their way to the Metropolitan Museum in New York, where the writer examined them in 1956. He gained the impression that although some of the fragments can be joined together, it is quite impossible to restore the statues to any semblance of completeness, too many pieces are missing. It was apparent that the statues had suffered two kinds of damage, a preliminary mutilation of features and cartouches, and a more violent smashing later, when they were probably demolished to retrieve the massive blocks of stone that formed their pedestals. It would appear that in design they followed the examples that flank the Boundary Stelae, and are shown as standing in colonnades or flanking the sanctuary of the temple in the tomb reliefs of Huya and Ahmose.

cf. Pl. 64

Among the fragments recovered by Carter were reliefs which Petrie published as parts of stelae. Some of these are now divided between the Brooklyn and Metropolitan Museums, and careful study by John D. Cooney and W. Kelly Simpson has shown that in fact they come from the balustrades of offering-places within the sanctuary of the Great Temple as well as within the Great Palace. The slabs in question are carved on both faces with the familiar scenes of the royal family making offerings to the Aten; but only figures of the king and queen survive, carved in the grotesque style of the earlier years of the reign. As the name of the queen is given in the short form which also appears on Stela K, and which was abandoned thereafter in favour of the expanded version, it is probable that these fragments come from one of the earliest monuments to be erected at Akhetaten, perhaps the altar for the great oblation which the king offered up on the occasion of the founding of the new city.

Pl. 6

The private houses built of mudbrick proved something of a disappointment to Petrie. It is true that he recognized that they were of a different character from the simple modular units of the workmen's village he had found years previously at the pyramid-city of Sesostris II at Lahun. The Amarna houses had belonged to the official classes and gave Petrie an opportunity to study ancient domestic buildings of a superior standard which had not been found in Egypt before. He noted their main features, the front steps leading up to a porter's lodge, the entrance lobby, reception rooms, a loggia generally on the north side open perhaps to cool breezes, and the central hall, square in plan, with its mastaba and fire-pan, and curious red-painted niches the exact purpose of which baffled him. Some rooms he designated quite arbitrarily as the master's room, the women's quarters, the men's quarters and the storerooms. Petrie was obliged to adopt this means of identifying the various apartments, because the houses proved to be remarkably denuded of household goods, not a single scrap of papyrus and scarcely even a potsherd. Although he searched for buried objects that might have been deposited for safety or concealment beneath the floors, he found nothing, though subsequent searchers were to recover hidden treasures by this means. To him it was evident that the town had been gradually deserted: the remaining inhabitants had abstracted from each house, as it became vacant, every object that could be put to any possible

cf. Pl. 22

use. Hence, nothing was found in place, except some stone tanks and column bases to indicate the purpose of a particular room. Despite this total clearance Petrie was able to study the domestic architecture for the first time in Egypt and his conclusions have been largely confirmed by later investigations on a more elaborate scale.

A fruitful discovery was found in another area of the town, apparently devoted to cottage industries, where Petrie lighted upon the remains of three or four glass factories and two large glazing studios. The actual workrooms had almost vanished, but the waste-heaps yielded material of the highest importance which enabled him to trace every stage in the manufacture of ancient glass and faience. Petrie's pioneer work in this field is the basis upon which subsequent researchers have been able to add very little. The technique of making brilliant, polychrome glass vessels, inlays and jewellery, and the cognate craft of manufacturing faience objects covered with various coloured glazes, reached its peak in the late Eighteenth Dynasty, and was greatly *Pls. 9, 10* exploited in the reign of Akhenaten when, as we have seen, it vied with painting in architectural decoration.

A prime target for investigation by Petrie, however, was that part of the ruins where the Amarna Letters had been found. He was able to pin-point the spot as the remains of an office block opposite the eastern end of the King's *Pl. 23* House, and when he came to dig there he found a fragment of a clay tablet in one room, and others in two rubbish pits beneath the foundations. As brick walls had been built over one of these at least, he was of the opinion that the tablets had been discarded earlier in the reign before the offices had been extended. But this is by no means certain, having regard to the frantic rummaging and upheaval that the friable sand foundations had suffered by the time Petrie dug into them. He cleared the adjacent ground and recovered only one other stray portion of a letter. Of the 18 fragments and 1 clay cylinder retrieved by this operation, 7 referred to letters from Abdi-Ashirta of Amurru, Ribaddi of Byblos and Shutatarra of Kadesh, all princes of northern Palestine and southern Syria. The remainder were portions of word-lists and syllabaries used by the cuneiform clerks in their work of translation. Nothing of importance was found, and none of the fragments fitted tablets already *cf. Pl. 13* retrieved; but the exact finding-place of the letters had been identified and was to receive further attention later.

Perhaps the most important discoveries, however, throwing a steadier light on the history of Amarna, arose from Petrie's interest in the unconsidered trifles that other excavators tended to overlook as the discarded rubbish of antiquity. He made a deliberate search for the middens and wasteheaps of the Great Palace, and eventually found them in extensive mounds southeastwards of the Smaller Temple of the Aten. By sifting the spoil, Petrie preserved everything found except the rough pottery. It was in this way that so much of the broken glass vessels and imported Aegean pottery was recovered. More significant, however, were the many examples of scarabs, bezels of broken faience finger-rings, and elements from costume jewellery and amulets, most of them bearing the names of kings and queens, which threw some light on the activities of royalty at Amarna. Similarly, sealings from discarded amphorae, and fragments of broken wine, beer, honey, oil and meat jars bearing hieratic dockets written in ink, gave a wealth of information not only about the commodities brought into the town, the estate of which member of the royal family they came from, or other details of their origin; but also, most importantly, the year and sometimes the month and day in which they were prepared. The hundreds of dated jar-fragments, brought back by Petrie, *cf. Pl. 67* Carter and others, and deciphered by Griffith, allowed a plausible history of the site to be reconstructed. Six inscribed shards from wine-jars showed that seventeen was the highest regnal year attained by Akhenaten, when presumably he died. His ephemeral successor, Smenkhkarē, was credited by the same method with a reign of no more than three years. As there were no ring-bezels found with names of kings who ruled after Tutankhamun, it must have been in his reign that Amarna was abandoned.

Petrie did not confine his attention wholly to the objects below ground. He *cf. Fig. 8* also surveyed the entire region of Amarna, making a triangulation in the plain, and tramping the bounds of the site some 25 kilometres a day. The chart he produced as a result of this inspection was the only reliable map of the district available for the next thirty years. During the six vacant days that he could devote to this work, he discovered seven more of the Boundary Stelae and devised a system of identifying them by letters of the alphabet from A onwards, but introducing gaps where it seemed possible that other examples might come to light later. His system of nomenclature is still followed, though only one stela (X) has been discovered since his survey in 1892.

He also mapped the various ancient routes that were still visible on the desert sands, especially in the evening light, and distinguished between tracks made by the police patrols for guarding the area, roadways to the various quarries and tombs, and the chariot-ways to stelae and other focal points. He came upon two more quarries among the eastern hills in a region where limestone which had the appearance of alabaster had been abstracted since the days of the Old Kingdom. In one of these, he found the name of Queen Tiye, mother of Akhenaten.

Another of Petrie's finds was the plaster mask of the king, which he *cf. Pl. 16* uncovered in a workshop of the Great Palace where it had evidently served as a model for the portraits of Akhenaten carved on his shawabti figures used among the funeral furniture at his burial (see Chapter 10). Such an object of

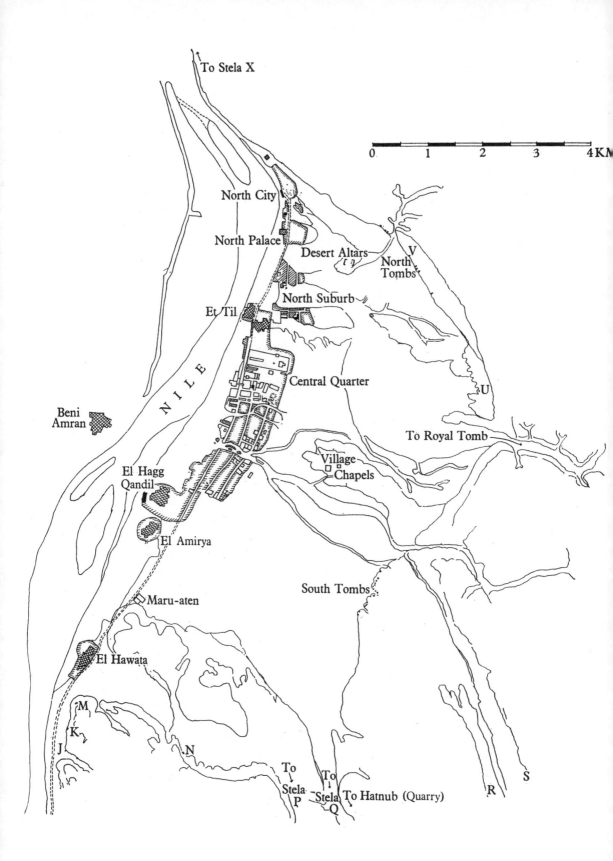

8 Sketch-map of the Amarna region.

this date had not been uncovered in Egypt before, and so impressed was Petrie by the realistic treatment of the king's features that he persuaded himself that he had found the death-mask of Akhenaten. With commendable speed Petrie published the results of his operations and stimulated a general interest in the archaeological potential of the site.

But it was another fifteen years before his promising beginning was continued by his successors. In 1907 the Deutschen Orient-Gesellschaft under the direction of Ludwig Borchardt began excavating at Amarna on a more thorough and systematic basis, spending several seasons on the preliminary survey and making trial digs. They carefully prospected the site, and mapped the entire area under their cartographer Paul Timme, whose map, however, did not appear until 1917, three years after they had been obliged to relinquish their operations on the outbreak of the Great War. The plan of the area of the town ruins was divided up by a 200 metre grid in which buildings could be located by a letter-and-number reference, and subdivided by additional numbers if necessary.

Borchardt's excavations did not get fully under way until the season of 1911 when he began digging to the north of Hagg Qandil in the southern part of Akhetaten, a district occupied by the mansions of high officials, such as P.47, 19, the residence of the General Ramose, the owner of Tomb No. 11, who was found to have changed his name from Ptahmose in deference to the prevailing fervour for sun-worship at Amarna. The door-jambs of house M.47, 3 were inscribed with the name and titles of Ma'nakhtuf, a Master of Works in Akhetaten, and were removed to Berlin. But the most spectacular discovery was made in December of the following season when a complex of house and studios was uncovered in square P.47, 1–3. The owner was identified as 'The King's Favourite and Master of Works, the sculptor Djhutmose', inscribed on the upper half of an ivory horse-blinker disinterred from a rubbish pit in the courtyard. In a sealed magazine of the house, the Germans found a number of plaster casts, sculptors' studies, half-finished statues, heads and busts, which gave an entirely new and impressive aspect of the scope and methods of portrait sculpture in Egypt. The most astounding piece in this miscellaneous collection *Pl. 17* was a life-size painted limestone bust of a queen, which had fallen from a collapsed shelf riddled with termites. It had landed upside down among debris on the floor of the storeroom, and happily was found to be little damaged. This piece, later cleaned and identified as a master study by the chief sculptor of Queen Nefertiti for lesser sculptors to copy, was not brought to general notice until after the Great War, when its appearance in Berlin created the liveliest stir by its timeless interpretation of regal grace. It has since become the most publicized portrait from the ancient world, though other sculpture from the same find rival it in achievement.

Pls. 18, 74

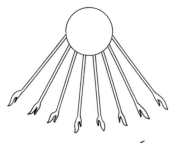

CHAPTER 6

The Buried Evidence: the Later Finds

The exploratory work of the Germans was continued by the British from 1920 onwards. For the next sixteen years the Egypt Exploration Society under its different field directors, notably Leonard Woolley, Henri Frankfort and John Pendlebury, was to uncover most of the central area of the site and to extend its operations into the northern regions of the township.

The objectives of the Society were tersely stated by its first director, T. E. Peet, as follows:

1 The systematic clearing of the town-site begun by the Germans, so as to gather details of the architecture and arrangement of the houses, to learn more of the daily life, and to secure objects for museums.
2 The throwing of fresh light on the numerous difficult problems raised by the so-called religious revolution of Akhenaten.
3 The investigation of the question of dating, and in particular to determine whether the site had been occupied before the reign of Akhenaten, and whether it was ever reoccupied, either partly or wholly, after the great abandonment.

These aims were only partially achieved. More was indeed learnt of the daily life of the inhabitants of Akhetaten, and of the domestic architecture, despite the paucity of material objects and the heavily ruined condition of the official buildings; but less information was secured than was desirable. A few items of museum quality were brought to light to enhance the collections of Cairo, London and New York; but as Petrie had remarked a generation earlier, the township had been thoroughly cleared out by its inhabitants before they evacuated it, and little was left behind of the everyday domestic furnishings so characteristic of similar abandoned sites elsewhere in Egypt. Akhetaten, too, proved to have an elementary stratigraphy, but no evidence was found of its previous settlement, and nothing to refute Akhenaten's claim that he founded his city on virgin ground. The problems raised by his religious innovations were, however, scarcely elucidated by fresh discoveries, and in fact the additional evidence that was uncovered tended to confuse the picture even further with conflicting detail, as we shall describe later.

The work that the Germans had begun in the southern quarter of the ancient city was extended sporadically by the British. In the process, they excavated the large mansion of the vizier Nakht with its reception halls, bedrooms, *Pl. 22* bathroom, lavatory and offices, and were able to reconstruct much of its interior details and decoration. In the same area they found a house adjoining the sculptors' studios, excavated by Borchardt over twenty years earlier, and uncovered in it statue heads in various stages of completion and plaster casts which have greatly enriched the collections of the Cairo Museum.

The main thrust of their explorations, however, was directed to the area that extended between the modern villages of Hagg Qandil and Et Til. Its western side was almost entirely occupied by the Great Official Palace in which Petrie had found the painted pavements. This vast structure, which sloped down to a colonnaded corniche and gardens on the river bank, was less of a royal residence than a great administrative centre for the conduct of the king's affairs. On the other side of the wide road that skirted its eastern boundary, lay the King's House, and the Mansion of the Aten (the Smaller Temple). The *Pl. 2* northern boundary of this insula was formed by the vast compound of the Great Temple. All these buildings with their gardens, magazines, bakeries and workshops occupied most of the central area. In addition, on its eastern flank were other government buildings such as the House of the Correspondence of Pharaoh, the House of Life (or scriptorium where official inscriptions were composed and copied), and the Police Headquarters with its offices and stables. Some of these buildings could be identified with certainty because, although their contents had been entirely removed, the mudbricks of which they were built had been stamped with their names.

All the official constructions, such as the palace and temples, had been *Fig. 7* extensively ravaged by stone-robbers, and the modern excavators had to recover their ground-plans from what evidence remained in the markings on the initial plaster sealing that covered the entire area of the precincts, well below the vanished floor-level. When even such vestiges had been obliterated, they had to depend upon the depressions left in virgin sand whence heavy masonry foundations of walls, columns and podia had been removed.

The excavators also turned their attention to a long and narrow depression in the ground, behind a spit of rock that extended from the limestone cliffs almost in the centre of the site. Here they uncovered the ruins of the walled mudbrick village occupied by the workmen who hewed and decorated the royal and private rock-tombs at Amarna. A similar village with a comparable function had been found by the French at Deir el Medina in Western Thebes, whence the necropolis work-force was almost certainly transferred by

Akhenaten. But the wealth of remains found in the Theban village, with its mass of hieratic documents, is far more voluminous than the meagre spoil gleaned from the seventy-four standard houses at Amarna, which had been cleared of everything but some modest stone furniture and broken pottery. Recently the stone-built, on-site hutments of these workers have also been found about a kilometre to the east of the village towards the entrance of the Royal Wadi.

In the southern area of Akhetaten, between the modern villages of El Hawata and El Amirya, what had been identified by the Germans in the course of a brief inspection during one rainy day in 1907 as 'palace ruins', proved to be something quite different. Alexandre Barsanti of the Antiquities Organization of Egypt had removed from this spot in 1896, mostly to the Cairo Museum, parts of a painted pavement. When Woolley came to examine it in 1921, he was able to expose the remains of an unusual *maru* or 'viewing' temple, with its pools, quays, gardens, tanks, offices and hypaethral kiosks, or 'sunshades' for the daily rejuvenation of members of the royal family by the sun's rays; this was despite the almost total removal of the stonework in antiquity, and the destruction of the mudbrick by modern seekers after *sebakh*. Sufficient fragments of various stones and faience were recovered, however, to reveal that while some of the decoration was modest as compared, for instance, with the gilding and glass inlays of the Great Official Palace, the material of other kiosks was of the richest quality: alabaster, sandstone and granites inlaid with coloured stones and faience. Such *maru* temples are referred to in the texts of the period, and one was built by Amenophis III, evidently in the vast palace site at Medinet Habu (see Chapter 15).

cf. Pl. 37

It was in the Amarna *maru* that the excavators recovered evidence which gave them some disquiet. Here they reported that, unlike anywhere else, the queen's name had in nearly every case been carefully erased from the inscriptions, and that of her eldest daughter, Meritaten, written in palimpsest upon the stone; Nefertiti's distinctive attributes had been blotted out with cement, her features recut and her head enlarged to the dropsical cranium of the Princess Royal. The alterations were the most thorough-going in the case of a group of buildings which seemed to have been called 'the sunshades'.

Similar changes were later found in other damaged reliefs at Akhetaten. In some fragments from the Great Temple, for example, Nefertiti's name had been erased, and references to her maternity of Meritaten obliterated. These surprising alterations encouraged speculation by the somewhat bewildered scholars that the domestic idyll of the royal family was perhaps less than perfect.

The British also extended their excavations to that part of the site lying immediately north of the Great Temple, where they uncovered a suburb built between two wadis and bounded on the east by the desert and on the west by the Nile. It had one or two official buildings but for the most part was a somewhat crowded residential district of modest houses with no great space for gardens. Some of the buildings, however, had an exceptional number of corn-bins and magazines, suggesting that this was a merchants' quarter where commodities brought by river to nearby quays north of the Great Palace could be stored and officially inspected. This suburb was still being developed when the town was abandoned and its new houses were left in various stages of construction.

Lying about a kilometre and a half further north of this suburb stretched a series of greatly ruined structures, evidently part of a great palace area, though the excavations are by no means complete, and the details have not yet been fully published. One building, however, the southernmost of the group, has been more completely revealed, and proves to be an unusual complex of palace and zoological garden, with a throne-room, hypostyle halls, courts, chapels,

9 *Kingfisher and dove in the marshes, from a painted frieze in the North Palace at Amarna.*

administrative offices and a pool. Its novel features were a courtyard for cattle, ibex and gazelle. There were also aviaries with access through a large open window to a garden court. The walls of one of these latter rooms were cut with nesting-niches and painted with a continuous frieze of birds among the marsh plants, one of the masterpieces of mural painting from the ancient world. Fortunately it was copied almost immediately after its discovery, despite its extremely fragile and disintegrating condition. Some surfaces were subsequently consolidated with celluloid solution and the remains successfully removed to Cairo and London.

Fig. 9

About 200 metres north of this palace is a curious, isolated mudbrick structure which was at first described as a granary, but has now been more plausibly reinterpreted as a ramp leading up to a bridge which crossed the nearby ancient road, similar to the one that spanned the same road 3 kilometres to the south, and connected the Great Palace with the King's House. The northern bridge apparently gave access to the southern end of an enclosure, which is almost totally destroyed, but which probably extended for about 800 metres to the north and contained a complex of buildings comprising another great palace built on terraces along the banks of the Nile. If this was the palace that is represented in the tomb of Mahu, the Chief-of-Police, as the destination to which the royal chariots are returning from a visit to the Great Temple, it would seem that its entrance may have resembled the fortified gatehouse or 'migdol' that is an equally striking feature of the much later mortuary complex of Ramesses III at Medinet Habu. To the east of this Northern Palace at Akhetaten lay substantial mansions in their own grounds, which await further examination, but which appear to have been occupied by members of the royal family, or their most intimate courtiers. The damaged titles and names of Queen Tiye and King Smenkhkarē were found on stone door-jambs from these structures but have since been lost.

About 300 metres beyond the palace compound, with its massive double boundary wall partly surviving on the east, stands the most northerly terminus of Akhetaten in another ruinous complex virtually reduced to little more than a confused ground-plan. The name of Northern Administrative Building has been given by the British excavators to this structure. Here the eastern cliffs curve round in an arc to approach the river, leaving a triangular tract of ground with the roadway that verges the river as its only thoroughfare. The Northern Administrative Building straddled the roadway and probably constituted a massive ornamental gatehouse to regulate entry into Akhetaten, forming a kind of *khan* and customs house for the reception of traders and their goods.

The great straggling site of Akhetaten still awaits complete excavation. Areas to the north and south of the central township have not yet been thoroughly investigated, though new explorations have been made annually since 1977 by the Egypt Exploration Society under the field director, Barry J. Kemp. Sondages have been conducted in selected areas in the hope of elucidating old enigmas and finding fresh evidence or confirming conjectures. A comprehensive archaeological survey has been carried out, and maps prepared on a scale of 1:2000 are to be published shortly, thus providing a tool for further research which has long been desired. Further excavations are envisaged in places which give promise of a satisfactory outcome; but spectacular results are not to be expected. Further progress in our knowledge of this ancient city and its story is more likely to come from the meticulous recovery of what clues still remain, though perhaps only of a very modest nature, rather than from any sensational discoveries.

Nearly a century of archaeological exploration has revealed that the design of Akhetaten, built from scratch on a virgin site and extending for about 10 kilometres, was largely conditioned by the nature of the terrain on which it stood. The wadis that score the plain in an east–west direction become charged with storm-water from tempests over the high desert on the east about once in fifteen years. These flash torrents are often severe enough to do considerable damage to ancient and modern structures. They have also determined the division of the long straggling town into separate units between the wadis – the northern town with its administrative building and palace complexes, the northern suburb, the central city and the southern suburb. The central city, *Fig. 7* with its great official buildings and offices, was evidently the 'Island Exalted in Jubilees' referred to by Akhenaten in his Boundary Stelae, and not an island in the river. It appears to have been, in fact, purely an administrative centre which was probably deserted at night, apart from concierges and police patrols. Its day population of clerks, priests and artisans probably commuted to it along subsidiary roads from the northern and southern suburbs. The high officials whose duties brought them to one of the palaces, temples or offices of the centre, would reach it from their mansions in the southern environs. Such great residences stood in extensive grounds, surrounded by the lesser habitations of ministrants who provided them with goods and services.

The ruined buildings for the most part survive only within a few feet from the ground, but their mudbrick is of a special kind owing to the lack of suitable deposits of alluvium along the eastern bank at this point. It consists largely of the local limestone pebbles and marl which can be bound together by water to form a sort of concrete brick. This, however, decays in time releasing the limestone chips and particles which are so prominent on the surface of the ancient ruins at Amarna. Despite their extreme dilapidation, and their complete absence of wooden fittings such as columns and doors, the domestic buildings have yielded up a wealth of information about the ground-plans, design and decoration of the Egyptian house at this period. Stone fittings,

thresholds, window grilles, door-jambs, lintels, tables, stools and even a lavatory seat have been recovered; roofing materials and wall-paintings have survived in part, though wood has suffered from the ravages of the white ant.

Pl. 24
A feature of all such houses was the shrine in one of the principal rooms in the form of a false door with red-painted jambs, and a niche for a stela showing *Pls. 58, 60* the royal family engaged in some cultic activity. Similar religious foci have been found in ancient houses elsewhere, at Deir el Medina for instance, *Pls. 20, 21, 72* dedicated to the worship of major and minor divinities, or the family ancestor, but only at Akhetaten was it the king and queen with one or more of their daughters who were so adored. In one case at least, in the official residence of Pinhasy the Chief Servitor of the Aten, this domestic cult was observed in an independent hypaethral chapel within the central hall. Similar shrines, greatly damaged of course, are found in the gardens of other mansions, sheltering stelae or statues of the royal family, now reduced to mere fragments.

It was in the vicinity of Pinhasy's private residence in the southern suburb that a damaged stela was found which showed the figures of a royal pair, seated on their thrones before an altar loaded with food and flowers beneath the rays of the Aten. The relief, however, differed from similar examples found at Amarna in representing the old king, Amenophis III, and his chief queen,

10 Chariot-drive from a palace to the Great Temple at Amarna, Akhenaten leading with an armed escort of out-runners, and a following of Nefertiti, courtiers, princesses and ladies-in-waiting.

Tiye. Such a memorial of the older generation of rulers, apparently represented as living persons, gave rise to the belief in the minds of Griffith and other scholars that Amenophis III and Tiye had actually resided at Akhetaten until well into the reign of their son, to judge from the late form of the name of the Aten. The red-painted niches with yellow panels inscribed with hymns to the Aten and figures of the royal family making offerings became more intelligible in their design and purpose as the great mansions were excavated, and more fragments came to light of the architectural features that had puzzled Petrie.

Pl. 26

While the mounds of decaying mudbrick were prominent at Amarna, there was little to see of the great stone-built monuments that must also have been erected on such a capital site. The Great Temple of the Aten within its enormous compound was a devastated area. While a fair proportion of the mudbrick entrance pylon of the Mansion of the Aten was still visible, the stonework of the temple was almost entirely missing. It was obvious from the start of excavations that the buildings had been deliberately robbed of all stone, and that masons must have squatted in the town for a long time removing worked stone, right down to the foundations, for use elsewhere. Rough huts, for instance, with ovens and furnaces, had been run up within the walls of the Northern Palace and occupied by workmen concerned with this work of demolition. The dismantling of stone walls was not pursued, of course, without severe damage to the edges of the individual blocks and the plaster rendering between them. Inlays of polychrome faience and coloured hard stones set into the decoration fell out under such treatment and were trodden into the trenches at the foundation level, where reliefs used as models for the craftsmen to copy in the original construction had also been abandoned.

Pls. 9, 10

Pls. 1, 25

Another mystery that at first baffled the modern excavators was the absence of second-class cemeteries of a kind which exist in every ancient town-site in Egypt. The tombs of the high officials located in the southern foothills and the northern cliffs on the eastern margins of the city had been known for many years, but the burial grounds of the less affluent, though not impoverished dead, defied discovery despite the best endeavours of expert diggers, not to mention casual ransackers among the local population. Opinion has now hardened into the belief that any such burials made at Akhetaten during the lifetime of the city were taken up and removed to family burial grounds elsewhere when it was abandoned. On the other hand, rough burials of poor persons, particularly young children, have been found in stray locations among the ruins, but very few can be dated with much certainty and may have been later interments brought over from habitations on the west bank.

Most cities of any distinction, even in the ancient world, boasted a certain focal point or spatial feature that elevated them to a position of esteem and prestige in the eyes of their rulers and inhabitants, such as a palace, temple, acropolis, stoa or forum. A landmark of this character was not lacking at Amarna and has been remarked by successive travellers over the years, despite the fact that much of it lies beneath the cultivation. This is a great roadway 40 metres wide that sweeps from the Northern Palace area, with slight changes of course so as to follow the line of the river, until it makes an abrupt dog-leg between two buildings still awaiting further examination beneath mounds of concealing sand, at the southern end of the Great Official Palace. This road, the modern Sikket es Sultan (Kingsway), forms a great processional way for much of its length between the north and south bridges that once spanned it. As all the great buildings were orientated in relation to it, the conclusion emerges that it was planned as such from the beginning, and not as the result of some organic development. So wide a thoroughfare, stretched like the chord of an arc, suggests a course designed for chariots rather than by, say, the wayward wanderings of a pack-ass, and it may well be the first structure to be established at Amarna, running from the site of Stela X on the northern headland to Stela J on the southern boundary, and was that 'goodly road' that Akhenaten took at the foundation ceremonies. A town built around a processional chariot-way must have been a novelty in Egypt and the significance of this innovation will require fuller assessment later (see Chapter 12).

Pl. 2

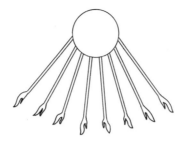

CHAPTER 7
The Karnak Talatat

Until the discovery of the cuneiform tablets at Amarna in 1887, few Nile travellers found any incentive to brave the rigours of such a dilapidated site. The violent winds that blew around the bluffs and pinnacles of the massive Gebel Abu Foda often discouraged the crews of their *dahabiyahs* from doing more than holding their course for the favoured sites upstream as happened, for instance, to Miss Amelia Edwards, the intrepid founder of the Egypt Exploration Fund, during her momentous journey in 1873. There was always the inducement to reach Thebes, 370 kilometres further south, the main tourist centre of the Valley, and the ancient capital of Upper Egypt. Unlike Amarna, the villages here on the eastern shore of the Nile were prosperous, and together with the vast necropoleis on the opposite bank, had a long, if interrupted, tradition of welcoming tourists since Roman days. The genial winter climate, the brilliant sunshine and the wealth of ancient remains attracted visitors throughout the season. The temple ruins at Karnak and Luxor were still extensive and awesome. Among sites on the western bank, at Qurna and the Valley of the Kings, at Deir el Bahri and Medinet Habu, all bathed in the luminous desert air, visitors found themselves no less 'among wonders'.

Thebes owed its importance to the favour of great pharaohs: the Montuhoteps, the Ammenemes and the Sesotris who comprised the Middle Kingdom rulers originating from the region. The shrines which they raised to their city gods, who were thought to have promoted their power and prosperity, were eclipsed only by the palaces and huge temples which the wealthier pharaohs of the New Kingdom built at Thebes in subsequent periods. These later kings greatly increased the importance of their birth-place by cutting their splendid tombs in a wild ravine on the desert margin of the western bank, the Valley of the Kings, and building their attendant mortuary temples a mile away in a row on the edge of the cultivation, where they were overlooked by the decorated tomb-chapels of their relatives and officials hewn into the adjacent hills.

With the rise in the fortunes of Thebes, the local gods also increased in power and wealth. Thus Montu, the god who was the *genius loci* of Armant on

Fig. 14

the western bank, about 11 kilometres south of Luxor, arose to predominance in the whole of the Thebaid where he was worshipped as incarnate in a falcon wearing a solar disk with uraei and twin plumes on his vertex. He fought the enemies of the sun-god and promoted the victories of kings, particularly in a warlike age such as the Eleventh Dynasty. But he steadily lost influence during the Twelfth Dynasty to Amun, the local god of Karnak, who became of paramount importance in the Eighteenth Dynasty, assuming the identity of the primal king, the sun-god Rē-Herakhte, taking his place in the solar bark, traversing the sky-realms from dawn to sunset and contending with the cloud-demon Apophis. Thebes became less the pharaonic residence than the holy city of Amun, the King of the Gods, and a focus of pilgrimages. These festivals of Amun were sufficiently important to bring rulers from their palaces at Memphis, Miwer and other centres to attend the joyous ceremonies at Thebes. Thus the feast of Opet during which Amun, his consort Mut, and their offspring Khons, were towed in their resplendent barks along the canal from Karnak to Luxor, was celebrated amid music, dancing, flowers and great rejoicing during the second month of Inundation. This was an occasion when the god gave oracular judgments on human affairs that were not otherwise capable of resolution, such as the recognition of a new king as legitimate and enjoying the right to rule, as happened to Tuthmosis III and Haremhab at their accessions.

The west bank of Thebes was equally under the sovereignty of Amun, though he also shared his power with the complex female divinity Hathor, originally the mother of the sky-god Horus, and therefore of the king, sometimes manifest as a vast cow, dappled with stars and spanning the vault of heaven. Among other attributes, she was the goddess of desert regions and foreign places and could prevail over the wastes of the Theban necropoleis.

Pl. 51

Amun on the west bank had first emerged at the creation of the world as a primaeval snake Kneph residing in a subterranean cavern at Medinet Habu. In this aspect he was a chthonic power and his annual feast, the Feast of the Valley, in a bay of the cliffs at Deir el Bahri, involved most of the denizens of Thebes both living and dead. Another festival of this primaeval serpent-ancestor of Amun, who had existed in Chaos at Medinet Habu, was held every ten years when the inhabitants of the world of the living and that of the dead were reunited in a communion of offering, worshipping and feasting. Around Amun was thus woven an intricate web of beliefs embracing the idea of a heavenly king, the omnipotent god of light and air in Karnak, and a chthonic power from the mysterious hidden world of the Theban necropoleis. So influential was this mortuary cult of Amun that it found no place for Osiris, the god *par excellence* of death and resurrection, until almost the last years of Dynastic Egypt.

The visitors to Luxor, Karnak and Qurna during the halcyon years of the last century were overawed by the ruined monuments of this great past that mostly reflected the grandiose architecture of the Ramesside kings of the Nineteenth and Twentieth Dynasties. The Eighteenth Dynasty was hardly in evidence in the greatly dilapidated pylons at Karnak and in the Festival Temple of Tuthmosis III on the same site, or in the vanished constructions of Amenophis III at Karnak, Ashru and Kom el Heitan. If the 'Disk Worshippers' had raised any monuments in Thebes, nothing would then have been visible to the average tourist blind to all but the flamboyance of 'Ramesses the Great' and his imitators. But there were among such visitors, one or two travellers who did not fail to spot the exceptional piece lying unremarked amid the debris strewn on the ruined sites. As early as the forties of the last century, Prisse d'Avennes and Richard Lepsius had noted loose blocks lying on the open ground on the south side of the Great Temple of Amun at Karnak near the Ninth and Tenth Pylons. These blocks were decorated with *Pl. 27* representations of the sun-god Rē-Herakhte, not as a radiant sun-disk, but in his old traditional aspect of a falcon-headed man. His name, however, was in that expanded form that was familiar to them from its appearance at Amarna, though at Karnak it was not always enclosed in two cartouches. The figure of the king who appeared with him also bore the prenomen Neferkheperurē, the same as that of Akhenaten at Amarna; but his nomen was different, Amenophis, with an epithet, 'Divine Ruler of Thebes', thus distinguishing him from his predecessor, Amenophis III. For this reason scholars were apt to call him in this guise Amenophis IV.

The reliefs seen by Lepsius, one of which was taken back to Berlin, were carved on the faces of large sandstone blocks of a kind that were characteristic of the massive masonry of Amenophis III. They were also drawn and carved in the style of that king, with delicate low relief, classical proportions and impeccable technique, entirely lacking the distortions of the Amarna monuments. The view gained ground, therefore, that such reliefs came from buildings which had been erected by Amenophis IV at Karnak during his first months of rule in the traditional style of his father's reign, before he had changed his name to Akhenaten, and moved the seat of government to Amarna. We may here anticipate later conclusions by disclosing that recent research suggests that the blocks came from the nearby southern gateway to the *Pl. 28* precincts of Amun at Karnak, planned by Amenophis III and decorated under Amenophis IV. They were subsequently demolished and used as fill in the Ninth and Tenth Pylons, and in the repair of the adjacent Festival Temple of Amenophis II.

But in addition to such substantial masonry, which had apparently fallen from the crumbling pylons, other isolated blocks of a much smaller size, about

Pls. 29–32 a cubit long (0.5 metres), half a cubit high and nearly as much thick, could be glimpsed, built into the interiors of other ruined structures. Most of these attracted attention for the peculiar nature of their decoration, since although they were also of sandstone, they were carved in sunk relief in the characteristically distorted style of the early monuments at Amarna; and on them, too, the many-armed disk of the Aten did indeed appear. Most of these blocks came to view as ruins, were tidied up and the ancient disintegrating masonry consolidated. The habit grew of referring to such blocks as 'talatat', an Arabic word of disputed meaning which, however, has become established not only in popular parlance among the workmen who handle them at Karnak, but also in the jargon of the scholars who study them.

From the eighties of the last century talatat were brought to light in a spasmodic flow as official campaigns were mounted to clean up the ruins at Thebes and strengthen their foundations. At Karnak, not only was the ground around the Ninth and Tenth Pylons cleared and examined in some detail, but also the tottering towers of the pylons themselves were partly consolidated. Such operations yielded their quota of talatat and large architraves and other massive elements bearing the names of Amenophis IV and his immediate successors. Much of this stonework bore the familiar marks of desecration. It was mostly fragmentary, the names and features of its original owners often hacked out and their inscriptions obliterated.

The Temple of Luxor, a mile to the south, was also cleaned and reinforced during the campaign of restoration, during which operation very many talatat were recovered, most of them from the interior of the great pylon of Ramesses II. Excavations at Medamud, to the north of Luxor, retrieved additional hundreds of talatat, and it became evident to archaeologists that the temple, or temples, that Amenophis IV had erected on Theban soil during his reign had not entirely vanished but had been demolished and used in the substructures of later buildings in the vicinity.

As the magazines at Karnak and Luxor began to fill with hundreds of these rescued blocks, the Antiquities Service conceived the ambitious plan of emptying the sites in which such talatat were known to be located and to essay the task of reconstructing the loose blocks into entire wall-reliefs, if not complete buildings. In this programme, spread over several decades, pylons were dismantled, their reused interior blocks recovered and replaced by new stone and unworked talatat, while their exterior skins were replaced. Other buildings were dismantled and their foundations examined before being consolidated and the superstructures rebuilt. In this way, the Second and Ninth Pylons and the foundations of the Hypostyle Hall at Karnak have rendered up a vast hoard of sculptured blocks, most of them from the temples of Amenophis IV.

15 *Limestone relief excavated by Petrie in 1891, and now in the Louvre; part of a stela (cf. Pls. 26, 58, 60 and 71) found in a private house chapel where the intimate and relaxed life of the royal family was a theme of the domestic cult. This fragment shows the queen in the lap of her husband enthroned in a light garden arbour while their two eldest daughters clamber upon them. The sensitive drawing and carving of the queen's dangling feet were noted by Petrie.*

16 (below) *Plaster cast of a life-size head of Akhenaten excavated in the studio of the master sculptor Djhutmose at Amarna in 1912–13. The head was cast in a two-piece mould, the joint running vertically down the centre line of the diadem, forehead, nose, lips and chin. This feature, and the parietal bulges in front of the ears, reveal that the cast was made from another portrait head of the king wearing the Blue Crown in the naturalistic mode of the later years of the reign.*

17 (right) *Limestone bust of Queen Nefertiti, reinforced in places with plaster, and painted, the left eye missing, also found in the studio of Djhutmose. The artist has elongated the neck to balance the mass of the crown, an idiosyncracy which is found in other studies of the queen, and suggests that this bust, which conforms to none of the ritual requirements of Egyptian sculpture, was a model for the guidance of lesser craftsmen concerned with getting a likeness of the queen in other art-works.*

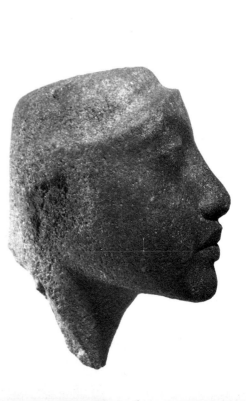

18 *Quartzite head from a composite statue of one of the senior princesses, found in the studio of Djhutmose at Amarna. The gem-hard stone has been handled with consummate skill and finished with a skin-like polish. Below the neck is a tenon for slotting into a limestone body imitating the linen of her dress; and the eyes and brows have been hollowed to receive glass inlays.*

19 *Head of a queen or princess from the same workshop. The unpolished areas of the cheeks and forehead would have been hidden by a close-fitting wig in another colour of stone or faience. But the work is unfinished, perhaps because it was broken at the neck during manufacture and discarded. The portrait has been identified by Rolf Krauss with great probability as that of Kiya (cf. Pl. 37).*

20, 21 *Painted limestone pair-statue of Akhenaten and Nefertiti with a late version of the Aten name painted on the rear of the back-pillar. It doubtless came from a house shrine and was used in the domestic cult at Amarna in place of the more usual ancestor* lares, *or in addition to them, and was abandoned when the city was evacuated.*

22 (above) *View in the mudbrick house of the vizier Nakht in the southern city at Amarna (see Fig. 8) soon after its excavation in 1922, looking south from the central hall to an inner reception room with stone lustration trough and splash-back. The stone bases supporting wooden columns were removed by the owners when Akhetaten was abandoned.*

23 (below) *Site of the House of Correspondence of Pharaoh at Amarna during excavation in 1933. The area where the cuneiform tablets were found is to the right of the picture.*

24 *Restored jambs and façade of the small stone shrine built in the central hall of the official house of Pinhasy as Servitor of the Aten outside the boundary wall of the Great Temple excavated in 1927, and restored in the Cairo Museum. The scene shows the royal pair with their daughter Meritaten offering to the sun-disk bearing the later name of the Aten.*

25 *Sculptor's model in limestone (cf. Pl. 1) carved in sunk relief with distinguishing portraits of two kings, almost certainly Akhenaten on the left and his putative co-regent, Smenkhkarē, on the right. The model, which had doubtless been for the guidance of craftsmen engaged on the royal commissions, had been discarded in a trench where a wall of the Great Temple had been demolished, and came to light during the excavations of 1933.*

26 *A painted limestone stela excavated in 1924 in the ruins of the private residence of Pinhasy in central Amarna, showing Amenophis III and Queen Tiye seated together on thrones spread with rugs before altars loaded with food and flowers, and positioned beneath the rays of the Aten bearing the late version of its name. The prenomen of the king is here repeated in place of his nomen, thus avoiding the name Amun in the city of the Aten. The royal pair are shown in the costume of the living and the mutual embrace of any husband and wife. Some scholars, however, have maintained that because of the late date in the reign of Akhenaten, this icon must represent a posthumous cult of the old king, despite the absence of any epithet to show that he is no longer alive.*

During the inter-war years over 40,000 talatat, sculptured in sunk relief and often bearing traces of brilliant colour, as well as a rather greater number of plain blocks of similar size, were recovered by the Antiquities Service under their inspectors, Maurice Pillet and Henri Chevrier. These retrievals were stored in open magazines on the south side of the temple of Amun at Karnak, where in their jumbled parts reposing on wooden racks, like so many pieces of several huge jigsaw puzzles, they invited solution.

The hope of the Antiquities Service that they would respond to the solver's manipulations, proved forlorn. Unlike a jigsaw puzzle, the various pieces did not interlock. Each sculptured face was originally rectangular or square in shape though the edges had been abraded and lost, together with their plaster pointing, by demolition in antiquity. The piecemeal nature of their discovery, as a result of limited and sporadic excavations, had resulted in a haphazard allocation of blocks among the various magazines, so that talatat from different parts of the site became jumbled together. Moreover, the shortage of funds and lack of an adequate staff of specialists had the consequence that records were not kept as fully as was desirable. It was also clear from the greatly ruined condition of several of the secondary locations, particularly the pylons, that many of the talatat that comprised their fill had been irretrievably lost. Most visiting scholars who saw the talatat in store recoiled in dismay from the prospect of trying to reconstruct in a reasonable span of time any scenes from thousands of fragments of relief that were in confusing disorder. Sometimes an isolated block would yield a significant inscription or part of a scene that could be copied or photographed and perhaps published. But, for the most part, the hoard languished on its wooden racks in almost total obscurity. The system of storing many of the talatat, as well as the more massive fragments, in the open, resulted in the occasional theft of a block, and its subsequent reappearance, sawn into a slab, in the private and public collections of Europe and America.

In 1965, however, a new dynamic was introduced into the situation. Ray Wingfield Smith, a retired officer in the foreign service of the United States, and a knowledgeable amateur of ancient arts and technology, became interested in the problem of reassembling the talatat, and resolved to do something about it. He succeeded in bringing together, under the auspices of a number of international Egyptologists, the Antiquities Organization of Egypt, the University Museum of Pennsylvania, and IBM, the International Business Machines Corporation, in a determined effort to achieve results. Thanks to his energy and enthusiasm, the Akhenaten Temple Project was inaugurated, largely as an American enterprise funded initially from private sources and the Foreign Currency Program administered by the Smithsonian Institution, although it employed Egyptian and British specialists on its staff. In 1972, after the preliminary phase of the project had been completed, the Canadian scholar,

Donald B. Redford of the University of Toronto, took over the directorship of the enterprise; and from 1975 it was financed by grants from the Killam Program of the Canadian Council and from the Social Sciences and Humanities Research Council of Canada, in addition to contributions from private donors. The scope of the Project has also been widened to include investigations in the field, conducted by a team under Professor Redford at East Karnak, to a very high degree of professional competence.

The procedure adopted by Ray Smith and pursued vigorously by him and his coadjutors over six seasons, involved the photographing to a uniform scale in black and white, and in colour, of each sculptured surface of the talatat, not only in Egypt, but also in those collections elsewhere in which they had come to rest. The particulars of each scene were entered on special punch-cards by expert cataloguers, and included such details as exact dimensions, colours, types and sizes of human figures, measurements of all features intersecting each edge, angles of solar rays, inscriptions, architectural settings and many other particulars, under eighty headings. Such data were fed into an IBM computer, and under its guidance individual photographs could be matched with contiguous possibilities and built up into mosaics. Units so formed could be assembled into complete scenes where no extensive runs of talatat were missing, and sooner than anyone dared to hope, destroyed reliefs of the Aten temples began to emerge from the wreckage of time. The work was done on paper, in the offices of the Project, but if necessary the physical reconstruction of selected reliefs could be undertaken, and in fact an assembly of 283 talatat has been built into a wall in the new Luxor Museum, and shows a coloured relief of offering-bearers and servants at their duties in the temple offices.

This reconstructed portion of a wall, however, is the work of a separate organization, the Franco-Egyptian Centre at Karnak, which has continued the operations of the former Antiquities Service, now the Antiquities Organization of Egypt, on the dismantling and rebuilding of the Ninth Pylon. This undertaking, which was intended to consolidate a dangerously crumbling structure, revealed that layers of talatat had been deposited to form the mass of its towers from the systematic dismantling of three of the buildings of Amenophis IV at the same time as the pylon was being built. For the first time talatat could be retrieved in an orderly fashion to make contiguous scenes, a reversal of the procedure by which they had been taken down from their original walls. Moreover, undecorated blocks, hitherto disregarded, which were more numerous than the sculptured ones but all part of the same shrines, were also recovered by the Centre and stored apart.

Owing to the loss of many talatat in their secondary positions by dilapidation over the centuries, a complete recovery of all the decorative elements of the demolished buildings of Amenophis IV, and their reconstruction, cannot be expected. Nevertheless, it has been possible to reassemble notable scenes, some of them of an unusual character, and to visualize the appearance of others from significant samples. The iconography of the Karnak reliefs can be reconstructed with a fair degree of certitude not only from parallel scenes at Amarna, but also because a few themes are often repeated and one or two critical extracts are sufficient to determine the appearance of whole scenes. But the restoration of the actual buildings which were embellished with such reliefs is an entirely different proposition in the absence of sufficient structural members, architraves, columns, cornices, shafts, jambs, thresholds, lintels and the like. Inscriptions on the talatat are meagre and repetitive, but give the names of half a dozen different buildings at Karnak which were concerned with the cult of the Aten. Unfortunately, such information is not explicit enough to determine whether some of these structures are not divisions of the others. Thus it is known that one building at Karnak, the Rud-menu (*Rwd-mnw-n-itn-r-nhh*, 'Enduring in Monuments of the Aten Forever') also existed at Amarna where it was evidently a part of the Great Temple. Talatat from the Rud-menu were found in the lowest internal courses of the Ninth Pylon, and also in the area of the Luxor Temple.

Similarly, another temple or shrine, 'The Mansion of the Ben-ben' (*Hwt-bn-bn*), which can be identified from its remains, was evidently part of a much larger structure, the Gempaaten (*Gm(t) p3-itn-m-pr-itn*, 'The Aten is found in the Estate of the Aten'). The Mansion of the Ben-ben housed, as the focal point of the rites, some aspect of the Ben-ben stone, the ancient fetish of the sun-cult in Heliopolis. Such a shrine and its staff of choristers and musicians is frequently mentioned in some of the tombs at Amarna, where the owners pray that they may hear eternally the sweet voice of their king in the Mansion of the Ben-ben.

On the other hand another building at Karnak, the Teni-menu (*Tn-mnw-n-itn-r-nhh*, 'Exalted is the Monument of the Aten Forever'), is unknown at Amarna, and its form and function at Karnak are equally obscure. Its talatat were found in the middle layers of the fill of the Ninth Pylon.

Although the reliefs on the talatat, like those in the tombs at Amarna, often show pictures of palaces and temples, they are invariably schematic and incomplete, according to Egyptian ideas of architectural drawing. They convey an impression rather than an explicit plan or elevation, and are of very limited use in trying to reconstitute the proportions and appearance of the ancient temples. Without an actual ground-plan, any reconstruction is apt to be highly conjectural. Unfortunately, it is only too evident that these temples were deliberately razed to the ground and their sites must now lie concealed beneath the remains of later buildings. It is to be suspected, for instance, that the Rud-menu and the Teni-menu originally stood somewhere in the southern quarter

Pls. 65, 66

83

of Karnak in the vicinity of the Ninth Pylon, to which their dismantled talatat were transferred, but the foundations of these two temples have not so far been identified.

The search for the actual sites of the constructions of Amenophis IV at Karnak was, however, facilitated by a fortuitous discovery. In 1925, while a drainage ditch was being dug beyond the eastern boundary of the enclosure wall of the Great Temple of Amun, workmen uncovered a row of fallen *Pls. 33–5* sandstone colossi bearing the name of Amenophis IV, which in the following year became the concern of Henri Chevrier, the chief inspector of antiquities at Karnak. For some twenty-five years he periodically dug the area in the hope of further elucidating this partly revealed colonnade; but although he succeeded in tracing the foundations of a wall and identifying its southwest angle, and in exposing a parallel row of twenty-eight adjacent bases of rough masonry which he interpreted as the pedestals of the fallen colossi, he was disappointed in his ambition. A modern village barred further progress on the west, and elsewhere the obliteration of other vestiges seemed complete.

Nevertheless, the discovery of the remains of this enigmatic monument aroused the liveliest stir amongst Egyptologists. The broken colossi, of which fragments of twenty-five were eventually brought to light, were of a startling character, carved in a bold, assured style, unlike any statues that had been found in Egypt, with their distorted representations of the traditional, idealized, heroic image of the pharaoh. They were hailed by some authorities as 'grotesque', 'appalling' and 'frankly hideous'. Others thought them 'expressionistic', 'vital', 'daring' and 'compelling'. To the French scholar Jacques Vandier, they revealed 'a true grandeur, an expression of an interior life made up of suffering and disillusionment more than joy'. The general opinion, however, was that what had been discovered was the remains of a peristyle *Fig. 24* court in the Gempaaten, a temple erected by Amenophis IV and known to have been built at Karnak from references to it in a quarry at Gebel es Silsila, on the talatat themselves, as well as in the tomb of the vizier Ramose at Western Thebes. A rival view, however, claimed that the ruins were all that survived of a palace that the king must have built at Thebes, and the balcony of which was *cf. Fig. 12* represented in the same tomb of Ramose.

In the season of 1975 the Akhenaten Temple Project began excavating at East Karnak beyond the Gate of Nectanebo I in the eastern boundary wall of the Great Temple of Amun where Henri Chevrier had toiled sporadically from 1925 to 1952. Using the most exacting and meticulous techniques upon a heavily devastated and churned-up site, the Canadian Expedition have succeeded in extracting a great deal of information from a most unpromising locale. They have established beyond any doubt that the remains are those of the Gempaaten, and have been able to define some of its archaeological features

84

and an unusual scheme of decoration, even though its ground-plan has not yet emerged except to a very limited extent.

The temples of the Aten at Karnak will be considered more fully later, here it must suffice to summarize the conclusions of the Project as a result of their careful investigations which are still in progress.

The Gempaaten was the largest of the group: its talatat, uncovered mostly in the foundations of the Hypostyle Hall and the interiors of the Second and Ninth Pylons, outnumber those from any other structure. It was evidently orientated on the north side of the west–east axis of the main temple of Amun, and it is presumed that in conformity with Egyptian ideas of architectural symmetry, a corresponding building lay on the south side, although it has not so far been traced. This is probably the Royal Palace which is mentioned in inscriptions as being within the Gempaaten. The earliest of the Aten temples to be erected at Karnak was apparently the Gempaaten, to judge from the style and treatment of the reliefs, and the iconography of the growing family of Amenophis IV and Queen Nefertiti. The Rud-menu and the Teni-menu followed soon afterwards and the Mansion of the Ben-ben towards the end of the fourth regnal year. After the fifth year when the king changed his name to Akhenaten, and the new city of Akhetaten began to take shape, no further building was undertaken at Thebes during his reign.

It is clear that the dismantling of the Aten temples at Karnak was the work of King Haremhab some fifteen years or more after the death of Akhenaten, since he was responsible for laying the foundations of the Hypostyle Hall of the temple of Amun west of the Third Pylon, and those of the Second Pylon at its proximal end. He also raised the Ninth and Tenth Pylons on the processional way on the south side of Karnak. But it is evident from the state of several of the talatat that some of the scenes had been vandalized before the demolition began, particularly the figures, faces and names of Amenophis IV and Nefertiti. The destruction of the Aten temples was very thorough and a large stock of talatat was left over from Haremhab's demolitions to be used in the buildings of later kings at Luxor, Medamud and elsewhere in the neighbourhood.

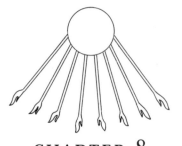

CHAPTER 8

The Other Monuments

The excavation at Karnak of talatat from the early buildings of Amenophis IV, had a parallel find elsewhere. In 1939, during their seventh season at Hermopolis, near modern Ashmunein on the west bank opposite Amarna, the Expedition of the Pelizaeus Museum of Hildesheim made an unexpected discovery. In the last days of their campaign they uncovered layers of talatat in the foundations of a greatly ruined pylon in the temple built there by Ramesses II. The blocks were retrieved in such profusion that there was no room to store them in the Expedition's magazine, nor was there time to photograph them all, nor to measure and copy their scenes and inscriptions before striking camp. The excavators had no option, therefore, but to bury them on the site in the expectation of dealing with them the next season. The German archaeologists at Hermopolis were no more fortunate than their predecessors at Amarna: war broke out a few months later, and they never returned to their dig.

During the war, supervision on archaeological sites became slack, and it was not long before local pilferers dug up the buried blocks, and for good measure another deposit of similar talatat in the foundations of the other tower of the ruined pylon. About 1942, the blocks, now sawn into slabs for ease of handling, some partially restored in plaster and tricked out with modern watercolour paint, began to appear in the art market. By the end of the war almost all of the plunder had vanished, to reappear in America, dispersed among private and public collections.

Pls. 36, 37   The Hermopolite talatat, however, differed from the Karnak examples in several particulars. While they, too, were carved in sunk relief, they were in *Pls. 40, 41*   limestone which was finer and more compact than the sandstone of the Karnak talatat. The carving too was less bold and experimental, and more delicate and *Pls. 59, 61*   subtle, like the later style of the Amarna tomb reliefs. It was clear, in fact, from some of the inscriptions, that these blocks had come from destroyed temples, and perhaps palaces, at Amarna. They represented the most sophisticated development of the Amarna style, whereas the sandstone talatat revealed the first essays in the new revolutionary art of the period. Unlike their Karnak counterparts, however, few if any fitted on to contiguous blocks, and it was evident that they had been reused at Hermopolis by a system of dismantling which was different from that employed at Karnak. Whereas the Karnak talatat had been taken down and re-employed in a continuous operation, the tops of walls, for instance, forming the lower courses of fill, and the foundations appearing among the uppermost courses, the Amarna talatat had been reused at random. The reason for this difference in building technique is doubtless a matter of logistics. The Amarna blocks had to be taken by ship across the river to Hermopolis, and during the loading, unloading and reallocation of blocks, cargoes probably got out of sequence, and a thorough mix-up of the various consignments resulted. Moreover, talatat were sent from Amarna to other sites in the region, to Asyut and even as far south as Abydos. An orderly removal of blocks cannot be envisaged, but rather the creation of a vast dump of spoil on the quays of the eastern bank at Amarna for dispersal by boat to other sites in Egypt. Furthermore, the severe denudation of the Ramesside pylon at Hermopolis suggests that most of its fill has long ago disappeared into the furnaces of the local lime-burners.

While the scenes from the Hermopolite talatat lack the large compositions that have been recovered in many of the Karnak examples, and are in a more restrained and traditional style, they also show some remarkable innovations in the development of ancient art. Unusual and attractive representations of the activities of the royal family are found, and new personalities appear. The princesses are seen in a more mature stage of development and a few of the inscriptions have cast a somewhat flickering and lurid light on the history of the last years of the reign and the actors in the drama. Other scenes are of enigmatic import largely because they are mere samples of novel compositions which have not survived except for one or two examples in the following reign. The proper recovery of these talatat has been frustrated in modern times by unhappy strokes of fate; but the German scholars, particularly Günther Roeder and Rainer Hanke, have been assiduous in tracking down the present location of the scattered blocks, and in publishing them worthily.

The stray blocks found at Asyut and Abydos appear to have come from the same sources at Akhetaten, but other limestone reliefs which have been dug up on various sites in the Nile Delta apparently originated in demolished temples in Lower Egypt, especially at Memphis and Heliopolis. Monuments of the reign have been discovered on sites at various points in Egypt. Apart from the city of Gematen which was established by Amenophis IV at Kawa in Nubia, between the Third and Fourth Cataracts of the Nile, temples or shrines dedicated to the Aten appear to have been founded elsewhere, evidently at towns such as Hierakonpolis and Balamun, dedicated to falcon-gods identified with Rē-Herakhte. These sites, however, have yielded up little more than mere vestiges.

Monuments of greater significance, since they refer to the king's building enterprises, are found in Upper Egypt where there was a great burst of activity in the sandstone and granite quarries from the first months of the reign. This industry continued unabated for the next five years when the limestones of Middle Egypt were exploited for the building of the new capital at Amarna. High officials were dispatched to Gebel es Silsila and Aswan to direct operations for securing good stone immediately in ample quantities. Two of them, a certain Iby and the chief of the quarrymen, Neferrenpit, erected memorial stelae on the rocks near the Upper Egyptian village of Zarnikh, on the east bank almost opposite to Esna. These are dedicated to Nekhebet and Amun-rē as the gods of Upper Egypt and are wholly in the style of the previous reign. Despite the great damage they have suffered, the early name of the Aten, not enclosed in cartouches, can be made out, and is almost the only indication that they date to the reign of Amenophis IV.

But the most important memorial of this earliest phase of the reign is the great stela, about 4 metres high, that is carved in the cliffs north of the quarries at Gebel es Silsila. It is also in the orthodox style and iconography of his father's reign, and shows Amenophis IV wearing the White Crown of Upper Egypt, making an offering to the King of the Gods, Amun-rē, both standing beneath the winged solar-disk of Rē-Herakhte. The surface has been much damaged, at a later period in the reign, by agents anxious to suppress all references to Amun, and again later still by traditionalists no less eager to expunge the vestiges of the heretical king. Nevertheless, the text can be restored, and gives the names and titles of the king in their earliest forms, denoting him as 'The Chief Prophet of Rē-Herakhte Rejoicing in the Horizon in his Aspect of the Light which is in the Aten', another early appearance of the didactic name that was soon to be enclosed within two double-bordered cartouches. The other god commemorated is Amun-rē in his solar aspect, as Lord of the Heavens and the Ruler of Eternity, thus emphasizing his dominion over the world of the dead as well as the living. Apart from this brief nod in the direction of tradition, the declaration is concerned with:

... the first time of His Majesty's giving command to the Master of Works ... to undertake all constructions from one end of the country to the other; and to the commanders of the soldiery for mustering a large corvée in order to hew sandstone for making the great Ben-ben of Rē-Herakhte in his Aspect of the Light which is in the Aten, in Karnak. Verily, the nobles, the courtiers and the leaders of the superintendents [will act] as the controllers of the labour force in transporting the stone blocks.

The fact that the stela is undated, and the mention of a 'first time', presumably indicate the monument commemorates the innovative decree of the king's reign. The old name for Karnak, 'Select of Places', is retained, though its other version, soon to oust it from favour, 'the Heliopolis of the South', is already present in the king's Golden Horus name. The Ben-ben is to be installed at Karnak in a building evidently not yet named but shortly to be called 'the Mansion of the Ben-ben'. The sandstone is presumably for this building and not for the Ben-ben itself, which in the inscription is determined by the picture of an obelisk, and not the pyramidion at its summit. An obelisk sufficiently high to be called 'great' could hardly have been made of sandstone which would have fractured under the strains of erection and must have been of a hard stone, granite or quartzite, perhaps sheathed in gold. A fragment of a granite obelisk of Amenophis IV has been found at the Tenth Pylon at Karnak, and another has been unearthed in the First Court but whether from the same monument is not disclosed. An excised portion of the text on the stela refers to a Master of Works who is made responsible for all the new constructions of the king, and the most likely candidate for this office is May, whose tomb at Amarna (No. 14) shows him to have been the Superintendent of All the Works of the King, and in addition to other duties, the Scribe of the Elite Troops and the Commander of the Soldiery of the King, offices that would have put him in charge of the labour-corps. Most of the inscriptions referring to the name and titles of May in his tomb have also been erased, evidence of a vindictiveness attributed to his fall from royal favour. But what this stela most vividly discloses is that from the first days of the new reign the populace of Egypt, the peasantry, workmen and nobility, were to be united in a great and pious undertaking, a labour of devotion to the king's new god.

Other monuments of the reign concern the king less than the king's men, and of these officials two have left memorials of their time in their tombs at Thebes. The most important is the southern vizier and Mayor of Thebes, Ramose, a member of the influential family which included not only his older half-brother, Amenophis, the High Steward of Amenophis III in Memphis, but also a greatly distinguished relative, Amenophis-son-of-Hapu, the favourite of Amenophis III. The tomb of Ramose (No. 55), once known as Stuart's Tomb after the quixotic Irish MP, Villiers Stuart, who in the eighties of the last century first brought it to general notice, was restored by Sir Robert Mond in the late twenties and is now one of the showplaces of the Theban necropolis. The exquisite reliefs with which the eastern wall of its great columned hall is adorned, show Ramose and his near-relations in all the perfection of immortals, not a hair out of place, their transcendental beauty purged of all earthly blemish. That they are transfigured is evident from the epithet 'justified' (or 'deceased') which is attached to all their names since they exist with the vizier himself in an eternal heyday, and no longer in the world of the living, even though he had in some instances pre-deceased them.

11 Copy in line of a relief in the tomb of the vizier Ramose at Thebes, showing Amenophis IV newly installed under the royal baldachin with the goddess Maet presenting a good-wish symbol of an eternity of rule.

The dominant feature of this sculptured hall, however, is the equipoise of two reliefs on either side of a central doorway which pierces the opposite wall.

Fig. 11   On the left is a scene carved in the classic style of the preceding reign showing the young King Amenophis IV enthroned under a baldachin and receiving the vizier at his advent. On the right is an entirely new icon of Amenophis IV, and his chief queen Nefertiti, at the Window of Appearance in the palace within the Gempaaten, honouring Ramose by bestowing *shebu* collars and other golden awards upon him. This is the first appearance of an icon which was to have great prominence in the tombs of similar functionaries at Amarna. In contrast

Fig. 12   to the scene on the left-hand half of the wall, the Award of Collars is represented in the style of the revolutionary art of the Karnak talatat, albeit the sculptor's chisel seems to have followed the drawing of a draughtsman already versed in the new mannerism, but exercising the restraints of an artist of traditional outlook. The tomb of Ramose was unfinished at his death, or disappearance from the scene, and the vizier Nakht replaced him at Amarna. But more has to be said later about the wall-reliefs and drawings of this important tomb.

Another Theban tomb that belongs to the same transitional period is that of the Steward and King's Cupbearer, Parennefer, who had another tomb at Amarna (No. 7) whither he had followed his king. His tomb, No. 188 in the Khokha area of the Theban necropolis, is also sculpted with scenes in relief and

12 *Copy in line of a relief in the tomb of the vizier Ramose, with the royal pair on the palace balcony in the Gempaaten at Karnak bestowing golden gifts upon the tomb owner.*

others finished off in paint. All have been badly damaged, and his name carefully excised, but close scrutiny has succeeded in deciphering it. Among pictures of traditional design in the style prevailing towards the end of the previous reign, such as scenes of the grain and fruit harvest, and the presentation of temple-staves at the inauguration of the new king, the owner appears before the royal baldachin to be rewarded with the gold *shebu* collar of honour. There are other details which show that a new iconography is being explored: but instead of the Window of Appearance, the venue of the Ceremony of Awards is the royal baldachin with its canopy penetrated by the rays of the Aten which fall upon the royal pair beneath. These are Amenophis IV and Queen Nefertiti, but as yet no infant princess is in evidence.

Amenophis IV appears in scenes within a third tomb nearby, that of Kheruef (No. 192) who was a Royal Scribe and First Herald of King Amenophis III. In the later years of his career, Kheruef was appointed the Steward of Queen Tiye in the Estate of Amun, and presumably therefore discharged his duties at Thebes. The tomb he prepared in the Asasif area of the necropolis is unfinished, and in a great state of disrepair through the collapse of the rock, and the spiteful desecration inflicted upon the figure of the owner, as well as on some of the texts; yet it contains unique records of events in the first and third jubilees of Amenophis III, carved in low relief, which is arguably the

cf. Pl. 50

finest of all such decoration in the tombs of this period.

Amenophis IV is shown in scenes at the entrance to the tomb making offerings to his parents, and with his mother offering wine to Rē-Herakhte and other solar gods. He also appears in the same guise with his mother on the outer lintel of the doorway that leads into the first columned hall beyond the large open court which is such an unusual feature of the tomb. The reliefs, both at the forepart and rear quarters of the decorated chambers, have been completely carved and painted, and were evidently among the first scenes to be finished in the tomb: yet they are designed and carved in the orthodox style and proportions of the sculptures of the preceding reign of Amenophis III, and show nothing of the distortions of the Karnak talatat. Amenophis IV, too, appears alone without his consort Queen Nefertiti who is so prominent in the Karnak scenes, and in such early icons as those of Tombs 188 and 55 already mentioned. His presence here, accompanied by his mother but not by his chief wife, has been interpreted, therefore, as showing that his youthful figure represents him in his earliest years on the throne, or even as a co-regent to his father, before his marriage to Nefertiti and the eruption of the religious and artistic revolution that he promoted. Further comment on this must be reserved until later.

Fig. 13

The penultimate monument in this group is a great stela, surely too elaborate to be described as a graffito, carved on a giant granite boulder below the Cataract Hotel on the eastern river bank at Aswan. The relief is virtually invisible except at certain times of the day when the sunlight falls at a raking angle and shows, under a common sky-sign which forms its upper border, an equipoise of two Masters of Works and Chief Sculptors, Men who served Amenophis III on the right, and his son Bek who served Akhenaten on the left. Both officials are shown on a diminutive scale, dressed in festal garb with gold collars of honour, worshipping their kings. Men offers at a triple altar before a colossal statue of Amenophis III which bears the name 'King of Kings, Lord of Might'. The statue not only acts as a substitute for the presence of the king, but evidently represents one of his notable colossi which Men extracted and fashioned in the quarry of the Red Mountain near Heliopolis.

In the other half of the scene, Bek adores Akhenaten who burns incense at an altar below the radiant Aten which is said to be in the Great Temple at Akhetaten. The figure of the king, his names, and those of the Aten have been expunged from the relief. The effigy of Amenophis III, on the other hand, is intact but his prenomen is repeated in place of his nomen, thus avoiding the mention of his name compounded with the proscribed Amun. The titles given

13 The stela of Bek and Men at Aswan.

to the Aten in this relief show that it was carved about the ninth year of the reign of Akhenaten, when Bek was evidently still alive and probably undertook the cutting of the double scene on behalf of his father as well as himself.

Adjacent to this stela is another and similar graffito, unfortunately more heavily damaged, which when intact would have shown Amenophis IV censing Rē-Herakhte, rejoicing on the Horizon in the Aspect of the Light which is in *cf. Pl. 27* the Aten, represented not as a radiant disk but as a falcon-headed man. The cartouches of the god are not accompanied by titles, and they thus belong to the earliest months of the reign. The name of the official responsible for this graffito has evidently been obliterated together with the figure of the king and part of the inscription; but it is not too daring to suggest that it may have been Bek himself in the first days of the new reign when he had doubtless come to Aswan to superintend the cutting of granite monuments for the Mansion of the Ben-ben, mentioned in the stela at Gebel es Silsila, and chose this same location eight years later to record another stage in the progress of the mighty works of the Aten cult.

On the larger stela, Bek describes himself as 'the apprentice whom His Majesty instructed', and this is usually taken to mean that he was responsible for the 'deplorable' colossi at Karnak which no sculptor brought up in the idealistic concept of pharaonic portraiture would have dared to produce without the sanction of his king. Bek also gives the name of his mother as Roy of Heliopolis in the North, and it is probably from this site that an unusual quartzite stela came to light in the eighties of the last century and is now in Berlin. It shows Bek very much in the build and fashion in which he appears in the Aswan relief, with his wife Taheret standing beside him; and again he takes pride in describing himself as 'the apprentice whom His Majesty taught'.

With the stela of Bek, now reposing at Berlin among so many of the sculptures which he and his colleagues designed and executed in their day, we may fittingly conclude our tally of the monuments of Akhenaten which have somehow survived the hand of time and the malice of his detractors.

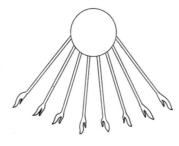

CHAPTER 9

Personalia

Until recently, the mummies of the great pharaohs of the New Kingdom, and their relatives, have received only summary medical attention. The pioneer work was done by the anatomist Grafton Elliot Smith in 1907 when he prepared necroscopic studies for the catalogue of the Cairo Museum which was published four years later. He worked under difficulties, having to limit his investigations to visual examination. The Röntgen-rays (later termed X-rays) were employed in only one case, that of Tuthmosis IV, and did not prove fully effective. Subsequent studies have been made on individual mummies by Armand Ruffer, Douglas Derry, R. G. Harrison and other experts. The most recent survey was made in the 1970s by a team of specialists from the Universities of Alexandria and Michigan in collaboration with the Antiquities Organization of Egypt. Using advanced techniques and specially designed radiographic equipment, they have produced a more accurate X-ray atlas of the royal mummies under somewhat adverse conditions. Other medical studies have been concerned with the recognition of blood-groups from samples of necrotic tissue, in the hopes of establishing close familial relationships. Such investigations are extremely intricate and as yet somewhat experimental, so they have not been carried very far.

Another controversial aspect of such enquiries and one that concerns particularly the historian of ancient Egypt to the exclusion of much else, is the age of the subjects at death. In no case at this period does the record survive of the exact age that a pharaoh attained before he died; and except in one or two cases the length of his reign is also unknown. In this predicament, Egyptologists have to depend upon medical opinion for estimates of the length of time a particular king occupied the throne. On the accuracy of such data depends the chronology not only of Egypt but also of the entire ancient Near East. Unhappily, in late years, the estimates of medical experts have increasingly failed to win the approbation of Egyptologists. Forensic scientists still seem unable to give clear verdicts on the exact age of a cadaver. New techniques, such as those recently perfected by two American doctors of determining the age of a subject at death by measuring the extent of the transformation of the amino-acid L-aspartate into D-aspartate in a tooth, may eventually produce results which can be accepted with confidence. At the moment such trust does not prevail: and because the recent estimates of the Alexandria-Michigan team have so far failed to convince the Egyptologist, he is now obliged to question the reliability of the individual identification of the mummies made in antiquity.

The royal mummies were ruthlessly plundered, and badly damaged in the process, at the end of the New Kingdom. The necropoleis officials concerned with putting their stripped and broken bodies into some kind of order, and writing their names on their rebandaged remains before reburying them, may not always have correctly identified the human wreckage when all possessions, including their coffins, had been stolen or destroyed. It is clear in one or two cases no evidence survived, and the anonymous bodies were left unwrapped and unidentified in the two mass-burials which contained the royal corpses. In the seventies of the last century, one of these caches was discovered by the Abd er Rassul family in the tomb of Queen Inhapi at Deir el Bahri, but not disclosed to the authorities until 1881. The other repository was found in the tomb of Amenophis II in the Valley of the Kings in 1898. In these circumstances it is little short of miraculous that the human remains of several members of the family of Akhenaten should have survived and can be recognized without cavil, apart from his father and grandfather, to go no further back among his paternal antecedents. The doyens are his maternal grandparents, Yuya and Tuyu, who were discovered in a modest non-royal tomb (No. 46) in the Valley of the Kings in 1905 by James Quibell working for Theodore M. Davis. Though the tomb had been rifled in antiquity, the opulent funerary furniture was largely intact, and there was no doubt as to the identity of the pair who were found resting among their torn linen wrappings within their nests of coffins. Yuya proved to be a man of striking appearance, fairly tall for an Egyptian, with a large head of wavy white hair, a prominent beaky nose and thick fleshy lips. His unusual physiognomy, and the various spellings of his name, which was probably a pet form of a more orthodox name, induced some earlier Egyptologists to accredit him with a foreign origin. As Yuya was the Commander of the Chariotry, it is not improbable that he may have inherited some Asiatic blood, together with his calling, for Asiatics had had the reputation of being skilled in the government of horses since the incorporation of chariot forces into the Egyptian armies from the beginning of the Eighteenth Dynasty. His wife, Tuyu, was typically Egyptian in appearance and held very important positions in the hierarchy of the gods Amun and Min. Their daughter, Tiye, was the chief wife of Amenophis III, and the mother of Akhenaten, a woman of immense power and influence who has left her mark upon the map of Africa by perpetuating her name in two of its modern toponyms (Chapter 15).

Pl. 39

27 (top) *Sandstone block sculptured in low relief in the style of Amenophis III, from Karnak, brought back to Berlin by the Prussian Expedition in 1845. It shows on the left, Rē-Herakhte as a falcon-headed god wearing on his vertex the Aten or sun-disk encircled by a uraeus. His name is in his earliest didactic form, but not yet enclosed within two cartouches. Facing right is the figure of Amenophis IV making an invocation to the same god.*

28 (above) *A block in the Louvre, of slightly later date, carved in sunk relief, from the same dismantled monument, showing confronted figures of Amenophis IV censing the Aten who is now symbolized as a radiant sun-disk shining upon an altar. The nomen of the king has later been recarved to read Akhenaten in place of Amenophis. There is also an evident attempt to represent the peculiar anatomy of the king, but in a discreet manner.*

29 (left) *Talatat from Karnak, sandstone with traces of red colour, representing Queen Nefertiti wearing the short Nubian wig with a streamer hanging from the nape of the neck. The queen's features have been rendered in a bold angular style perhaps as a foil for the heavier features of the king with his pendulous chin, long nose and fleshy mouth as adopted for his earlier representations.*

32 (above) *Painted sandstone relief, part of a talatat from the Teni-menu monument to the Aten, found dismantled in the middle internal courses of the Ninth Pylon at Karnak. Akhenaten, wearing the* afnet *wig-cover, followed by Nefertiti in a long wig with double plume, elevates different offerings to the Aten. The exaggerated appearance of the king's physique, with a lean jaw, thick lips and wide hips, is characteristic of the artist who designed the reliefs of the king on this structure.*

30, 31 *Sandstone talatat (left) from Karnak of Amenophis IV bearing sceptres and wearing the crown of Lower Egypt, taking part in the Jubilee procession on 'a day of the Red Crown'. He is followed by Nefertiti, also under the rays of the Aten, wearing the tall double plumes on her crown. A retinue of bowing priests and officials follow them.*

An adjacent talatat (far left) shows two of the escorts in the jubilee retinue, wearing military plumes in their hair. They carry staves for clearing the path and guarding the procession.

33–35 *Painted sandstone colossi excavated from the site of the Gempaaten temple at East Karnak between 1926 and 1932 and now in the Cairo Museum; part of a series which had been toppled by breaking them at the knees of their spindle shanks and leaving them where they fell (cf. Fig. 24). Most of them bear the name of Amenophis IV upon their belts and have therefore been identified as representations of the king in a eunuchoid guise, suggesting an endocrine disorder.*

Other opinion claims that they are hypostases of the primal sun-god as 'the mother and father' of creation. A third suggestion tends to the view that the example on the left is of Nefertiti wearing the heavy artificial beard and a close-fitting gown as Tefnut, the daughter of the sun-god. Other statues in the series (e.g. centre and far right*) represent Amenophis IV as Atum, the demiurge in the sun cult, wearing the Double Crown as the First Ruler of the universe, and as Shu the god of the luminous Void, with plumes upon his head (broken in the central example) as the son of the sun-god, and a manifestation of the light that dispelled the darkness at the creation of the universe.*

36 *Scene from a limestone talatat found at Hermopolis, and now in the Brooklyn Museum, of Nefertiti wearing a short curled wig and a diadem with uraeus, kissing the lips of her eldest daughter who must be standing upon her lap (cf. Pl. 60). The block had been subjected to desecration before it was dismantled, for the features of the queen have been hacked out and her name removed from the inscription. The fragment is a rare example, not only in Egyptian sculpture but also in the whole field of antique art, of royalty embracing each other. Such a pose is found only in the Amarna period, when Nefertiti and Akhenaten are shown kissing each other as well as their children.*

37 (right) *Detail from a talatat from Hermopolis, now in Copenhagen, carved with a figure of 'The Favourite' Kiya, wearing a large ear-stud with a short Nubian hairstyle. The pose with the head lightly raised as though she is gazing at an object on high is slightly unusual (cf. Fig. 2 & Pl. 59). The inscription referring to her behind her head has been effaced and altered in favour of the eldest princess, Meritaten, and the wig recut to portray the peculiar coiffure that the princesses affected in the last years of the reign. It is difficult to decide whether it was at the same time, or later, that the eye was obliterated, since all concealing plaster has been lost.*

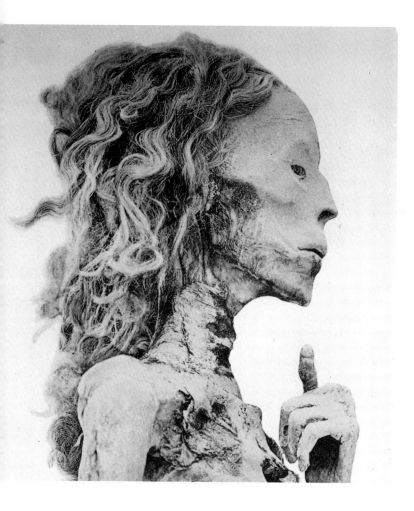

38 *The upper part of an unwrapped and nameless mummy of a woman found in 1898 with other plundered royalty in the tomb of Amenophis II in the Valley of the Kings. Catalogued as 'No. 61070, the Elder Woman B', she has recently been identified as Queen Tiye, but this conclusion has since been challenged.*

39 *The head of the mummy of Yuya, the father of Queen Tiye, who was found in 1905 with his wife Tuyu in a tomb in the Valley of the Kings. Their virtually intact burial equipment, supplied by their son-in-law Amenophis III, was the most opulent found in Egypt until that of Tutankhamun seventeen years later.*

Tiye was missing from the roll-call of members of her family until 1975, when she was purported to have been found by a process which, if correct, was as extraordinary as any in the annals of Egyptology. Among the mummies *Pl. 38* found in the royal cache in the tomb of Amenophis II in 1898 was that of a woman whom the necropoleis officials were evidently unable to identify, so they left her unwrapped and undocketed. Elliot Smith gave her the No. 61070 in his catalogue, and named her as 'The Elder Woman B' to distinguish her from a younger and greatly damaged younger Woman A. He described her as middle-aged and as having long brown wavy, lustrous hair without any trace of grey. He also noted that her left hand was tightly clenched, but with the thumb fully extended and placed in front of the breast-bone, the forearm being sharply bent at the elbow. He might also have described her for all her shrivelled state as a woman of imposing mien with her distinctive hair and firmly rounded chin.

The unusual pose, as though she were grasping a sceptre, suggested to Edward Wente of the Oriental Institute, Chicago, who was collaborating with the Alexandria-Michigan radiological team, that Woman B was a subject of great importance, a queen regnant no less, perhaps Hatshepsut or Tiye. The latter is often represented in her statuary as carrying a 'lily-sceptre', or fly-flapper, in her left hand.

Her X-ray cephalogram when compared with those of the other royal women showed that her skull resembled Tuyu's most closely. The correspondence was confirmed when an electron probe was used to compare a clipping of the hair of the mummy with a sample from the lock of auburn hair, found sealed in a wooden coffinette and inscribed 'Queen Tiye', among the heirlooms deposited in the tomb of Tutankhamun. Such probes provide an exact analysis of the chemical constituents in the hair, which it is claimed vary from one person to another. The two samples were identical. Unknown Woman B has now been removed from the side-room in the tomb of Amenophis II, where she had remained since its discovery in 1898, and as Queen Tiye placed among her fellow royalties in the Cairo Museum. Recently, however, objections against these findings of the Alexandria-Michigan team have been raised by Dr Renate Germer on several grounds, including what she regards as defective methodology. The age of mummy No. 61070 at death is against its identification as Queen Tiye. The blood group of the mummy shows that while in theory it could be a daughter of Yuya and Tuyu, this is not very probable. Further, the process of identifying family relationships on the basis of skull measurements is considered too uncertain for any proper conclusion to emerge. Lastly, the hair analysis provides no proof that the mummy is Tiye. Until further investigations have confirmed its identity beyond conjecture, the verdict, in the words of Scots Law, will have to remain 'not proven'.

Amenophis III, the husband of Queen Tiye, was cached in the tomb of his grandfather. But it was his father, Tuthmosis IV, who evidently introduced an innovation in royal burial by selecting the impressive western branch in the Valley of the Kings as the site of his son's large, well-cut and opulent tomb, No. 22. This departure from dynastic tradition did not spare Amenophis III from the attentions of robbers who plundered what must have been an exceedingly rich deposit, hacking his mummy to pieces in the process in order to steal his *cf. Pl. 52* amuletic jewellery. Nearly all the soft parts of his head had disappeared under this treatment, exposing the bones of the face and revealing to Elliot Smith that the king had lost his upper incisors some time before his death, and another tooth in his last days. There was also evidence of alveolar abscesses and, like his father-in-law Yuya, he must have suffered miserably from dental disorders in his later years. In the case of both men, who by Egyptian standards were of advanced years, their teeth had been worn down to the pulp by a lifetime of masticating the staple of Egyptian diet, bread made from flour with a high percentage of grit from the milling process.

Amenophis was about 1.58 metres (5 feet 2 inches) in height and at death was almost completely bald, having only scanty hair on his temples. It is evident that special measures were taken by his embalmers to restore to his corpse some semblance of his appearance in life by packing a mixture of natron and resin under the skin, an innovation which was not repeated until four centuries later, when other kinds of padding were used to plump out the mummies of the ruling grandees of Thebes in the Twenty-First Dynasty. This peculiar feature of the embalment is one of the reasons that have induced some scholars to question whether this mummy is really of the Eighteenth Dynasty and not in fact of Twenty-First Dynasty date. They claim that it was incorrectly identified by the officials who rewrapped it in Year 13 of King Smendes of the Twenty-First Dynasty (1057 BC) and wrote the date and the prenomen, Nebma're (Amenophis III), on the outer bandages. Recently the Alexandria-Michigan team have added their voice to the chorus of doubt as to the date of this mummy. They argue that from the craniofacial skeletons it is difficult to accept that a close relationship exists between the mummy of Amenophis III and that of his father Tuthmosis IV. They have not, of course, been able to make any comparison with the craniofacial skeleton of his mother, Mutemwiya, whose mummy has not so far come to light. They further confuse the issue by claiming that his craniofacial skeleton resembles more closely the portrait of Akhenaten, whose mummy has not yet been identified beyond a wild surmise.

In this contretemps it seems best to accept, for the present anyhow, the opinion of Elliot Smith who could distinguish better than most between a mummy of the Eighteenth Dynasty and one of the Twenty-First, just as an official of the period was unlikely to confuse a mummy four centuries old with one of his own day. The mummies of the Twenty-First Dynasty magnates were not so richly equipped, or so brutally pillaged as those of the pharaohs of the New Kingdom, and although some of their coffins had suffered the loss of gilded external parts, from opportunists among the burial parties, they were otherwise intact. The Er Rassul family limited their depredations to helping themselves to the funerary papyri, shawabtis and other trivial items included in the Twenty-First Dynasty burials in order to sell them to tourists in Luxor across the river.

The military administration that governed Thebes after the end of the New Kingdom ruled the region with a firm and ruthless hand. They saw to it that the royal mummies were repaired, rewrapped and reinterred in groups over an extended period whenever arrangements had to be made for one of their own major burials. Eventually, by the end of the dynasty, they had disposed of the entire stock of rehabilitated mummies in three or four caches.

The embalmers who plumped out the corpse of Amenophis III may have taken such exceptional measures in his case because the king at death was grossly obese. Several representations of him in his later years show him as corpulent and elderly, though with the traditional idealism of court art, such *cf. Pl. 26* portraits are discreet and restrained. Elliot Smith was undecided in his estimate of the king's age at death as 'nearer forty or fifty'. Ruffer at first made it fifty-two, but later opted for forty-five: the latter figure accords well with the documentary evidence (see below).

Amenophis had other wives, both native and foreign, besides Tiye, and must have fathered a numerous progeny. Child mortality rates, however, were also very high; and a generation after his death none of his descendants was apparently living. No mummy of his children has been identified for certain; but in two cases human remains have survived which may well be of his sons or grandsons, and one day histological and genetic investigations may settle the question decisively.

The two cases in question concern discoveries made in the first decades of this century in Western Thebes. Between 1902 and 1912 the concession for excavating in the Valley of the Kings was held by Theodore M. Davis, a wealthy American lawyer who employed professional Egyptologists, principally Howard Carter, James Quibell and Edward Ayrton, to direct his operations. As a result of such investigations, a number of royal deposits were found, including the burial of Yuya and Tuyu already mentioned. In the season of 1907, Davis and Ayrton succeeded in finding another tomb, now catalogued as No. 55, which though not of such a design and size as to qualify as a *Pls. 53, 55–7* king's tomb, yet contained rich burial furniture that had been made for royalty in the Amarna period. The kernel of the deposit was a decayed mummy, reduced to a virtual skeleton, resting within a rotting wooden coffin. It was found impossible to identify the remains with certainty since the name and titles of the deceased had been excised from the equipment. Since the time of their discovery, the bones have been examined by medical experts on four separate occasions, but opinion has oscillated between the view that they are of Akhenaten himself, and the belief that they belong to Smenkhkarē, Akhenaten's possible co-regent and successor. We shall have to return to the problem of Valley Tomb No. 55 in a later chapter.

Davis's concession passed to the Earl of Carnarvon in 1914 and over the next eight years he employed Carter to continue the work of exploration which culminated in the discovery of the tomb of Tutankhamun in 1922. Although the tomb consisted of a mere four chambers of modest size, it was crammed with treasures of every kind and proved to be the most opulent discovery ever made in the history of archaeology. Paradoxically, the body of the king had suffered grievously as a result of avoiding the spoliation that had been the fate of the other pharaohs. His wrappings, drenched with sacramental oils and unguents at his entombment, had not been torn off soon afterwards by impious hands, but had remained hermetically sealed over long centuries. In these conditions great heat had been generated by spontaneous combustion reducing his bandaged remains to a cracked, brittle and carbonized integument. A full anatomical examination using X-rays has only recently been possible, and then in circumstances not wholly ideal. It has, however, been sufficient to reach the conclusion that the king died at an age which did not exceed seventeen years at the most, and not the eighteen previously suggested.

On a granite lion from Sulb in the British Museum, Tutankhamun refers to Amenophis III as 'his father', which if it is to be taken literally means that he was a younger brother of Akhenaten; but this degree of consanguinity between Amenophis III and Tutankhamun is regarded as impossible by an influential body of opinion. We shall therefore have to examine this relationship more closely in due course.

Among the furnishings of the tomb of Tutankhamun were two miniature gilded coffins, each containing an embalmed human foetus of indeterminate sex, who are almost certainly the children of the king, though buried under his own name since they never lived to be given ones of their own. The somewhat extravagant suggestion has been advanced that these stillborn infants are somehow substitutes for the placental fetishes of Khons presumed to be used in the burial ceremonies. Why stillborn babes should replace the placenta either of the king or themselves in such a ritual is not explained. The Khonsu fetishes found in the tomb of Haremhab, to which they have been compared, are made of resin-coated blocks of wood, not human tissue. There seems no reason to doubt that these foetuses were the last of the line of Amosis, the founder of their dynasty, the prematurely born children of the pharaoh, entombed with their father according to a practice for which there is ample precedence in the Eighteenth Dynasty. Perhaps one day a careful serological scan will establish the relationship for certain.

A comparable biological analysis might be equally profitable in determining the identity of the bones found in the tomb of Haremhab at North Saqqara. This great private tomb in the New Kingdom area of the necropolis of Memphis has been rediscovered and cleared in recent years by an Anglo-Dutch team, after having been deprived of many of its fine limestone reliefs in the early years of the nineteenth century, and subsequently lost to view beneath the invading sands. In the main shaft No. IV, the excavators have found human bones which have encouraged them to believe that they might be the mortal remains of the chief wife of Haremhab, Queen Mutnodjme, who, unlike *Pl. 77* her husband, was not buried in the Valley of the Kings, but at Saqqara, perhaps because at the time of her death, about Year 14 or 15 of their reign, his Theban tomb had not been planned.

There are Egyptologists who adhere to the venerable belief that Mutnodjme *cf. Fig. 20* was the sister of Nefertiti. A full autopsy of the remains might help to decide not only her age at death, and perhaps the cause of her demise, but also if there is any blood relationship with Queen Tiye, who may have been her aunt (see below).

The existence of so many remains of the royal family, even in a vestigial state, from this particular period of Egyptian history, provides an opportunity for research into their physical relationships, which, however, must be the province of the medical expert rather than the Egyptologist. But there is still one notable absentee from the assembly who would be worth all the rest. The historian of ancient Egypt would sacrifice much to be able to examine the authentic mummy of Akhenaten, and replace the many conjectures about him with even a few hard facts. So far, his remains have never been proved to exist, and most students are now convinced that they were destroyed in antiquity. Nevertheless, there persists a small but stubborn core of opinion which claims that they have survived under a false identification, and this is yet another problem to which we must address ourselves in due course.

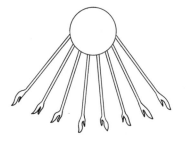

CHAPTER 10

Interpretations

In 1894, after his pioneer explorations at Amarna, Flinders Petrie attempted to bring his discoveries to bear upon the historical problems of the reign of Akhenaten. He had indeed uncovered much, including seven of the Boundary Stelae. His examination with Griffith of the hieratic dockets on fragments of pottery vessels that had contained food and drink, showed that Akhenaten had ruled at Amarna for seventeen years and may have died in his eighteenth regnal year. Petrie settled the succession of rulers after Amenophis III as Akhenaten, Smenkhkarē, Tutankhamun, Ay and Haremhab, in that order, an arrangement that has withstood the test of time. He also correctly read the name of Smenkhkarē from the many bezels of faience finger-rings that he had collected on the site, and dated the co-regency of this king with Akhenaten to the latter's seventeenth regnal year.

Petrie was able to affirm that Amenophis IV and Akhenaten were one and the same person, married to the same Queen Nefertiti, and having two daughters bearing the same names. The reign of one king had ended in his fifth year, while the reign of the other had begun in his sixth (*sic*). He dismissed the earlier suggestions of Mariette and Lefébure that Akhenaten was a eunuch or a woman in masquerade, believing that such theories were flatly contradicted by the king's uxorious behaviour, appearing with his wife on every monument, riding with her in a chariot, kissing her in public and dandling her on his knee. He also pointed to their steadily increasing family and tried to show that the physiques of Akhenaten and Nefertiti, as revealed in a statuette which he had excavated at Amarna, were essentially different. It cannot be claimed, however, that this last judgment is at all convincing.

Slowly out of the mists of time a figure of Akhenaten was dimly and spasmodically emerging, thanks to Petrie's discoveries: but the excavator of Amarna went even further and provided an appraisal of the character of the king and the nature of his reign. Petrie's views on racial types, which reflected the ethnological ideas of his day, are somewhat vitiated by his delusion that the plaster portrait-study that he had found in the Great Palace was the death-mask of the king. Thus from the assumption that Queen Tiye was a

Pl. 15

Mesopotamian wife of Amenophis III, he argued that the peculiar facial features of Akhenaten were inherited from an Asiatic mother; but his comparisons are based upon wrong identification and need not detain us. When he wrote, the tomb of Yuya and Tuyu had not been discovered, and still more remote was the finding of the conjectured body of Tiye herself.

Petrie did recognize, however, that the innovations of Akhenaten's reign amounted to a revolution in Egyptian art, religion and ethics. He was fascinated by the personality of a man who could initiate such radical changes in a very few years, and he identified the motivating force for them in the king's use of the epithet, everywhere proudly proclaimed, of *Ankh em maet*, 'Living in truth'. According to Petrie, this phrase was not redolent of the violence, power and vainglory of the king's conquering forebears, but a devotion to a steadfast philosophic aim to live in a true spirit.

The distinctive and novel feature of his religious ideas was the emphasis he placed upon the rays of the sun, ending in hands which operate to bring life to each person and to accept offerings from each. Petrie saw in this a unique concept of the power of the radiant energy of the sun, in contrast to the idea of the sun as only a distant intangible body. The traditional cult of the sun as a personal deity was rejected, together with all its human and animal connotations. The Aten or disk was adopted to replace such anthropomorphic concepts with the idea of a supernatural personality. It is the rays of the sun that act among men and bring life that are the special subject of representation. In no other sun-worship have the rays been so clearly emphasized as the source of life and action. The distinction thus made shows a scientific approach not found again until the present day. 'It was a philosophic view and determination, which anticipated the course of thought some thousands of years.'

Time has not dealt kindly with some of Petrie's conclusions. A more profound examination of the 'maet' in which Akhenaten professed to live has shown that its earlier translation as 'truth' is an over-simplification, and it refers rather to that harmony prevailing when the universe left the hands of the creator at the beginning of time. The idea, too, that a philosopher king had replaced an all-conquering pharaoh will not stand up to examination, in view of the traditional icon in the porch of the Third Pylon at Karnak of Amenophis IV executing the foreign rebel. Fragments of similar scenes, showing the decorations on the sides of the cabins of the royal barges, have also been recovered among the talatat from Karnak and Hermopolis. Here Queen Nefertiti joins in the ritual slaughter of the national foe, albeit in a feminine guise.

If Petrie, too, had looked a little more closely he would have seen that the rays of the Aten do not give life to each person, but bring its breath only to the nostrils of the king and queen. The rays may also embrace the bodies of the royal pair exclusively, and support their crowns in a daily act of coronation.

Petrie goes on to discuss the principle of 'Living in truth' as far as it concerns the art of Amarna, which he defines in painting and sculpture as characterized by the fullest naturalism. We shall examine this thesis more critically below (see Chapter 20).

In ethics, too, he notes a distinct departure in the public behaviour of the pharaoh. No other king is so dedicated to an ethical ideal, which is to be seen in the conduct of his private life. He was devoted to his one queen, appearing with her on all occasions, and the domestic detail of their family life is frankly displayed:

> His affection is the truth, and as the truth he proclaims it. Here is a revolution in ideas! No king of Egypt, nor of any other part of the world, has ever carried out his honesty of expression so openly. . . . Thus in every line Akhenaten stands out as perhaps the most original thinker that ever lived in Egypt, and one of the great idealists of the world.

Petrie's admiration is unreserved. He sees Akhenaten as the philosopher, moralist, religious reformer, art innovator and idealist, almost anticipating the nineteenth-century scientist and pacifist. It is not difficult to understand how such advocacy should have arisen. The historian of ancient Egypt, searching the conscious and unconscious propaganda that serves as the official record, is often at a loss to project the personality of the ruler beneath the trappings of power, the man beneath the divinity. Seldom, except in folk tales with their element of sardonic ribaldry, is the pharaoh ever represented as having human foibles. In the official utterances he is larger than life, a personification of absolute power. Only the office has any individuality and the temporary holder of it is cast always in the same mould, as the incarnation of the god who created the Egyptian world at the beginning of time. In the case of Akhenaten, the historian fastens with relief upon a king who clearly departs from the stereotype and shows himself as a human being in the intimate circle of his family and friends. Above all, here is an individualist who abandoned the worship of the bizarre multifarious gods of Egypt and substituted for them an abstract symbol, the radiant disk, busy with its many hands, by which to represent it.

Petrie's unstinted praise influenced a whole generation of scholars, particularly the American Egyptologist, James Henry Breasted, who was one of the most distinguished pupils of the Berlin School under Adolf Erman. He had made a close analysis of the hymns to the sun-god inscribed in the Amarna tombs, and in 1909 he summed up a classic study of Akhenaten's reign in these words:

... there died with him such a spirit as the world had never seen before – a brave soul, undauntedly facing the momentum of immemorial tradition, and thereby stepping out from the long line of conventional and colourless Pharaohs, that he might disseminate ideas far beyond and above the capacity of his age to understand. Among the Hebrews, seven or eight hundred years later, we look for such men; but the modern world has yet adequately to value or even acquaint itself with this man who, in an age so remote and under conditions so adverse, became not only the world's first idealist and the world's first individual, but also the earliest monotheist, and the first prophet of internationalism – the most remarkable figure of the Ancient World before the Hebrews.

Where so eminent an authority expressed such approbation, it would be surprising if less judicious enthusiasts should have held back. Similar partial studies have provoked their own reactions, resulting in a spectrum of opinions which obscure as much as they illuminate. To Sigmund Freud, Akhenaten was the mentor of Moses and the instigator of Jewish monotheism. Others have dismissed him as a mere henotheist – the promotor of the belief in a supreme god without any assertion of his unique nature. The most recent judgment sums him up as a literal atheist. The king's social and political innovations have been denied him. His pacificism and internationalism have been exploded. The domestic idyll with Nefertiti and her daughters has suffered cruel blows. Another queen, Kiya, has turned up; and although not a chief wife, bids fair to *Pls. 37, 57* outrival Nefertiti by reason of the unbridled attention that has been paid to her. There have been suggestions of serious political differences between Nefertiti and her husband during the last years of the reign. Another opinion canvasses a change of sex-role for the queen in this later period, and envisages the interaction on the scene of two ostensible kings in contrast to the conviction of the early investigators that two ostensible queens were functioning together.

At the same time, those thinkers who see modern pressures operating even in the Bronze Age have not been slow to assert that the general trend of events would have been no different if Akhenaten had been a sack of sawdust. The historical process, they believe, would have advanced even without the main actor on the stage. The interpretation of events at Amarna which once seemed so solid with Breasted has now resolved itself into a morass where any firm standpoint is difficult to find.

The swing of opinion, and the violence of the partisanship among scholars, owes much to questions of interpretation, since the ancient records of Akhenaten's reign have come down to us in an even more tenuous form than those of most other kings of the dynasty. The researcher has to contend not only with the chance obliterations of time but also with the malicious suppression of man himself. Thus the plain facts upon which any reconstruction of the period must depend are scanty enough, and that they exist at all is due to the ingenuity and industry of generations of Egyptologists who have patiently tracked down and assembled scattered clues after the ancient Egyptians had deliberately effaced most of Akhenaten's memorials, expunged all mention of him from their official records, and done their best to blot out of their consciousness the recollection of a pharaoh who had apparently not conformed to the centuries-old tradition of repeating the primal pattern of kingship which had come down from the gods.

During the course of such investigations, it is inevitable that errors should have been committed. Inaccurate data and incomplete reports have been responsible for misinterpretations. Increased knowledge, however, has led to the correction of details here and there, but whether a juster appreciation of the Amarna period as a whole has emerged, is problematic. Petrie saw Akhenaten as a great thinker and idealist, far in advance of his time. To Breasted he was the world's first individual. More recent opinion, while recognizing a certain poetic interpretation of nature, and innovations which Akhenaten stimulated in the arts of his day, denies much of the revolutionary thought that has been attributed to him, and takes a somewhat jaundiced view of the man and his followers. Each generation, in fact, tends to reinterpret the *disjecta membra* of the past from its contemporary standpoint.

We would do well, then, to suspend judgment for the moment on Akhenaten's ideas, in so far as he has expressed them, and to consider him strictly within the context of his own time and place. In the next section, therefore, we shall attempt to outline the main features of the civilization of the Eastern Mediterranean in the middle of the second millennium BC, in which Egypt played a particularly influential role, and which Akhenaten dominated as the god-king of an immensely rich and powerful land.

PART II

THE
MILIEU

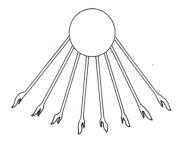

CHAPTER II

Egypt in the Eighteenth Dynasty:
Foreign Affairs

The great watershed in Egyptian history is reached in the seventeenth century
BC when the nation woke up to the realization that its government had fallen
into the hands of a line of Asiatic princes ruling in Memphis with all the
authority of the pharaoh. Long afterwards, the Ptolemaic historian Manetho
could only explain this take-over as the result of the irruption of a conquering
horde, like the Persians of his own day, though it was also the echo of a legend
that dated back to the time of Queen Hatshepsut. The Egyptians in fact had
long been acquainted with these foreigners. A painting in the tomb of the
nomarch Khnumhotep at Beni Hasan, dating to *c.* 1890 BC, shows a trading
party of them, men, women and children, in their leather buskins and long
coats of many colours being received by Khnumhotep in his capacity as
governor of the Eastern Desert. The Egyptians referred to the tribal chiefs of
these nomads as *Hikau khasut* or 'Rulers of desert uplands', a term which
Manetho rendered as *Hyksos* or 'Shepherd kings'. This name has clung to them
stubbornly ever since, applying to the entire people, mostly Semitic bedouin,
rather than to their rulers.

Despite the chain of fortresses along the northeast frontier that regulated the
influx of Hyksos into the Delta during the Twelfth Dynasty, Asiatics entered
Egypt peaceably as merchants, or took service as cooks, brewers, seamstresses,
vine-dressers and the like. The story of Joseph reflects the manner in which
many of them arrived, sold into slavery for silver or corn in time of famine, to
exchange a frugal and uncertain existence in return for food and shelter. The
records show that a large proportion of these immigrants arrived as young girls,
doubtless because they were generally less cherished than their brothers, and
took service as needlewomen or grinders of corn. Such traffic continued well
into the Eighteenth Dynasty as paintings in the Theban tombs reveal. These
menials were classed as 'slaves', a comparatively new element in Egyptian
society, but one which was an established institution in the Levant, and one
which prevailed for a long time as wholesale migrations and foreign wars
brought refugees, captives and other aliens into Egypt. Their children often
took Egyptian names and so vanish from our notice. Some reached positions of

responsibility and trust; others won their manumission by the simple statement of their owners before witnesses that they were being made freedmen of the Land of Pharaoh. Nor were these newcomers confined to the Delta. The number of Asiatics even in Upper Egypt was considerable: one official for instance had no fewer than forty-five such slaves in his household.

The impact upon the civilization of Egypt of such foreigners, even as a subject people, was considerable, and will account for a number of changes in religious ideas, and for innovations in the material culture, even perhaps in the ethnic composition of the governing class in later years; for mostly such immigrants did not join the closed family ranks of the toiling peasantry, but developed the more specialized skills, particularly in the luxury crafts, which have ever been among the resources of enterprising refugees.

The official propaganda of the victorious Thebans later dismissed the Hyksos as barbarous marauders, whereas it is clear that many of the Asiatics were from urban cultures that were literate and as advanced as that of Egypt. They were familiar with the machinery of bureaucratic scribal government, and quickly adapted themselves to the special conditions of the Nile Valley. Their rulers wrote their Semitic names in Egyptian hieroglyphs, or even assumed Egyptian names, such as Apophis. They also adopted the titularies of the pharaohs, and coined prenomens for themselves as the sons of the sun-god. *Pace* Queen Hatshepsut, they worshipped Egyptian gods, such as Rē of Heliopolis, and Seth or Sutekh of Avaris in the Eastern Delta, a town which from *c.* 1700 BC became their chief seat of power. From this centre they extended their grip until Memphis, the ancient religious capital, fell into their hands, and with it presumably the whole of Lower Egypt.

About 1660 BC, according to Manetho, there appeared among the Hyksos chieftains a leader of more dynamic stamp, a characteristic *condottiere* of the time among those who were carving out kingdoms for themselves in the turbulent conditions of the Near East. This was Salatis, a king who ushers in a new era of the rule of the military leaders with their paladins, their professional soldiery and new-fangled weapons. Such men were thereafter to dominate the politics of the ancient world. Salatis appears to have assumed power over the whole of Egypt, imposing taxes upon the entire population. But the Hyksos preferred to govern their realm from Memphis and Avaris through the agency of loyal vassals in Middle Egypt, Upper Egypt, and Nubia (Kush). The latter had become independent under a prince who referred to himself as a 'son' of his overlord, the Hyksos king.

Despite the imposts that were levied, the Hyksos yoke does not appear to have lain heavy upon their vassals. Theban courtiers considered themselves fortunate that although all Egypt was loyal to the Hyksos as far as Cusae, they in their portion of Upper Egypt were at peace as far as their strong fortress of

Elephantine on the southern frontier. The best of their fields were still cultivated for them and they continued to exercise grazing rights in the rich pastures of the Delta, and corn was sent to feed their hogs.

It would appear that some kind of pact existed between each dependant on one side, and the Hyksos on the other, which was cemented by intermarriage. Enough evidence survives to arouse the suspicion that Asiatic wives lived in the harims of the Theban princes, and doubtless the Hyksos kings received in exchange Theban princesses as pledges of the loyalty of their southern vassals. Under this benign hegemony, the fiery Theban princes with their contingents of warlike Nubian mercenaries were eventually inspired with the ambition to challenge the pretensions of the Hyksos pharaoh in the north. In the middle of the sixteenth century BC, the assay of arms broke out in earnest under Kamose, the last ruler of the Seventeenth Dynasty in Thebes.

What began as an insurrection developed into a war of national liberation when the struggle was continued by Amosis, the infant nephew and successor of Kamose. The nature of the terrain in Egypt with its many irrigation canals and the branches of the Nile, both large and small, in the Delta, dictated that the campaigns would be mainly ship-borne operations; and in point of fact our slender knowledge of this contest is largely derived from the laconic reports that an officer of marines inscribed in his tomb at El Kab. The struggle must have been as heroic and protracted as that around Homeric Troy, and it has been suggested that it was not until his tenth regnal year that Amosis reduced Avaris to a plundered ruin and expelled the Hyksos.

In its latest phases the conflict changed its character and adopted all the elements of the new mobile warfare that had developed in Western Asia during Hyksos times. The Egyptians were quick to employ the superior military skills of the Asiatics, doubtless assisted in this by deserters who took service with their captors, particularly in the novel chariot arm, with its special weapons such as the composite bow, the javelin hurled by a spear-thrower, the heavy-crushing falchion, and bronze or leather armour. The levies of young men raised on an *ad hoc* basis were developed into a standing army imbued, particularly as the struggle against the Hyksos wore on, with a new-found patriotic fervour. Such an army, divided into three or four divisions named after the principal regional gods, had its hard core of veterans and trained professionals besides the new recruits.

A class of military scribes formed a general staff; and tactics and strategy became the concern of a war council with the pharaoh or his deputy at its head. The old clash of armed men in a general melée was replaced by organized forces trained in the arts and disciplines of war. Awards and decorations for valour were instituted and veterans were pensioned off with grants of land, prisoners as serfs and a share in the plunder.

Such a professional battle-trained army enabled Amosis to follow up his capture of Avaris with a campaign in Palestine as far as the town of Sharuhen, which was destroyed after a three years' siege. The same army also took the field against the tribes of Nubia and Kush, restoring the old southern boundary at Buhen, the point it had attained in the Middle Kingdom near the head of the Second Cataract. Subsequently the army thrust even further south, until it had stabilized the extreme southern frontier at Napata near modern Gebel Barkal.

In Asia, the semi-nomadic and pastoral society of earlier times had been replaced by an urban culture similar to that prevailing in Syria during the Middle Bronze Age, though still retaining elements of the old patriarchal society. By the Hyksos period, Palestine and Syria had been settled by Amorites and Canaanites, Semitic-speaking peoples who had adopted a settled agrarian way of life in place of their erstwhile nomadic existence. They formed small principalities centred around townships in the more fertile areas such as the Jordan Valley and the coastal plains. The population was thinly spaced but comparatively prosperous, each group consisting of an industrious peasantry governed by an aristocracy with a king or princeling at its head, generally of a different ethnic origin.

The Hurrians, a people living around Lake Van in Armenia, had pressed south, establishing a feudal state of the Mitanni, in the area of Naharin, between the Upper Tigris and Euphrates. They were ruled by an Indo-European élite, speaking an Aryan language, which had brought into its ambit the Amorites of North Syria. To the west of the Mitanni and the north of Syria was Hatti, the lands of the Hittites, a mixed people occupying most of Anatolia, also ruled by an Indo-European caste, speaking a tongue akin to Greek and Latin. It was roving bands of Indo-European adventurers, invincible with their new weapons and methods of warfare, who seized principalities, great and small, and made themselves masters of the situation in Palestine and Syria.

During the Eighteenth Dynasty such petty states were in constant conflict with each other, having inherited the tribal feuds of their ancestors. Occasionally, under the leadership of a prince more energetic and crafty than his fellows, a coalition of states would win some temporary ascendancy; but the federation would all too quickly dissolve and re-form in another direction. The proximity of Egypt, Hatti and Naharin exerted a magnetic effect upon these princes, drawing them into the orbit of the great power that lay nearest to hand, and whose assistance could be sought in furthering their own local ambitions. What the vassals required of their overlords were troops to assist them in their squabbles and jockeyings for power; and they therefore set up a constant clamour for armed help to save them from an impending or actual attack from some reprobate neighbour. Assurances that unless such aid were forthcoming immediately the town or state which they were so valiantly holding for their lord would be lost forever, were combined with protestations of their own loyalty and integrity, and the treachery and chicanery of their rivals. Very often their accusations were contradictory, and included in their censure were the commissioners who were supposed to be carrying out Pharaoh's orders. There is more than a suspicion that the Egyptian governors on the spot were taking advantage of the local rivalries in order to prevent any one state from becoming too powerful. 'Divide and rule' was as much their motto as that of Machiavelli. Such is the state of affairs revealed by the Amarna Letters.

Amosis campaigned in Asia principally to deter any fresh incursions by roving bands into the Eastern Delta, and in the process he found himself involved in the suppression of unrest in the coastal area from Byblos to Ugarit, which from earliest times had been an Egyptian sphere of interest since her supplies of good constructional timber came from this region. By the reign of his son, Amenophis I, the phrase sending an army 'to extend the frontiers of Egypt' is heard, suggesting that the taste for warfare and the pre-emptive strike, provoked by the Hyksos wars, had developed into an appetite for imperial adventures. Egypt joined in the rivalry of the other great powers, Hatti and particularly Naharin, for dominion in Palestine and Syria. In fact it is probable that the spirit of aggression in the military sphere was sustained by its own momentum, since Amosis and some other kings were too young when they assumed the leadership of their armies to have had any experience of campaigning in the field.

In the next reign, that of Tuthmosis I, the Egyptian armies made a victorious sweep along the valley of the Orontes to throw down the gage on the threshold of Naharin, and proclaim to the entire region the arrival of a new dynamic upon the scene. This challenge, however, was allowed to decline until by the twenty-third regnal year of Tuthmosis III a dangerous confederation of Asiatic princes, under the leadership of the king of Kadesh on the Orontes, and doubtless incited by the Mitanni, prepared to drive Egypt from the field and invade its lands. The chosen place for the contest was Megiddo (Armageddon) in the plain of Esdraelon: and this first decisive battle of which any record survives was an overwhelming defeat for the Asiatics whose routed forces were cooped up in Megiddo and besieged for seven months. The eventual fall of the city, as Tuthmosis declared, was the capture of a thousand towns of the northern federation. This striking success was consolidated by another victory ten years and eight campaigns later when Tuthmosis transported prefabricated boats on ox-waggons to the Euphrates and crossed that river into the heartland of the arch-enemy, the Mitanni.

In after years the Egyptians looked back to the long and prosperous reign of their military genius Tuthmosis III as a golden age in which their arms had everywhere been successful, from Napata near the Fourth Cataract in the

Sudan, to Naharin beyond the Euphrates. The material wealth in tribute, plunder and slave labour that poured into Egypt as a result of these campaigns stimulated all kinds of enterprises, notably grandiose and widespead temple building in many towns in Egypt, but particularly at Thebes.

Amenophis II, the vigorous and ferocious son of Tuthmosis, attempted to repeat his father's successes particularly in North Syria. Here the neighbouring great powers, Hatti, Babylon and the Mitanni, sought to control a corridor to the coastal ports of Western Asia, with access to the timber of the Lebanon and the trade with Egypt, Crete and the Aegean world. Despite Amenophis's contemptuous boasts, Naharin was able to bring its vassals back into allegiance whenever the Egyptian forces were withdrawn. In time, the pharaoh came to realize the futility of campaigning so far from home on the doorstep of powerful rivals. An arrangement was reached with other potentates in the region to define their spheres of interest. A treaty with Hatti had been made early in the reign of Tuthmosis III, when the Mitanni were the common foe, and was still in force later in the dynasty. Babylonia also had a pact of mutual assistance with Egypt, and invoked it to deter the Canaanite dynasts from attacking the territory of its ally. Such treaties were cemented by marriages between the daughters of the royal houses and the pharaoh, the best documented of such alliances being the series made between princesses of the Mitanni and Tuthmosis IV, Amenophis III, and Akhenaten. The daughters of less exalted princes, however, also entered the royal harims in Egypt and played their part in the diplomacy of the age. The traffic was all in one direction, for when the king of Babylon asked for an Egyptian royal bride, he received the haughty dismissal that as of old it had not been the custom for the daughters of pharaohs to be married to foreigners.

The treaties between the great powers brought a period of comparative peace and stability to Palestine and Syria during the reigns of Tuthmosis IV and Amenophis III, when Egyptian garrisons at key points were able to reinforce local levies in police actions to curb the more turbulent vassals, and control the Semitic Shasu bedouin, who posed a constant threat to law and order. Included among such elements were the Apiru banditti, who appear to have been displaced persons of different ethnic origins and speech, wandering about Palestine and Syria in robber bands. They kept to the unfrequented tracks, living by rapine and mercenary service according to their opportunities. Groups of Apiru were hired as soldiers of fortune by the local rulers, and occasionally even by the Egyptian district commissioners.

Most of these client princes bear Aryan names and were the descendants of Indo-European adventurers mixed with Hurrian components who had seized power from the Semitic-speaking Amorites in the Late Middle Bronze Age. They were divine war-lords, the sons of the supreme god such as Baal or

Shamash, living in splendid palaces with a staff of scribes and officials to form an administrative corps which organized trading ventures as much for prestige as for profit, exchanging their corn, oil, copper, timber and wine for such luxuries as gold and silver, lapis lazuli, rich jewels, fine furniture and ivory carvings, intricate embroideries, ornate chariots and spirited horses. They were supported by their *maryannu*, an aristocracy of chariot-using warriors dedicated to the service of their leaders. The heroic character of these stratified societies is as much revealed in the epics of Homer as in the Amarna Letters. They were feudal, contentious, boastful and aggressive, obsessed by a *folie de grandeur* encouraged by their wealth and pride.

They observed a strict diplomatic protocol by which they regulated the relations between their equals, their vassals, and their overlords. The Amarna Letters reveal that in the literate world of the fourteenth century BC, messengers travelled from one court to another bearing despatches by which *Pl. 13* kings, queens, and even their high officials communicated with their counterparts in other states. By such means marriage alliances were arranged, trade goods exchanged, treaties negotiated, extradition requested, protests submitted, demands made, warnings administered, aid solicited – all the features, in fact, of a well-established system of international relations which compares favourably with that functioning in modern Europe.

The messengers, part couriers, part ambassadors, both Egyptians and foreigners, were important functionaries in their own countries and evidently enjoyed some kind of diplomatic immunity, for a passport has survived which was issued by a North Syrian ruler to allow his envoy to pass safely through Canaan on his way to attend a state funeral, probably of Amenophis III in Egypt. In time of war the journeying of these envoys was particularly hazardous. Amenophis II boasts of capturing in the Plain of Sharon a messenger of the king of the Mitanni with a cuneiform tablet 'at his neck', where presumably it was carried in a satchel. Ambassadors could sometimes encounter a cool reception and be detained in the country of their hosts as a sign of displeasure with their masters. On the other hand, envoys who brought good news could expect to be well entertained, being allowed to sit in the presence of their host, even to dine with him, and to receive rich rewards.

The kings of Egypt, Babylon, Naharin, Assyria and other great powers which regarded themselves as equals, addressed each other as 'brother' and accompanied their letters with valuable gifts: lapis lazuli, gold, silver, chariots, horses, weapons, worked garments and the like. Tushratta of the Mitanni, whose relations with Egypt were especially close, was lavish with such presents to which on one occasion he added a boy and girl from booty he had captured from the Hittites. At another time he included thirty women who were no doubt skilled in music-making, or embroidery, or other Asiatic arts. It was

cf. Pl. 44

probably such immigrants and gifts which were boastfully referred to in the official texts as tribute exacted by Pharaoh from the 'Chiefs of Retenu'.

A more aloof and even peremptory tone is employed by the pharaoh when writing to his vassals in Palestine and Syria. The preamble is brief, and the ending often contains an implied threat with the assurance that the king is mighty and his chariots many and ready. The reply of the vassals is couched in a suitably servile form, and invariably refers to the pharaoh as their 'sun', their 'god', even while rebellion was being actively fomented.

The picture which these fragmentary records give us of the world that lay to the north of the Egyptian border in Asia is confused in its details. Chapter 17 will be concerned with some of the problems of historical interpretation that the Amarna Letters pose: here we shall sketch the broad outline of the story which is rather clearer.

While Egypt was too remote for its living-space to be seriously threatened by the struggle for dominance that obsessed the Mitanni and the Hittites, with the Assyrians waiting to intervene, and the Babylonians staking their own claims, these nations were concerned to keep Egypt from engaging in their dynastic wars on the side of their foes. Burnaburiash of Babylon was sensitive to any favours that an Assyrian deputation might have received at the Egyptian court, and asked the pharaoh to reject them. The king of Alashia, thought to be Cyprus, or Enkomi in Cyprus, also requested that the pharaoh should not make a treaty with the Hittites and North Syrians.

The few surviving drafts of letters which the pharaoh addressed to his fellow monarchs are mostly concerned with negotiations for his marriages with their daughters. The practice was of long standing: both Tuthmosis III and IV contracted marriages with the daughters of Asiatic princes, and their examples cannot have been unique. Amenophis III espoused Gilukhipa of the Mitanni in his tenth regnal year, and later in the reign wedded her niece Tadukhipa. Such marriages were a tangible expression of a diplomatic alliance, and the negotiations that preceded the dispatch of the bride and her retinue were often protracted. The extent and nature of her dowry had first to be agreed; and then the pharaoh himself had to offer a bride-price which gave a further chance for haggling. The inventories which have survived of the trousseaux of these princesses read like the catalogue of the contents of a state treasury of the time – gold, jewels, gold and silver vessels, horses, chariots, weapons, bedsteads, chests and other furniture overlaid with gold, mirrors and braziers of bronze, bronze vessels and implements, elaborately embroidered clothing, bedclothes, stone vessels full of oils, spices and so forth. The weight of gold and silver used in the manufacture and decoration of the various items is always carefully stated, just as in the case of other royal gifts, perhaps to ensure that a proper bargain will be struck, but also to insure against pilfering *en route*.

In return, the pharaoh sent similar gifts, particularly ebony furniture overlaid with gold and silver and inlaid with coloured stones and opaque glass, objects in ivory, stone vessels, oils, gold and silver statues, clothing, fine linen, and above all the gold in worked and bullion form for which Egypt was so renowned. These marriages, which were negotiated not only with the Hittites, the Babylonians and the Mitanni, but also with local dynasts, were in the nature of important state trading enterprises at a time of autarky when private commerce was evidently sparse and marginal.

The foreign kings wrote to their brother in Egypt to request that good relations should be maintained between them, or to complain of misdemeanours against their nationals in the territories subject to Pharaoh. Thus Burnaburiash twice had to deplore that his caravans had been plundered and their merchants slain on Egyptian-held lands. He asked that Pharaoh should make good the loss, and punish the culprits. The king of Alashia asked for the price of a consignment of wood that was taken from his people by Egyptians. He also requested that the property of one of his subjects who had died in Egypt should be returned by the hand of his messenger, since the man's wife and child were still in Alashia. Ashuruballit of Assyria was vexed to hear that Pharaoh's messengers had been molested by bedouin in his territories, and did not rest until he had pursued and captured the miscreants.

But the one demand which all these foreign rulers alike made of the pharaoh was for gold. 'Send gold, quickly, in very great quantities, so that I may finish a work I am undertaking; for gold is as dust in the land of my brother' – this was the burden of nearly all their letters; and when they were not begging for gold, they were complaining about the niggardly quantity that had been despatched, or about its quality which was not up to standard when assayed. It is clear that the large deposits of gold which Egypt could mine in her Eastern Deserts made her respected and wooed by the nations of the Near East.

As far as can be judged by the Amarna Letters, the great powers were cordial enough in their relations with Egypt in the earlier years of Amenophis III. The vassal princes appear to be in their usual state of endemic bickering and intrigue. A display of force had been deemed advisable earlier in the reign when Pharaoh had visited Sidon; and troops were also sent to help Ribaddi of Byblos against his rival Abdi-ashirta of Amurru. Notorious trouble-makers, like the latter, were violently removed when admonitions had failed to curb their conspiracies. Immediately, however, new dissidents took their places; but the general impression left by the letters is that even if the mutual accusations of perfidy, rapine, menace and mayhem are accepted at their face value from the vassals, Pharaoh's commissioners, with the aid of Egyptian troops from the garrison towns and local loyalists, were able to keep the situation in hand, and by playing off one ruler against his rival, to keep both in check.

With the accession of Suppiluliumas to the Hittite throne, however, about the second decade of the long reign of Amenophis III, a new and vigorous actor appeared upon the scene who was to remould decisively during his reign the political structure of North Syria. The struggle that now developed between Hatti and the Mitanni for the supremacy that the Hittites had lost in the reigns following the murder of Mursilis I, *c.* 1520 BC, involved the vassal states of Egypt on their borders with these two powers. Inevitably the pharaoh was drawn into the turbulent politics of the region; and that pharaoh was fated to be Akhenaten.

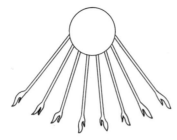

CHAPTER 12

Egypt in the Eighteenth Dynasty: Home Affairs

From the time of the first pharaoh, it was the founder of a dynasty who had so often given Egyptian culture its impetus and character. This was certainly the case with Amosis whose warlike operations put a military stamp upon the civilization of the New Kingdom. Although a son of the Seventeenth Dynasty, he was regarded by subsequent generations as the architect of a new epoch, the first king of the glorious Eighteenth Dynasty. Not only did he develop a formidable fighting force, he also initiated the same logistic organization in the machinery of government, thus ensuring that his instructions would be carried out effectively, and his authority loyally maintained.

The three districts into which Egypt had been divided by the end of the Middle Kingdom, each under a reporter and a herald, were replaced by the old concept of the Two Lands, Upper and Lower Egypt, with Thebes and Memphis at their respective heads. Wawat (Nubia) and its southern extension, the land of Kush, which comprised Nilotic Africa beyond Elephantine, was organized under the same fiscal and administrative system as Egypt herself, and contributed a great deal to the prosperity and prestige of Egypt by supplying the products of tropical Africa – ebony, exotic pelts, minerals, ivory, ostrich feathers, apes, charcoal, cattle and grain. It was also its fierce bowmen and other fighting men who formed the backbone of the Egyptian infantry arm abroad, and her police force at home. But, above all, the gold of Nubia and Kush in the Eastern Desert was the chief product that made Egypt renowned and courted among the nations of Western Asia.

In this reorganized Egypt there was much that was traditional. The feudal governors who had shared their power with the pharaoh at the beginning of the Twelfth Dynasty had been replaced near its end by local mayors chiefly concerned with the collection of its taxes. In Hyksos times they had functioned under the direction of the great chancellors of Lower Egypt. This system, tested by wont and usage, was adapted by Amosis under the supervision of a vizier for Lower Egypt and another for Upper Egypt, each with his seat in the appropriate capital city. In Nubia and Kush the administration that had arisen during the Second Intermediate Period under an independent Prince of Kush,

14 Drawing of a relief on the body of the chariot of Tuthmosis IV showing the war-god Montu guiding the hand of the king as he shoots down Asiatics on the battlefield.

ruling with the aid of officials of evident Egyptian origin, was superseded by a bureaucratic government under a military ruler, who continued to be called 'Prince', soon to become 'Prince of Kush', appointed by the pharaoh as his viceroy. What was new in the form of government that now prevailed, was a group of high officials, such as the viziers, the Overseers of the Treasury, Granaries and Cattle, the Chief Steward, the Cupbearer, the heralds, and army commanders, who formed a council of management around the king, like henchmen around their war-lord.

For indeed, the office of Pharaoh had changed its character during the rivalry that developed between the Hyksos kings and the princes of Thebes. While the age-old divinity of the pharaoh was not in doubt as 'the mother and father of mankind alone by himself without a peer', he was predominantly the incarnation of a triumphant warrior-god like Seth, Baal, or Montu, at the head of a caste of professional soldiers, the heroic champion of the Egyptian state. In this the pharaoh was conforming to the pattern of rule that was dominant in the Eastern Mediterranean at this period, where royal heroes had their aristocratic entourage of *maryannu* (chariot fighters).

Fig. 14   Profound changes had taken place in the structure of society by the introduction of a light but strong and supple chariot drawn by a span of horses, the weapon *par excellence* of the fighting élite. It was developed in the lands of Mesopotamia and still retained the Canaanite names for its various parts: but the tactics of its use, massed in squadrons, may have owed much to Indo-European innovations. Many of the drivers of these armoured vehicles were of Asiatic descent, such as the charioteer of Tuthmosis III who was the son of an Amorite, and are often delineated with Semitic features. Chariots were among the most precious gifts that could be sent by Asiatic potentates to their 'brother', the pharaoh, and were embellished with gold and other precious metals, and made brilliant with opaque glass and faience. The actual state *Pls. 42, 43*   chariots of Tutankhamun, and the stripped carcase of another example found in the tomb of Tuthmosis IV, have revealed how splendid such vehicles must have appeared drawn by a pair of stallions with gorgeous trappings and nodding head plumes.

When Akhenaten describes his epiphany at the ceremony of demarcating the city of Akhetaten, 'mounted in a great chariot of electrum like the sun-god when he rises on the horizon and fills the land with his beneficence', he not only describes the dazzling appearance of such equipages, he reveals how deeply their imagery had entered into the Egyptian consciousness, since from time immemorial the gods in Egypt had travelled over the waters of heaven in ships. In the reliefs on the chariot of Tuthmosis IV, the war-god Montu had stationed himself in the chariot to assist the king in bending his bow, the only known representation where the pharaoh is not shown alone in his fighting vehicle, in accordance with the new myth of the divine war-lord, unique and triumphant, the reins tied around his waist so as to leave his arms free to use his unerring bow.

The chariot was the preferred conveyance for Akhenaten at Amarna as distinct from the state palanquins in which he is carried for traditional ceremonial occasions such as his jubilees. The wide, straight, royal road through the centre of Akhetaten (see Chapter 6) seems to have been deliberately planned as a processional way along which the state chariot of the king, accompanied by that of his queen and followed by those of their retinue, would canter as a glorious manifestation, like the rising of the sun-god, while the adoring townsfolk prostrated themselves on the sidelines. This is a theme which is illustrated not only in the later tombs at Amarna, such as those of Meryrē I (No. 4) and Pinhasy (No. 6), but also in the earlier reliefs on talatat   *Fig. 10* recovered from the Ninth Pylon at Karnak, and appears to have a vital ritualistic meaning, just as the sun rising and shining upon the temple brings it and all creation to life every day.

The chariot with its costly woods and embellishment was an exceedingly expensive item, and could be afforded only by the wealthier families. The satirist speaks of the youthful charioteer spending his patrimony upon a chariot and a span of mettlesome horses and tearing around his home town with them learning to drive and showing off his prowess. The wealthy aristocratic charioteers formed a *corps d'élite* around the divine kings of the period. In Egypt they were often related to them, being the 'children of the court', the offspring and connections of the pharaohs by subsidiary wives, and they played an important role in the government, men like Yuya the Commander of the Chariotry under Tuthmosis IV, or Ay the Master of the Horse under Akhenaten.

The development of the professional standing army, and particularly its chariot arm, brought other Asiatic influences to bear upon traditional Egyptian culture and society. Foreign gods, like their peoples, were introduced into the Nile Valley and became naturalized. The Canaanite warrior-god Baal was established wherever military forces had spread, and the worship of the Syrian storm-god Reshop was introduced under Amenophis II. The cult of nude goddesses, Ashtoreth, Qedesh and Anath, appeared early, a naked female deity figuring prominently on Hyksos scarabs, and it may be the worship of such goddesses that was responsible for a steady increase in eroticism in the arts of   *Pls. 69, 70* the period. The love poetry, such as that contained in the various miscellanies, is known from Ramesside copies, but must have been created earlier, the sentiment being redolent of the middle years of the Eighteenth Dynasty, when the maidens attending even upon the male guests at the banquets in painting and sculpture are shown unclothed, and an elaborate symbolism of courtly love is also identified. The cult of the nude reached its apogee in the reign of Akhenaten, when a royal personage appears without her robe. The musicians, in particular, played upon foreign patterns of lutes, harps and oboes, discarded their outer garments in the accompanying dance, or sang love-lyrics of which only a scrap has survived. At Amarna, scenes in palace and temple sometimes show orchestras with musicians dressed in Anatolian attire, like the priests of Cybele of a later day, playing on a foreign type of standing harp.

Such arts of leisure and luxury belong to the aristocratic milieu of the royal courts of the day, whose tastes were for the exotic and opulent. Novelties in gold and ivory were greatly prized and eagerly trafficked. The king of Babylon sent orders through the pharaoh for such work from Egyptian craftsmen. Toilet vessels in brilliant glass or faience were traded as far as Crete. Granular work in gold, some of it coloured in shades from pink to purple, makes a somewhat barbaric appearance. Fine clothing was worked with elaborate decoration in coloured threads applied by the busy needles of Asiatic embroideresses. The objects found in the tomb of Tutankhamun, from his *Pl. 54* anthropoid coffins overlaid with gold, or entirely of gold, and inlaid with polychrome glass, to jewels carved in ivory or hardstones, have given the modern world an unrivalled conspectus of the wealth and luxury of such royal possessions in the Late Bronze Age, traded among the nations of the Near East. It was a commerce equally concerned with objects of utility as with knick-knacks and bijouterie. We have already spoken of the chariots sent as gifts to the pharaoh. Bows were also richly worked with coloured barks and the iridescent elytra of beetles, and mounted in gold filigree. The armour recorded by Tuthmosis III as having been recovered from the field of Meggido, was of bronze damascened with precious metals, more for display than reinforcement, like the armour of Achilles stripped off the corpse of Patroclus.

This Homeric echo is found also in the concepts of the sporting king, the pharaoh who is pre-eminent in hunting the animals of the wild, whether they be the asses and gazelles of the Egyptian wadis, or the miniature, red-haired elephants of Niy in North Syria. No one can bend the royal bow among the rival nations. With it the pharaoh shoots arrows clean through heavy ingots of copper. No one can equal him in rowing or managing horses. Both Tuthmosis III and Amenophis II vaunted their prowess in the hunt; and although Amenophis III did not go quite so far as the latter in boasting of his sporting achievements, he did issue a set of scarabs to commemorate a great round-up of wild cattle in his second regnal year, when he was hardly more than ten years old; and another series when he claimed to have shot with his own bow 102 wild lions during the first ten years of his reign.

In truth, it is probable that this skill in war and the chase is wholly mythical. The physiques of the pharaohs, as revealed by their mummies, are unlikely to have been as athletic in every case as their boasts profess. Amosis was slight and must have inaugurated the war against the Hyksos when he was still an inexperienced youth. Tuthmosis I, who until a few years ago it was customary to regard as a mature and experienced soldier at his accession, was little more than a mere stripling at his death if the mummy hitherto accepted as his has been correctly identified, a conclusion, therefore, which several scholars now question. Only Amenophis II in his height and physique, and what is known of his character, approximates to the quintessence of the hero. It would seem in fact that the military might of Egypt was sustained by a general staff who united in according their divine leader the sole palm of victory.

In the superhuman achievements accredited to the king, he stands well above the stature of his courtiers whose chariots follow his in the chase at a discreet distance. The rivals for the throne who had beset Amosis in his struggle against the Hyksos, had been eliminated. The king was a god by whom men lived, as the vizier Rekhmirē reported of Tuthmosis III, a myth wholeheartedly believed in by his powerful entourage. His pronouncements were oracular, his instructions followed to the letter as the divine will. In such a physical and spiritual milieu, no change could be made in opinion except by the pharaoh himself.

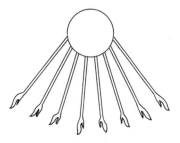

CHAPTER 13

The God's Wife and the Chief Queen

The Theban royal house, who challenged the power of their overlords, and initiated the liberation of Egypt from the Hyksos yoke, was not only fortunate in the fire and courage of its kings, it was also exceptional for a series of outstanding queens who won the veneration of later generations. Queen Ahhotep, for instance, the mother of Amosis, took over the reins of government on the sudden death of her husband Sekenenrē, probably at the hands of assassins. Evidently at this critical juncture she rallied the Theban forces, since a large stela, later erected in her honour by Amosis, speaks of her as cherishing Egypt by having tended her soldiers and succoured her fugitives, 'she has pacified Upper Egypt and cast out her rebels'. But destined to be even more influential was her daughter-in-law, Ahmose-Nefertari, the chief queen of Amosis and his probable cousin. She owed her renown, however, less to her political leadership than to her exalted position in the Theban religious establishment and especially in that of Amun, the god of Karnak.

Amun was of ancient origin, though he does not come into any prominence until the rise of the Theban kings of the Eleventh Dynasty at the beginning of the second millennium BC. Originally he seems to have been closely associated with the old prehistoric fertility god Min who thundered over the Eastern Desert, bringing the storm rains that occasionally filled the wadis and cisterns of that barren tract, and allowed a modest subsistence to its bedouin and their starveling flocks. Amun in this guise has the same ithyphallic form, with the flail and tall plumes of Min, showing his sovereignty over the region of the air, for he was also the 'Lord of the Sweet Breeze' that tempers the summer heat and refreshes the wilting spirit. The twin plumes he wore on his cap, like those of Shu the solar god of the Void, signified that he was also identified with the god of the luminous air which is a peculiar feature of the desert environs of Thebes.

The promotion of Amun by the Middle Kingdom pharaohs, not only at Karnak but also at Western Thebes and other foundations in the area, led to his pre-eminence by the beginning of the Eighteenth Dynasty when his solarization was complete. His role as a fertility god, like Min, was now overlain by his assumption of the divinity of the sun-gods of Heliopolis, Rē, the active god of the daylight, sailing across the heavens in a bark and contending with the cloud-dragon Apophis; or Atum, the ithyphallic demiurge of the solar cult who created the universe by an onanistic act.

The princes of Thebes, who successfully rebelled against their Hyksos overlords, regarded themselves as especially favoured by their city god Amun-rē, whose oracles had instigated their challenge and assured their triumph. They gratefully heaped their devotion and treasure upon him, building great temples to him at Karnak and Luxor as well as their mortuary temples on his territory on the western bank, appointing his four prophets or high priests and a host of sacerdotal officiants, and filling his estates with hundreds of captives as serfs. They also attended his periodic festivals at which he gave oracular judgments on all manner of problems great and small: above all, they ensured that their eternal habitations, and those of their entourages, would be hewn in his domains among the western hills in which they would rest after death. By the end of the New Kingdom, Amun-rē had become not only the supreme god of the Theban area, ousting Montu from his position of authority, but the state deity of all Upper Egypt, founding new enclaves for his cult even in Lower Egypt, and increasing his power and wealth until they far surpassed those of any other god.

The beginning of this ascendancy can be traced in the reign of Amosis, when his chief queen Ahmose-Nefertari took the title of 'God's Wife', a distinction borne by the High Priestess of Amun. Until her assumption of this office, the position had been in the hands of a woman of rank, probably a virgin incumbent who bore the title of the 'Wife of the God', or the 'Hand of the God', the god in this case being Amun, and the latter title referring to the act by which the demiurge Atum, the primordial god of the sun-cult, fashioned the universe by ejecting from himself a male principal Shu, the luminous Void, and a female deity Tefnut, or Moisture, and so initiated the process of creation. The origin of this belief is lost in the myths of the sun-religion to which it belongs and was assimilated by Amun when his cult was solarized during the Middle Kingdom. The marriage of the priestess to the god, in this case Amun-rē, perpetuated the idea of the cosmic myth and ensured the continuance of the work of creation which according to Egyptian belief was an everlasting cyclic process.

In the reign of Amosis the power and influence of the God's Wife was greatly enhanced, in step with the increase in the prestige and wealth of Amun, by the foundation of a college of 'recluses' or priestesses, and a choir of musicians and singers around her person, to which most of the high-ranking wives and daughters of the court dignitaries belonged. But the system is seen with greater clarity in the eighth century BC when all the features of a well-organized theocratic institution had emerged, with the king's eldest daughter as the virgin God's Wife inheriting a large and wealthy estate, espoused to Amun and filling the office of his chief vestal. As a celibate, she adopted her successor from the daughters of the pharaoh, and governed the whole of the Thebaid and Upper Egypt with the aid of an influential High Steward or major-domo. How far such a system prevailed in the Eighteenth Dynasty is not yet known; but the existence of such powerful queen's stewards as Senenmut and Kheruef suggests that the system may already have been established, at least in embryo. There are also other precedents which will be noted later.

Fig. 15 The first incumbent to have the titles of a God's Wife and a queen is Ahmose-Nefertari, who appears to have held the former title before she was married to Amosis. We are fortunate in possessing the account of the foundation of this harim of Amun under her direction as the God's Wife. A decree establishing the institution is recorded on three fragments from a temple wall subsequently demolished and used as fill in the Third Pylon of Amenophis III at Karnak. The inscription has come to be known as the Donation Stela, of which the opening date is damaged and uncertain. The scene in high relief shows Amosis and Nefertari before Amun of Karnak, and standing between them an infant prince whom the king holds by the hand, described as 'The eldest son of the divine flesh, Ahmose, may he live!' Evidently the boy, from his appearance as naked and wearing the side-lock, is a minor. The incised text which is almost complete records a solemn contract largely concerned with compensation to be paid to the queen in consideration of surrendering her office of Second Prophet of Amun. The indemnity in question consists of treasure in gold, silver and copper, clothing and unguents. In addition, she is to receive supplies of corn, and an estate and the labour to develop it. Her brother is to serve her, evidently as High Steward, 'so that she may be spared administrative troubles'. The donation is witnessed and sealed by the high dignitaries of Thebes and the palace, and is approved by the oracle of Amun who guarantees the transaction. The queen, thereafter, has the power of transmitting the office of God's Wife, and all the goods and services appertaining, to her heirs for pepetuity.

This important document incidentally informs us that the queen at some point in her previous career was appointed to the office of Second Prophet of Amun, a post which is not recorded before her time and is afterwards held by a male priest. The text does not reveal to whom the position was transferred by Nefertari, but there can be no doubt that it was her infant son Ahmose, and that was the reason for including him in the ceremony and depicting him in the relief. A funerary cone has survived showing that shortly after this occasion a Second Prophet of Amun, Ahmose, was buried in the Theban necropolis before Regnal Year 22 of Amosis. So it appears that this same Prince Ahmose died before his father, otherwise he might have inherited the throne. In any case, he could not have spent many years as Second Prophet and was probably not yet adolescent when he departed this life. The office of such priests, immediately thereafter, was held by incumbents who, seemingly, were unrelated to the royal family and the heirs of Nefertari. Nevertheless, towards the end of the dynasty, Anen, the brother of Queen Tiye, was the Second Prophet of Amun, in the reign of her husband Amenophis III; as was the nephew of another chief queen, Tey, in the reign of Ay, so perhaps some tradition survived that a member of the royal house should hold this important priesthood.

The Donation Stela commemorates the founding of the college of votaresses, or women of the harim of Amun, which appears to have been established in the 'house' or estate of Nefertari as God's Wife, probably on the west bank at Thebes. As well as being aided by a male steward, she was assisted, as the decree makes plain, by a female servitor who bore the title of

15 The 'Donation Stela' from Karnak with a relief of Amosis offering a white loaf to Amun, and followed by the 'King's Daughter, King's Sister, God's Wife and Chief Queen, whose every behest is done for her. . . Ahmose-Nefertari'. Between them stands their eldest son, the infant Ahmose who is still too young to hold the king's hand except by the forefinger.

16 Copy in line of a painting in the tomb of two sculptors at Thebes, showing the posthumous worship of Ahmose-Nefertari and her son Amenophis I as black resin-coated images clad in royal vestments within a kiosk or shrine.

'Superior of the Harim' and 'Adorer of the God' when she deputized for the God's Wife in her sacerdotal duties. The God's Wife is represented on the monuments of the early Eighteenth Dynasty as taking part in religious ceremonies, notably the scenes sculptured in relief on the dismantled granite shrine of Queen Hatshepsut, which has also been recovered from the filling of the Third Pylon at Karnak. There she appears as a slight, juvenile figure wearing a sheath gown and a close-fitting, rounded wig with a diadem. A curious ceinture confines her waist which, having regard to the conventions of Egyptian drawing, was evidently a girdle tied with ends falling loosely in front, and may have symbolized her virgin state.

It would appear that the title of 'God's Wife', once bestowed, could be claimed by the incumbent throughout her lifetime, though in the case of Ahmose-Nefertari as the first princess to be made a God's Wife, her position may have been exceptional, especially in view of the foundation which she established in Western Thebes. Certainly during her lifetime, others of her female relatives shared office with her in turn. It may well be on the analogy of the celibate nature of the office in the eighth century BC, that already at this early date in its development the God's Wife had to give up her duties, though not her title, on marriage. But it seems clear that the promise that the office would be handed down to the heirs of Nefertari in perpetuity was honoured as far as possible, and 'Heiress' was one of the constant elements in the full titulary of the God's Wives throughout the history of their office.

The accession of Tuthmosis I, however, marked a change in the pattern of dynastic inheritance during the fifteenth century BC; he was not the bodily son of his predecessor Amenophis I, but is generally regarded as belonging to a cognate line. His chief queen by whom he presumably acquired the kingship was another Ahmose who bore the modest title of a 'King's Sister', and is unlikely to be a child of Amosis, otherwise she would have claimed the additional and superior title of 'King's Daughter'. Queen Ahmose was not a 'God's Wife', so far as the inscriptions reveal, though documents of this period of her life are extremely scanty. But if she were not a God's Wife *de jure*, she certainly was *de facto*. The 'Birth Colonnade' of the mortuary temple of her   *Fig. 17* daughter Hatshepsut at Deir el Bahri shows the various stages in the procreation of the heir apparent. The god Amun in the guise of the reigning king visits Queen Ahmose and begets the future ruler by filling her nostrils with the breath of new life. Thus the fiction of the birth of the pharaoh by the union of the supreme god with a virgin priestess-queen is preserved and promulgated, the myth being only distorted to the extent that the newborn pharaoh is a female, with nevertheless the five great names of a male king and all his masculine trappings, even to a fictive beard on her chin. Whatever the exact status of Queen Ahmose may have been, her child by Tuthmosis/Amun was the God's Wife Hatshepsut, the Heiress, who became chief queen of the next king, Tuthmosis II.

The usurpation of pharaonic power by Hatshepsut on the death of her husband, during the minority of her stepson Tuthmosis III, is a drama that has provoked much discussion by Egyptologists in the past, although the elaborate scenario that was devised by the German scholar Kurt Sethe to account for all the vagaries in the altered monumental inscriptions of the time has now been quietly abandoned. The position of Hatshepsut during the short reign of her husband, as the influential and wealthy inheritor of a sacerdotal order that had been founded by the ancestress of the ruling family, would certainly prepare her mentally and materially for the assumption of supreme power.

There may well have been another reason for such arrogation of authority. Amosis in his first years on the throne had to contend with the pretensions of rivals for power, apart from his Hyksos opponents. This rivalry at the head of government has been diagnosed as the reason why many kings followed one another in rapid succession during the Thirteenth Dynasty, so bringing about the anarchy and weaknesses that allowed the Hyksos usurpers to seize control of Egypt. When Amosis had eliminated the last of the rebels who challenged his authority, he ensured that his family would continue to rule by making it a political as well as a religious tenet that the succession would be determined by an heiress princess, and the intervention of the god Amun.

In truth, the idea of the theogamous succession was not new. It has been encountered at least as early as the Fifth Dynasty when, according to a folk-tale, the sun-god had intervened to engender the first three kings of the new dynasty upon the wife of a priest of the sun-cult; and this fiction persisted to the end of pharaonic rule in Egypt. The sanctuary of the Birth House of Nectanebo I at Dendera, in the fourth century BC, shows scenes of the procreation of the divine child of the goddess-queen Hathor by Amun of Thebes which are duplicates, *mutatis mutandis*, of the reliefs of Hatshepsut at Deir el Bahri.

On assuming the insignia of a male pharaoh, Hatshepsut gave up the ornaments of a God's Wife in favour of Nefrurē, her daughter by Tuthmosis II. But this fair hope for the dynastic succession was dashed when the princess died prematurely, some time after her mother's eleventh regnal year, and possibly without marrying her half-brother, the co-regent Tuthmosis III.

Another hiatus in the prescribed order of succession of God's Wives may now have supervened until Hatshepsut Meritrē became God's Wife. She was the daughter of a priestess Huy who was not a God's Wife, but an Adorer of the gods Amun and Atum, and the Superior of the Harim of Amun. Her connection with the family of Nefertari is unknown, but it is possible that if she were not a descendant in the direct line, she may have been adopted into the succession. Who her husband was has not yet been discovered, but it is possible that he was a certain Yey who was Commander of the Chariotry (see below). Despite these uncertainties, there is no doubt her daughter was Hatshepsut Meritrē, and as the chief wife of Tuthmosis III she was the mother of the next king, Amenophis II. Her daughter Tia became God's Wife after her, and also in due course the chief wife of Amenophis II and the mother of Tuthmosis IV.

If the pattern of inheritance established by Huy was followed thereafter, Queen Mutemwiya, mother of Amenophis III and wife of Tuthmosis IV, should also have been a God's Wife in her time; but unfortunately very little of her career is known before the reign of her son. There may, however, have been another interruption in the line of descent when Tiye became the chief wife of Amenophis III. She does not bear the title of God's Wife, though she was certainly connected with the harim of Amun, her mother Tuyu being the Superior of that institution, and in fact holding the equivalent position that Huy enjoyed under Tuthmosis III. Tiye must have been married to Amenophis III very early in her career, and possibly had not reached a sufficiently advanced age to be initiated into the religious duties of a God's Wife before she assumed the position of chief wife of the king (see below).

It is, however, quite evident that the cult of Ahmose-Nefertari was greatly expanded during the early reign of Amenophis III. She became one of the great influential Theban deities, and together with her son Amenophis I and her husband Amosis was recognized as a patron of the necropolis on the west bank. Her worship was particularly prominent in the village of Deir el Medina *Fig. 16* where the workmen concerned with preparing the royal tombs were quartered with their families. Votive stelae and figurines carved with the features and fashion of dress peculiar to Tiye were dedicated to Nefertari on various sites in the Theban area. A statue of her in black, resin-coated wood was consecrated as the chief icon of her cult, probably in her temple on the estate she had founded at Western Thebes. It is also to be suspected that the great corn-bearing estate that Amenophis III established for Tiye in his Regnal Year 11 (see below) was as much for the enlargement of the harim of Amun which Nefertari had founded as for increasing the wealth of his chief queen. In short, it appears that this promotion of the cult of Nefertari owed much to the sponsorship of Tiye because she was a descendant, either directly or by adoption, of the earlier queen. It is noteworthy that members of her family bore names which refer back to the ancestors at the beginning of the Theban resurgence during the dawn of the Eighteenth Dynasty. Tiye is a pet name for Nefertari, in the same way that Nefertiti appears to be an allusive variant of it. Tuyu is a contraction of Ahhotep, a name of great significance at the beginning of the dynasty. Sitamun, the eldest daughter of Amenophis III and Tiye, was a name which was also given to a daughter of Nefertari and to a God's Wife in the reign of Amenophis II.

The importance of the part played by the God's Wife of Amun in the dynastic succession during the New Kingdom has only recently come to be appreciated, but will be found to influence profoundly the position of Queen Nefertiti, for instance, during the reign of Akhenaten. Whatever ambiguity there may be in the succession of God's Wives during the later half of the Eighteenth Dynasty, there is no doubt that the sons of such queens secured the throne in the case of Amenophis I, Amenophis II and Tuthmosis IV. The case of Tuthmosis III is a little ambiguous. His mother Isis, usually presumed to be a royal concubine, is shown wearing the double uraei of a God's Wife who had become a queen: but the oracle of Amun also played an equivocal part in his appointment, it would appear without the sanction of Hatshepsut, who therefore apparently felt herself free to intervene as Regent. The accession of Amenophis III is also problematic, the claim of his mother, Mutemwiya, to the position of a God's Wife being by no means clear. In his case, however, his procreation by the god Amun in the guise of Tuthmosis IV is represented in the 'Birth Room' of his temple at Luxor, in which event Mutemwiya, whatever her title, is seen to play the role of a God's Wife, exactly as Queen Ahmose did in relation to Tuthmosis I, as represented in the 'Birth Colonnade' of the temple of Hatshepsut at Deir el Bahri.

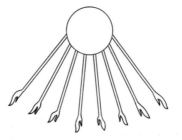

CHAPTER 14
The Reign of Tuthmosis IV

At the death of the sardonic old warrior Amenophis II, his son the youth Tuthmosis, Menkheperurē, succeeded to the throne of Horus. He may have been preceded by an elder brother who served his father as a co-regent but died before he could come into his own. Tuthmosis IV attributed his good fortune to the sponsorship of the supreme god of Lower Egypt, Rē-Herakhte, who in a dream promised him the crown if he would clear away the sands that engulfed his giant image of the sphinx at Giza. But his preferment may have owed much to the fact that his mother Tia was a God's Wife as well as a chief queen of Amenophis II.

The support accredited to the sun-god of Heliopolis, however, is but one indication of the increasing role that Lower Egypt was now to play in the government of the country after years of partial eclipse since the expulsion of the Hyksos. Amenophis II had been born in Memphis, where a great palace had been founded by Tuthmosis I, and had exercised authority in the supervision of the dockyards in the northern capital. Officials of Delta origin were to become more important in ensuing years, though they may have been buried at Thebes near the kings they had served in life. Tuthmosis IV seems to have been less concerned with Theban affairs and with promoting the welfare of its god. His monuments are scanty in the southern residence, which he may have visited but rarely, though he did complete and erect the great obelisk, now at St John Lateran in Rome, which had been planned by Tuthmosis III, and had lain at Karnak since the latter's death thirty-five years earlier. But this was as much a symbol honouring the sun-god of Heliopolis as Amun of Thebes. Another indication of the burgeoning influence of the sun-cult is seen in the issue of a large scarab during his reign in which the Aten is spoken of as a god of battles who makes the pharaoh mighty in his dominions and brings all his subjects under the sway of the sun-disk. This is the first notable mention of a new and universal aspect of the sun which was to achieve a supreme position under his grandson.

The reign of Tuthmosis IV also marks a turning-point in the fortunes of the dynasty in a wider context. The era of warring in Asia and extending the boundaries of Egypt was over. Police actions on the unsettled frontiers were the only foreign adventures that were called for. The rulers of the great powers in the Near East had agreed to stabilize their relations by treaties cemented by marriage alliances with the pharaoh. In particular, the rival king of the Mitanni, whose forces were dominant in North Syria at this time, entered into ever more cordial relations with his 'brother' the pharaoh; and after a long wooing, this understanding was consummated by the entry of the daughter of Artatama, king of the Mitanni, into the harim of Tuthmosis IV, doubtless with an opulent dowry commensurate with the wealth and status of her father, and a suitable bride-price from her Egyptian suitor. Egypt now embarked upon nearly half a century of peace and prosperity, when Asiatic influence in the Nile Valley became widespread and the arts of luxury were cultivated.

The reign of Tuthmosis, in comparison with those of his father and grandfather, was brief, most Egyptologists identifying him with a 'Thmosis', who in the middle of the dynasty is accredited with a rule of nine years and eight months, according to the extract by Josephus from Manetho. Recently, however, the scholars of the Oriental Institute, Chicago, have challenged this view to claim that his reign lasted much longer, since he appears to have celebrated a second jubilee, which according to them must imply that he ruled for thirty-two or thirty-three years. They also take into account a recent radiographic examination of his mummy by the Alexandria-Michigan team who argue that his age at death must approach thirty-five to forty years. In point of fact, their claims are not quite so decisive as might at first appear. Similar anomalous results in the estimates of the ages of the other royal mummies, as has been mentioned above, have aroused doubts about the correct identification of the subjects in antiquity.

In the case of the mummy docketed as that of Tuthmosis IV at the moment of its discovery in the tomb of Amenophis II in 1898, a contrary interpretation of the medical evidence presented by the Alexandria-Michigan team was made in a letter to the writer by the late Frank Leek, palaeopathologist. He pointed out that the bone of the skull was comparatively thin which precluded an advanced age. He detected no changes in the bones of the vertebral column, and the attrition on the teeth decreased from a flattening of the cusps of the first molar to no perceptible wear on the third or wisdom tooth. The alveolar bone, except between the lower first and second molars (which was probably caused by food packing), appeared to be normal. All the foregoing features, he concluded, indicated that in a time-span of twenty-five to thirty-five years, the subject was in the lower rather than the upper part of the range.

The chief argument for a long reign by Tuthmosis IV appears to depend upon a controversial graffito of a Year 20 chiselled by an unknown viceroy of Kush into the rocks near a quarry at Tombos above the Third Cataract of the

Nile. This inscription was seen and recorded by Breasted in 1907. He first read
the prenomen of the king as Menkheperurē and the name of the viceroy as Ari.
He subsequently modified this reading to take account of the prevalent view
that Tuthmosis IV ruled for little more than nine years, and concluded that the
king in question must be Tuthmosis III (Menkheperrē) who had a long reign
of over fifty years. The graffito has been damaged in places, the names of the
king and his viceroy being indistinct. The only clear fact to emerge is that the
year-number is twenty. The name of the king looks more like Tuthmosis III
than IV, and has not been queried by the recent experts who have examined the
actual inscription *in situ*. In the face of such ambiguity it is best to disregard
this graffito as providing any solid evidence.

There are other reasons for rejecting a long reign for Tuthmosis IV. The fact
that no dated monuments have survived from his reign after his Year 8, may be
dismissed as an argument *ex silentio*; but it would be exceptional if a gap of
some twenty-four or more years should have elapsed in the reign of a great
pharaoh at this period without some hint of activity on his part or by his high
officials. As it is, his monuments are particularly modest for a king enjoying the
blessings of peace and prosperity at the height of Egypt's greatness, and a
distinct contrast to the achievements of the following reign. Tuthmosis built
little at Memphis and scarcely more at Thebes, and that modicum was mostly
demolished soon after his death to clear ground for the Third Pylon at Karnak.
His most ambitious undertaking was a peripteral temple which was demolished
and incorporated in the mass of the Third Pylon. It awaits further study and
reconstruction but does not appear to be of great size. At Amada in Nubia he
interpolated a small peripteral kiosk in a larger temple built by Tuthmosis III
and Amenophis II during their co-regency. The decoration of these last two
temples, like that of similar kiosks on Elephantine Island and the Heb Sed
temple of Amenophis II at Karnak, has encouraged the view that Tuthmosis
IV celebrated a second jubilee, especially as the square pillars that form the
ambulatory of such temples have the standard text on each face to indicate that
a jubilee is being repeated. The inference (see above) is that in order to
celebrate two jubilees the king must have ruled for at least thirty-three years.
The writer, however, regards it as more probable that the jubilee in question
was being prepared for the senior co-regent, Amenophis II who, however,
appears to have died shortly before he could celebrate it. The decoration of
these temples was therefore completed by inscribing them for the junior
partner, most of the scenes serving for a coronation as well as for its repetition
in the jubilee.

The tombs of the courtiers and officials of Tuthmosis IV at Western Thebes
are relatively few, only eight being securely dated to his time. Others that have
been accredited to his reign on stylistic grounds, may have been started in the

previous reign of Amenophis II, or completed in the subsequent reign of Amenophis III. Moreover, at least three, those of Kha (No. 8), Haremhab (No. 78) and Amenmose (No. 89), show that their owners served all the kings during the middle years of the dynasty, from Tuthmosis III to Amenophis III, a total spell in office of more than sixty-four years each, on the Chicago reckoning. Such universal longevity is improbable when the average expectation of life, calculated by the Alexandria-Michigan team, scarcely exceeded thirty years for privileged royalty.

In these circumstances, the writer sees no reason for abandoning the long-accepted opinion that Manetho for once has been correctly reported in giving the length of the reign of Tuthmosis IV as nine years and eight months.

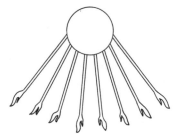

CHAPTER 15

The Reign of Amenophis III

The conclusion that the father of Amenophis III ruled for a few months short of ten years is important because it establishes that his son could not have been more than nine years old when he succeeded him, and was probably nearer seven years. This infantine aspect is very evident in early portraits of Amenophis, his features being chubby and unformed. Nevertheless he was married to an heiress-queen as part of the coronation rites; and his advent is commemorated in a novel fashion by an issue of large scarabs, an innovation that was to be repeated at irregular intervals during the first twelve years of his reign. Each series bore a lengthy inscription on the underside of the base announcing a notable event in the king's career.

cf. Pl. 47

The first issue was not dated because it initiated his reign, being a rescript of his names and titles for use in all official documents. Examples of this mis-called 'Marriage Scarab' have been found widely dispersed, even as far as the northern and southern extremities of his dominions. The styles and names of the king on this scarab are followed by those of his chief wife, her parents being identified as Yuya and Tuyu, without any titles. But it is known from other inscriptions that her mother Tuyu was the Superior of the Harim of Amun, and held a similar position in the harim of the cognate deity Min of Akhmim. Tuyu thus occupied an important position in the hierarchy of Amun at Thebes under the God's Wife. Indeed, if she enjoyed the same eminence as Huy in the reign of Tuthmosis III, there is no wonder that her daughter should have become the chief wife of the king.

Tiye, in fact, was far from being some attractive maiden from the royal harim who caught the king's eye, according to the romantic notions of some scholars who have been too much influenced by the king's negotiations for foreign wives and handmaidens later in his reign. At the time of his marriage to Tiye, he was not yet a teenager and his bride was even younger. We shall examine later in more detail the significance and ramifications of Tiye's family. Here we shall limit ourselves to the observation that her family was an important and influential one and probably closely related to the king himself.

Tiye had a township, Djarukha, in the vicinity of Akhmim, near modern Tahta which may enshrine her name, just as the village of Adaye near her temple at Sedeinga in the Sudan seems to do likewise. It was at Djarukha, on the first day of the third month in his eleventh regnal year, that Amenophis established for her an estate in the form of a huge irrigation basin, extending over 190 acres, that yielded corn to swell her revenues, as the so-called Lake Scarabs informed the world. This same inscription announced that the king inaugurated the flooded basin by sailing into it in his state-barge, *Radiance of Aten*; another mention of the solar deity soon to turn his realm topsy-turvy.

In the first decades of the reign there was no inkling of such a convulsion. From his early years, Amenophis III proved to be a mighty builder in the limestone of Lower Egypt and the sandstone of the south, though the full extent of his work is obscured by the mischance that much of it was unfinished at his death and taken over or adopted by later kings, particularly Ramesses II and Mineptah. The temples which he erected at Thebes alone must have changed the appearance of the southern capital beyond recognition. In 1896, Petrie, excavating in the ruins of the funerary temple of Mineptah in the row of such monuments on the western bank at Thebes, found a grey granite stela over 3 metres high which had been installed originally in the adjacent temple of Amenophis III but usurped by the later king. It gave a description of some of the mighty works that Amenophis had raised for Amun-rē in Thebes and Nubia, including the mortuary temple itself, the Third Pylon of the Great Temple of Amun at Karnak, the Luxor Temple, a *maru* or 'viewing' temple at Western Thebes, and a temple at Sulb some 80 kilometres north of the Third Cataract of the Nile. The description of the mortuary temple in this stela must also serve to give some idea of the other structures enumerated. It was built, we read, in fine white sandstone, embellished with gold throughout. The floor of its sanctuary was covered with silver, and all its doorways with electrum. It was made very broad and long, and adorned with a great stela embellished with gold and coloured stones. In it were numerous statues of the king and the gods in excellently worked granite of Elephantine, in hard red quartzite and every fine stone. They rose in their height more than the heavens and were beautiful to the sight like the Aten, or Disk of the Sun, at its rising. Its flagstaves were plated with electrum. Its sacred lake was filled by the Nile. Its offices were staffed with servitors both male and female, together with foreign captives, and its storerooms were full of countless treasures.

Its most abiding features, however, were the two giant monolithic statues of the king, over 21 metres high, that stood before the main portal. The northern colossus was famed in Classical times when it was identified with Memnon, the dead Trojan hero, who gave forth a mourning note at sunrise until an earth tremor silenced it in the reign of Septimius Severus. Both colossi won fame for the king's Master of Works, Amenophis-son-of-Hapu (see below), who had them carved in the quartzite of the Gebel el Ahmar, near Heliopolis, and towed nearly 700 kilometres against the Nile current to be erected at Thebes. Another pair, even a little larger, were positioned near the gateway of the Tenth Pylon that the king founded at Karnak, but were usurped by other kings, and now are almost totally demolished.

Other constructions of Amenophis III on the west bank were his extensive tomb in the western branch of the Valley of the Kings, and his large rambling palace city, extending over 80 acres, at the Malkata at Medinet Habu. This haphazard arrangement of palaces, courtyards, villas, offices and audience-halls was built of light materials, mostly wood and mudbrick. But it was gay with painted marsh scenes and decorative motifs on white-washed mud-plaster. Here an artificial basin, the Birket Habu, connected by a canal to the Nile, provided anchorage for ships and barges on the eastern harbour area fronting the entire palace complex.

Pls. 48, 49

Half a kilometre to the south, a hitherto unique feature has recently been reinvestigated, and confirms the earlier opinion that it was a kind of stadium for chariot racing, or exercising, with a straight course over 400 metres long. It was also on the west bank that the king constructed a *maru* on an east-west axis, a forerunner of one at Amarna, with pools, tanks, kiosks and flower-beds in which Amun in his aspect of a solar god could be viewed from his rising to his setting every day. The site of the *maru* has not been located for certain, but is believed to lie in the northern area of the Malkata palace.

At Karnak on the opposite bank, Amenophis added little to the Great Temple of Amun, but that little was spectacular. He raised a great triumphal gateway, the Third Pylon: and to make room for this he cleared away a lot of clutter, including several shrines of his predecessors, and incorporated their dismantled parts in the mass of its two towers. The approach to this monumental entrance to the temple was by means of a canal from the Nile leading into a docking basin now covered by the Hypostyle Hall. To the north of the temple of Amun he built on an ancient foundation a temple to Montu, the falcon-headed god originally of Armant who had extended his influence over the entire Theban region. This temple must have been a splendid building, complete and homogeneous, with a quay and a dromos flanked by sphinxes and a pair of obelisks over 18 metres high: but very little now remains except the ground-plan.

Another ruined edifice which Amenophis rebuilt and enlarged lies ½ kilo-metre south of the temple of Amun beside a crescent-shaped lake known as Ashru. This building was sacred to the goddess Mut, the consort of Amun, who here abandoned her aspect of a stately queen wearing the Double Crown of Egypt, and took the form of Sekhmet, a lion-headed goddess of Memphis and the chief companion of its god Ptah, thus bringing the ancient god of the Lower Egyptian capital into the adytum of the god of the Upper Egyptian capital. It has been estimated that over 700 granite statues of Sekhmet as a lion-headed woman, seated or standing, were installed on this site and nearly every Egyptological collection can boast of at least one example or a substantial fragment.

Recent research, however, has suggested that this huge collection was not originally positioned in Ashru, but removed thither from the king's mortuary temple across the river when it was plundered to provide material for constructions by Ramesses II and Mineptah. In their original state these hundreds of statues formed a kind of litany of the goddess under her various names and habitations, so providing a double prophylactic spell for the protection of the entire land during each specific day of the year, similar to later texts which were carved upon the temples of Edfu, Kom Ombo and Dendera. Sekhmet in her leonine aspect was a solar deity, the Eye of the Sun-god, a raging fire that could destroy mankind. Above all she was the goddess of war and pestilence. We shall later refer to the prevalence of plague at this time of prosperity in the Levant, perhaps a concomitant of the sudden expansions of population in over-crowded townships. As such visitations were thought to be the onslaught of offended gods such as Nergal and Reshop, the litany of Sekhmet in her role of a goddess of pestilence and war may be seen as an attempt to propitiate her and avert such calamities from Upper and Lower Egypt.

The most important of the Theban monuments of Amenophis III, however, must be sought not in the ruins of Karnak or Ashru but in the 'Southern Sanctuary', the ancient name for Luxor. Here rises the vast temple to the Theban trinity, Amun, Mut, and their offspring, a moon-god, the child Khons, which the king's architect was still building in Year 35 of his reign. Apart from a vestibule with a podium for the reception of the sacred bark of Amun during its sojourn there while the joyous festival of Opet was celebrated on the fifteenth day of the second month of the year, and subsidiary chapels for the smaller barks of Mut and Khons, the temple had an inner sanctuary with four columns, like a stone canopy, for housing a colossal statue of Amun upon a balustrade. Judging from the reliefs on the now ruined and empty sanctum, Amun was represented in his usual aspect of a divine king wearing a cap with *cf. Pl. 51* two tall feathers, seated upon a block-throne. But he was also worshipped in the special local form of an ithyphallic fertility deity like his *alter ego* Min, and thus with Mut of Ashru represented those other deities who were considered the patron-gods of the royal family at this particular period.

Around the two sanctuaries of the temple were rooms for storing the consecrated emblems, implements, garments, vessels and offerings used in the cult. In a columned hall flanking the vestibule, the (locally) western wall is decorated with reliefs of the theogamy or divine birth of the king in which appear all the elements seen in the better preserved scenes of Hatshepsut in her mortuary temple at Deir el Bahri. In Luxor, however, Amun enacts the part of Tuthmosis IV, and it is the king's mother Mutemwiya who is led by Isis and Khnum to the birth-chamber.

The temple was once gorgeously decorated with gold, silver, lapis lazuli and coloured opaque glass, and furnished with sculptures in hard and soft stones; but only a few dispersed and usurped examples of the statuary bear some witness to its former magnificence. Despite its ruinous state, however, and the alterations it has suffered, its grandeur is still impressive particularly at sunrise, the moment of the temple's awakening, when the Theban luminescence gives an almost translucent effect to the stone. The contrast between the rows of clustered papyrus-bud columns, where the diagonal shadows fall thick, and the broad areas of light in the open courts, the elegant balance of the proportions between the main structure and the soaring colonnade with its huge campaniform capitals, make it evident that within the rigid requirements of the Egyptian temple as a cosmological myth translated into stone, Amenophis III was able to call upon the services of a great architect whose work, however, was left unfinished at the end of the reign.

In addition to these works at Thebes, great buildings were erected in most of the larger centres during the long reign of Amenophis. At Memphis he founded a second mortuary temple for his posthumous cult, as a northern pendant to the vast structure at Western Thebes. He also raised temples at Athribis, Bubastis and Letopolis in the Delta. At Medinet Ghurab in the Faiyum he extended the palace-town of Miwer, founded by Tuthmosis III as a royal hunting-lodge and recreation-centre. Notable objects belonging to his family have been recovered from its ruins. On Egypt's border with Nubia, at the island of Elephantine, he built a charming peripteral kiosk for his first jubilee as the traditions of his dynasty required. It was completely destroyed early in the last century, so that its exact site is unknown, but happily not before the scholars of Napoleon's Expedition and some early travellers had made a provisional record of it. The ruins of the temple at Sulb, an outpost of the empire of Amenophis in the Sudan, are still considerable. Here the king dedicated the foundation to the cult of Amun who was represented by an avenue of couchant rams, his sacred animal, instead of sphinxes, guarding the approach from the quay on the river bank and leading to a vestibule in front of the pylon. Associated in the worship of Amun is the divinized king himself as Lord of Nubia. Nearby at Adaye, the companion temple of Sedeinga was built for Queen Tiye where she was worshipped in the form of a statue identified with the goddess Hathor as patroness of the foreign lands of Nubia and Kush.

17 The gods of conception conducting the pregnant Queen Ahmose into the chamber where her daughter Hatshepsut will be born.

All these works were notable for the lavish use of opulent materials, the exceptional quality of their design, the precision of their workmanship, and in most examples their great size. It is in this reign that statuary on a really enormous scale makes its appearance in great quantities. Whether this drive towards grandiloquence represents the king's own hubris in conformity with the spirit abroad in the Late Bronze Age, or whether it was but a manifestation by his artists and architects of their pride in the power and importance of Egypt of which their pharaoh was Lord, must be a matter of opinion; but that there was a climax in the belief in the divinity of the pharaoh during the reign of Amenophis III does not admit of much doubt. The theogamous nature of his birth had venerable precedents, and can be overstressed, but there is clear evidence that he was worshipped like a god in the form of a graven image at Sulb, Memphis, Hierakonpolis, Thebes and elsewhere during his lifetime. At Sulb he even adores his own image. This increase in the aura of majesty may have owed something to antiquarian research which was resolutely pursued during his reign, a harking back to a remote past when the pharaoh had been the Egyptians' greatest god. It was also prompted, however, by the steady growth in the idea of a single, universal, supreme divinity of whom the king was at once the offspring and the incarnation.

Paradoxically, his divinity had not quite the unique quality that Rekhmirē claimed for his king, Tuthmosis III, but was more a duality, even a trinity like the solar demiurge Atum. The female complement of Amenophis was his chief queen Tiye whom we have identified as the Heiress in the line of descent of the deified queen, Ahmose-Nefertari. Her name frequently accompanies that of her husband in ceremonial inscriptions, and her figure, sometimes on a huge scale, may appear equal to his in proportion, as on the colossal seated group from Medinet Habu in Cairo, and the upper part of a limestone statue in London. The reciprocal nature of her regal power is seen in the representation of the royal couple in the tomb of Kheruef, where she sits on a throne, the counterpart of the king's, but with arm-rests in the design of a female sphinx trampling down the traditional foes who also appear as bound African and Asiatic women supporting the seat. Her titles proclaim her might and status:

Pls. 45, 46

The Heiress, Greatly Favoured, Mistress of All Countries, Lady of Delight, who Fills the Palace with Love, Lady of the Two Lands, Mistress of Upper and Lower Egypt.

Her position in the government was recognized by foreign potentates with whom she might correspond; and in turn Tushratta of the Mitanni wrote to her after the death of Amenophis III as one who enjoyed the full confidence of her husband in matters of diplomacy. The importance of Tiye in the government of Egypt is therefore clear and unquestioned, and scarcely less ubiquitous than that of Nefertiti in the following reign, much as that queen's pre-eminence has been canvassed by some recent students of the Amarna period.

Besides Tiye, Amenophis had other wives both native and foreign. The Amarna Letters acquaint us with the negotiations that continued during his reign for foreign princesses to enter his harim, not only cementing diplomatic ties with brother rulers in Western Asia, but also redounding to his renown and wealth, and creating a legend that persisted thereafter in the imagination of the Orient. One of these alliances (see above) was sufficiently spectacular to be commemorated by a special issue of large scarabs in his tenth regnal year reporting the arrival of Gilukhipa, daughter of Shuttarna II the king of the Mitanni, with the chief part of her retinue consisting of 317 women, which would include many skilled needlewomen and musicians and other handmaidens proficient in the polite arts. Some years later, when Shuttarna had been succeeded by Tushratta in dubious circumstances, a new marriage alliance was necessary, and negotiations were completed for Tadukhipa, the daughter of Tushratta, to enter the pharaoh's harim together with an appropriately rich trousseau.

40 *Scene on a limestone talatat from Hermopolis showing a detail of the royal barge belonging to the king, a cabin decorated with a representation of Akhenaten smiting a foreign male captive in the presence of the queen.*

41 *A similarly decorated cabin on the queen's barge, with Nefertiti as the 'Divine Wife' engaged in the destruction of a state enemy in the guise of a female prisoner.*

42 *A light, but strong, open-ended chariot drawn by a pair of stallions yoked to the pole, driven by a groom, and carrying an aristocratic warrior, often related to the king, became a formidable arm of the Egyptian forces in the New Kingdom. Such armoured fighting-vehicles with a case for holding composite bows, and another for javelins*

strapped to the sides (cf. Fig. 14), were made of selected imported woods, or together with spans of horses were sent as gifts to the pharaohs by Asiatic rulers. Some were richly decorated with gold and polychrome glass, like this state chariot of Tutankhamun.

44 *Bearded Asiatics in their heavy embroidered robes making obeisance before Tuthmosis IV as they lay their precious gifts before his feet at his advent. Included in the tribute here are gold, silver and stone vessels, weapons and slave children. An eagle-headed rhyton on a dish, an object of Minoan design, was probably obtained by trade with the Aegean.*

43 *(left) Interior of the chariot in Pl. 42, lacking its ornate weapon-cases. The decorative panels are made of heavy gold foil worked in a repoussé technique, backed with gesso and linen, with scenes of the chastizing of foreign foes by the king as a sphinx. The gold is enhanced with bosses and borders inlaid with coloured glass, faience and similar ornamentation, to produce a gorgeous and dazzling appearance.*

45 (below) *Grey-green schistose head of a statue of Queen Tiye excavated in the temple at Serabit el Khadim in Sinai by Petrie in 1904. The characteristic features of the queen with her pouting mouth are more realistically rendered than in the official portraits that belong to the earlier years of her reign. The damage the lower part of the face has sustained has vitiated the effect of her firmly modelled and rounded chin.*

46 *The same features (above) as in Pl. 45, but rather less critically damaged, are found in this larger quartzite head from a composite statue which is reputed to have come from Amarna, perhaps from Queen Tiye's sunshade temple (see Fig. 29), wherein statues of the queen are shown holding offering trays.*

47 (right) *This basalt statue head of Amenophis III from an old European collection that was acquired before the middle of the last century is one of a series which shows the king in his youth wearing the* khepresh *or 'crown of victory'. This particular example appears to be the earliest in the group and in its chubby unformed features must represent the king as a child at his advent.*

48 *Fragment of a painted ceiling of a robing room in the palace of Amenophis III at the Malkata south of Medinet Habu. The interlocking spirals with bucrania and rosettes between the lattices may suggest Aegean influence, but such designs were of some antiquity in Egypt.*

49 *View across the harim quarters of the Malkata palace adjoining a columned hall with plastered brick shelf-supports in store rooms. The painted design of a bull emerging from a papyrus thicket may be a recollection of the king's momentous cattle-hunt in his Year 2.*

50 *(right) These elegant ladies, with elaborate coiffures and tall crowns, represented in low relief in the tomb of Kheruef at Thebes, are Asiatic princesses come to attend the first jubilee of Amenophis III in his Regnal Year 30, according to a custom that dated back to very early times. The rite was also observed for the jubilee of Amenophis IV at Karnak. The princesses had the duty of purifying the royal dais four times with holy water poured from gold and electrum libation vessels.*

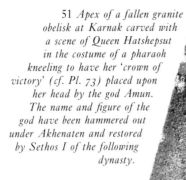

51 *Apex of a fallen granite obelisk at Karnak carved with a scene of Queen Hatshepsut in the costume of a pharaoh kneeling to have her 'crown of victory' (cf. Pl. 73) placed upon her head by the god Amun. The name and figure of the god have been hammered out under Akhenaten and restored by Sethos I of the following dynasty.*

52 *Bracelet plaque of dark sard torn from its original gold mount during the robbing of the funerary trappings of Amenophis III and discarded near his tomb in the Valley of the Kings. The restored gold mount as shown when it was in the Carnarvon Collection has since been removed. The openwork design evidently represents Queen Tiye as Tefnut, the daughter of the sun-god, in her leonine aspect as a winged sphinx (cf. Pl. 77) wearing a distinctive cap-crown and upholding the prenomen of Amenophis III. Tefnut accepts the king's name in some coronation scenes.*

In the tradition of his forefathers, Amenophis III did not hesitate to project himself in his official utterances as the all-conquering king. He vaunted his prowess as a 'fierce-eyed lion' and a 'raging fire' when smiting the rebel; and took his titles from the foes he claimed to have made captive, thus 'Destroyer of Naharin', and 'Sacker of Shinar'. He was particularly proud of his Nubian campaign in which he boasted of excelling above any other king; but as he was only just over twelve years old at the time, his assertion smacks of poetic licence, and the credit doubtless lay with Merimose, his viceroy of Kush, in what was evidently little more than a police action. His achievements as a sportsman are possibly more plausible, though his claim in his scarab of Year 2 to have rounded up, with the aid of a military detachment, a total of 96 bulls out of a herd of 170 wild cattle in the Wadi el Natrun, when he was scarcely nine years old, is probably to be understood as an operation by his army, with the king at their head, against a symbolic manifestation of evil invading the borders of Egypt. In the more numerous large scarabs of Year 10, in which is recorded the king's total bag of 102 fierce lions during the first decade of his reign, the quarry is said to have been brought down by his own shooting with the bow.

The last ten years of the reign was concerned with preparations for the king's jubilees and the ceremonies in connection with their celebration in his Regnal Years 30, 34 and 37. The Festival of the Sed, or jubilee, in its essentials was supposed to rejuvenate the ageing monarch and confirm him in his tenure of the throne. The locus of the main events, like that of the coronation, was at Memphis; and here the rites were associated with the Festival of Sokar, the falcon-god of death and resurrection in the ancient necropolis of Saqqara. But while the age-old mysteries of the Sed were largely concerned with Memphite usage, other observances appropriate to an Upper Egyptian milieu were enacted at Thebes, the now dominant capital of the south, and are represented in fragmentary scenes in the king's temples at Western Thebes and Sulb, and in the tombs of some of his high officials. It is from these sources that our knowledge of the chief events have to be gleaned, since nothing has survived of the jubilee scenes that were doubtless carved on the walls of his northern mortuary temple at Memphis, and on other monuments in Lower Egypt. Any attempt, however, to extract a coherent account from the representations of the progress of the ceremonies, from their inauguration to their conclusion, is fraught with difficulties, since the Egyptian artist was concerned with a number of significant impressions rather than a complete realization. Certain events were illustrated according to the taste and interest of the artist or his patron, and more intimate scenes were glossed over or excluded in favour of the public events in which the owner was directly involved.

The first jubilee in Year 30 is the most fully documented of the three festivals, and a text in the tomb of Kheruef tells us that the king celebrated it according to ancient writings, for generations of men since the Time of the Ancestors had never observed such traditions. If this was so, the ritual must have followed closely the usage of Memphis where the Festival of the Sed originated in the days of the first pharaohs. It is significant, perhaps, that a fragment of an early dynastic palette should have survived, evidently illustrating an archaic version of a jubilee ceremony, reworked with a figure of Queen Tiye carved on the reverse side some sixteen centuries later.

The high officials of Amenophis were closely associated with their king in the jubilee rites, and played different roles in the drama as illustrated in their tombs. It is from such sources that it has been deduced that the celebrations began on the anniversary of the king's accession and extended over a period of eight months. New statues of the king and queen had to be fashioned for all the sanctuaries that were built to commemorate each jubilee, and a large collection of these awaiting consecration are figured in the damaged tomb reliefs of the *Pl. 52* High Steward Surero. New clothing, jewellery and other equipment had to be specially made for the occasion. Obelisks were erected at Sulb and North Karnak, and large supplies of food procured from different areas of the land and as far afield as Syria and the Oases. At the private part of the celebrations, the coronation of the pharaoh would be re-enacted. Afterwards, dressed in a jewelled vestment imitating the plumage of the falcon Horus, under his short jubilee cloak, he would emerge from the great double doors of his palace and be carried in the state palanquin, accompanied by Queen Tiye in her litter, to the great dais where their thrones were set under the gilded canopy. There they would preside to receive the homage of representatives from Upper and Lower Egypt and the Oases. Delegates also came from Africa and Asia and the Aegean world of the Eastern Mediterranean. All paraded before the thrones bearing rich gifts which had been specially made for the occasion. As custom required, images of the gods were brought from their centres of worship, in the charge of their high priests, to assist at the functions.

At the Theban celebrations Queen Tiye was present as the incarnation of Hathor, and her daughters were in attendance as priestesses of that same goddess, shaking their sistrums and extending their *menyet*-necklaces to the king in token of their blessing. They were accompanied by the temple singers and musicians of Amun, a choir to which the wives of the high officials, as part of the entourage of the God's Wife of Amun, belonged. They sang hymns of *Pl. 50* jubilation in praise of the king and his god. The daughters of Asiatic princes also officiated, pouring libations before the king four times from gold and silver vessels. Acrobatic dancers, mummers and musicians performed their fantasia before the royal dais, singing to Hathor, incarnate in the queen.

In turn, the king entertained his court to a great breakfast of bread and beer, oxen and fowl, the basic menu of the offering repast. An investiture was held and the meritorious officials were anointed and decorated with valuable gold bracelets and collars of honour, and gold images of ducks and Nile fish. Green linen fillets to confine the hair were distributed to all those who took part in the ceremonies.

The Theban version of the jubilee rites involved many of the high dignitaries in rowing the royal barge on a stretch of water on the west bank, perhaps one of the lakes in the *maru* temple, and towing the boat of Sokar, like the day-bark and night-bark of the sun-god, miming his death at sunset when he traversed the womb of the sky-goddess Nut to a rebirth at dawn.

Such events are depicted in the wall-reliefs of the tomb of Kheruef, but their sequence and completeness are problematical. More concrete evidence for the enactment of the jubilee rites at Thebes are the many hundreds of dated labels from the jars which were ceremoniously broken after use and thrown on the mounds of rubble at the Malkata palace, the venue of the celebrations. These *Pl. 67* labels, and kindred objects, disclose the different foods and drink specifically contributed to the three jubilees, the dates of these festivals, the names and locations of the royal estates and other donors, and the names and titles of the various institutions and individuals concerned in the preparation and despatch of the provisions. Hieratic dockets, often written on the shoulders of the jars in ink, give details of the wine, grape-juice (*srmt*), meat, fat, fowl, various oils, milk, honey, fruit and incense that were supplied for the three jubilee celebrations. They far outnumber the quantities used in other years, probably because the pottery containers were ritually broken on the spot after emptying, and not sent away to be reused. Sixteen labels dated to Year 38, three to the last three months of the regnal year, are the highest in the reign and suggest that Amenophis III could have lived into his thirty-ninth regnal year, and died about the age of forty-five, as Elliot Smith deduced from the mummy believed to be his.

For the second jubilee of Year 34 we are wholly dependent upon such evidence as jar dockets, for despite the building of a special temple to Amun for the occasion, within the Malkata complex, no reliefs or paintings illustrating episodes from the event have survived. Nevertheless the testimony of the jar fragments shows that it was no insignificant affair. Of the 404 labels dated to Year 34, no fewer than 386 are qualified by the expression 'for the repetition of His Majesty's Sed-Festival', though most of them came from an area of the palace where little disturbance had occurred to the dumps of fragments since their discarding.

The archaeological evidence for the third jubilee is very scanty, only 27 jar labels mentioning the event, 25 of them dated to Year 37. This date has been confirmed by the inscription in the tomb of Kheruef, who has left the most detailed representation of the rites of this jubilee in his superb but damaged wall-reliefs. The royal pair in their resplendent robes again appear on their thrones beneath the gilded baldachin, while Kheruef exhibits many handsome souvenirs of the occasion commissioned by the king: pectorals, broad collars inlaid with lapis lazuli and other semi-precious stones, chased gold vessels and 'treasures never produced before'. In his capacity as the King's First Herald, he ushers the King's Companions, other courtiers and the High Priests of Amun into the royal presence. But the chief event represented was the erection of the Djed-pillar of the triune god, Ptah-Sokar-Osiris, by the king himself at the dawn of the day of jubilee. This rite, which was specifically a Memphite ceremony, presumably took place at the shrine of Sokar at Saqqara, the necropolis of Memphis, or it may have been observed in the chapel of Sokar in the king's mortuary temple at Western Thebes. Probably it was enacted at both places; but it has a distinct Memphite character, with the High Priests of Ptah officiating with the king and courtiers in hauling on the ropes that pull the fetish upright, and afterwards in driving cattle and asses around the ancient walls of the town four times. Other officiants were Queen Tiye and her daughters, propitiating the Djed with their sistrums and *menyet*-necklaces while musicians, the women from the Oases and dancers sang an anthem in praise of the king, and men engaged in festal games such as boxing and stick-fencing.

In all these events the king's courtiers and his high officials enthusiastically played their parts, and contributed supplies of food and drink to one or more of the jubilee feasts. Amenophis was served by dedicated and competent men whose pride in their position and authority is reflected in the high standard achieved during his reign in architecture, painting, sculpture and the applied arts. Foremost among them was Amenophis, the son of a certain Hapu, a man of no account, so we are asked to believe, from the Delta town of Athribis. Early in his career he was appointed Scribe of the Elite Troops, a post which made him responsible for a labour force as well as army recruitment. As such, not only was he concerned with the defence of the Nile mouths from piratical attacks, but he also saw to the conscription of labourers for quarrying, transport and building operations. He filled the post of Superintendent of All the Works of the King, and in that role has been credited, perhaps wrongly, with the design and construction of the Luxor Temple. He was certainly in charge of the quarries of the Gebel el Ahmar, whence came the Colossi of Memnon and other fine statuary during the reign. He also discharged duties in connection with the first jubilee of the king, and was probably responsible for the antiquarian research that animated it; he contributed supplies of meat and wine to the second. In his later years he was made High Steward of the estates of the king's eldest daughter Sitamun, who may have filled the role of God's Wife of Amun, and was allowed to install statues of himself, though a private person, at the entrance to the Tenth Pylon at Karnak. He was usually content with the simple title of King's Scribe, and the abbreviated version of his name, Huy. He died at the ripe old age of eighty, probably soon after the second jubilee. He had earlier been granted the unique honour of a funerary temple among the royal mortuary temples that lined the riverine plain of Western Thebes. His tomb was rediscovered in 1970 in the Asasif area of the necropolis, and found to be greatly dilapidated, having served for a long time as a stable. But he left behind him such a reputation for wisdom that he was deified as a god of healing in Ptolemaic times.

Closely related to him, and also hailing from the Delta, was the King's High Steward in Memphis, another Amenophis who held several important offices including Controller of Works in Memphis, and Treasurer and Overseer of the Double Granary of Egypt. He, too, claims that his parents were relatively humble in origin, but he studied as a scribe and his proficiency led to his appointment as one of the personal secretaries of the king. Like his namesake and near relation, he served as a Scribe of the Elite Troops, a post which resulted in his appointment as a treasurer, steward and architect. In the latter capacity he was responsible for the erection of the mortuary temple of Amenophis III in Memphis, which doubtless was an impressive and splendid structure, though nothing of it can be identified today. He was buried at Saqqara where his extensive tomb was pillaged in the early years of the last century and objects from it are scattered among museums all over the world.

Other Lower Egyptian officials of Amenophis III, such as another Amenophis, his northern vizier, and certain palace stewards, treasury functionaries and hierarchs of Ptah at Memphis, were also entombed at Saqqara, doubtless in sight of their king's northern mortuary temple. But others, such as Menkheper, the Mayor of Memphis, preferred to have their tombs at the southern capital in proximity to the king's sepulchre. Foremost among these was Ramose, who held the position of vizier of Upper Egypt and was a half-brother of Amenophis, the High Steward in Memphis. His important tomb (No. 55) has already been mentioned and will be further discussed below.

Other high officials who were granted tombs in the Theban necropolis on the west bank included the Overseer of the Granaries of Upper and Lower Egypt, Khaemhet, the Chief Steward in Thebes; Amenemhet, called Surero; and Kheruef, the Queen's High Steward (see above). In each of these tomb-chapels appears a representation of the owner reliving his finest hour on earth in the royal presence. Khaemhet submits the report of a bumper harvest in Jubilee Year 30. Surero presents new and splendid equipment for the same jubilee, and Kheruef officiates as the Master of Ceremonies at the jubilees of *Pl. 50* Years 30 and 37.

All these tombs, and less ambitious examples from the same reign, are cut in areas of the Theban hills where the quality of the rock has permitted the walls of their chapels to be carved in delicate low relief; they are drawn in the restrained and accomplished style of the period. Where such favourable conditions did not prevail, as in the tomb of the king's brother-in-law, Anen, glue tempera was used to decorate plastered areas of bad rock with pictures that are gay with bright yet harmonious colour, supplemented by an assured and fluid line. Both painted and carved decoration of these tombs enshrine the finest art of an era that had reached its grand climacteric and was soon to pass away forever, an autumn of richness and luxury, controlled by taste and high standards of fine craftsmanship. Into this milieu was born the prince, Amenophis, who was destined to change the direction and character of the culture he had inherited.

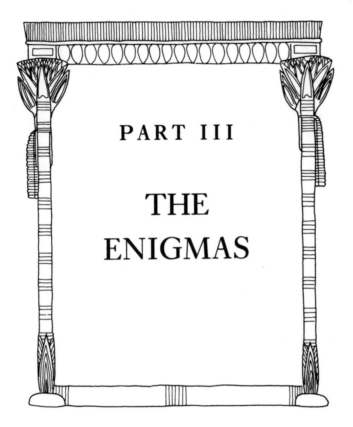

PART III

THE
ENIGMAS

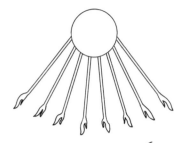

CHAPTER 16

The Question of a Co-Regency

The chief problem that has exercised the minds of students of the Amarna period in recent years has been the question of whether Akhenaten came to the throne immediately on the death of his father, or if he acted as his co-regent for a time before entering upon sole rule. As a corollary there is the further uncertainty of whether he also ruled with a co-regent during his last few years before he died. The matter is difficult and confused, with a mass of ambiguous evidence and a minimum of hard facts, so it is not surprising that a recent critic should refer to the 'hypothetical co-regency of Amenophis III and Akhenaten' as 'tedious'. Boring or not, it has to be faced as still an awkward problem of the period which so far from being hypothetical, decisively makes its presence felt from time to time, just when it has been pronounced dead.

The curious institution of co-regency is not explicitly mentioned in Egyptian writings, but that it existed is clear enough from evidence in the Twelfth Dynasty, all of whose kings from Ammenemes I to III each ruled for a time with a son as co-regent, and double datings exist to testify to the practice. During this period it seems to have been the custom for co-regents to be crowned on New Year's Day or to date each advent as though it had been made on such a day, thus bringing dates in the regnal year and those in the civil year into step. Double dates, therefore, can be harmonized, and a month and day in the reign of a co-regent correspond with the same month and day in that of the other partner.

In the New Kingdom, on the other hand, a different system was introduced by the vainglorious kings of the Eighteenth Dynasty whereby each regnal year was reckoned from accession day without reference to the civil calendar; and although Hatshepsut, for instance, said of her father Tuthmosis I that he knew the virtue of an accession on New Year's Day, not one king's advent during this dynasty fell on that particular day. The result is that the regnal year can change at any point in the civil year on the anniversary of the king's accession, whereas the calendrical year began on the first day of the first month of Inundation, which until recently began about the second week in June. This arrangement could lead to difficulties when a scribe, for instance, sought to place a series of dated documents in proper sequence. When two such systems had to be co-ordinated, the complications could have been even greater. Perhaps for this reason scribes adhered to one system or the other without trying to reconcile them. An exception holds for the reign of Tuthmosis III when the dates were expressed only in the years of the young king, presumably because Hatshepsut, despite all the trappings of a king, regarded herself as a regent rather than a ruling pharaoh.

With no double datings in the New Kingdom the evidence for co-regencies largely disappears. Yet this has not deterred Egyptologists from proposing that nearly every pharaoh of the Eighteenth Dynasty ruled with a co-regent for part of his reign. The only points at issue have been the choice of kings who ruled with partners, and the length of each period of co-regency. Some scholars have tried to avoid all the implications by assuming that each co-regent ruled with the older pharaoh for a very brief period only, as though the exact time of the death of the senior monarch had been nicely calculated in fixing the moment for the appointment of his partner. However much prescience or intelligent anticipation may have entered into the matter, there seem to have been several instances when the old king, rather than conveniently dying soon afterwards, outlived his young companion so that a new co-regent had to be appointed. In view of the fact that the expectation of life, even for royalty, was fairly low in antiquity, it may have happened that by the time a co-regent was old enough to be crowned his father had attained a comparatively advanced age, and they did not have to share the throne for long. Yet there is at least one instance, that of Ammenemes I, in the Twelfth Dynasty, who had a long ten-year co-regency with his son Sesostris I before his life was ended by assassination in somewhat mysterious circumstances; but not every monument during this joint reign bears a double date, which in point of fact is a rare occurrence.

The reason for the institution of co-regency appears to be a desire to avoid dynastic strife by firmly establishing an approved partner on the throne so that the succession could be recognized without ambiguity. We have already postulated that in the Eighteenth Dynasty the line of inheritance was by the eldest son of a king by a God's Wife who was a descendant of Ahmose-Nefertari, the chief queen of Amosis, founder of the dynasty. In time this sytem of inheritance would become so well accepted that the heir apparent would be appointed co-regent on reaching maturity, which certainly seems to have been the case when Amenophis II acceded at the age of eighteen, probably on the death of an elder brother.

There were, however, occasions when this system was set aside by other arrangements, largely it would seem as a result of interruptions in the line of descent. Thus Tuthmosis III, who was the son of Tuthmosis II by a concubine and not a God's Wife, claimed that he was recognized as the co-regent of his father by the oracle of Amun while he was officiating as a young neophyte in the temple of the god at Karnak. His father was sacrificing to Amun at the time and promptly crowned his son in the sanctuary. He was, however, married or promised to the God's Wife, his half-sister Nefruré, at the earliest possible moment. His step-mother took power by another violation of the established system on the death of Tuthmosis II a year later, and had herself appointed not so much a co-regent as regent. She justified this step by propagating the myth that she was the daughter of the God's Wife Ahmose by Amun himself (see above), claiming that Tuthmosis I, her corporeal father, presented her to the assembled dignitaries of his court and declared:

> This is my daughter Hatshepsut. May she live! I have placed her upon my throne. She it is who shall sit within my exalted baldachin. She shall direct the people in every office of the palace. She it is who shall lead you. You shall proclaim her edicts and be united under her commands.

Both these accounts are now taken to be largely fictitious, and there is little doubt that the latter is indeed so. A third report is that given by Ramesses II in the Nineteenth Dynasty when he discloses how his father Sethos I promoted him from the time he was a child until he became king:

> When my father made his state appearance before the people, I being a child in his lap, he said referring to me: 'Crown him as King that I may see his qualities while I am still living'. And he ordered the chamberlains to place the Double Crown upon my brow. 'Let him administer this land: let him show himself to the people' – so spake he through his great love of me.

Ramesses goes on to relate how he was provided with household women and a royal harim, so he evidently telescoped into one occasion a series of events: the time when he was proclaimed heir, probably at the advent of Sethos I himself; when he was appointed a commander of the armed forces while still an infant; and when, at the age of manhood, he was crowned as co-regent, given a separate household and provided with a chief wife and a harim. This memoir, like the accounts of their appointments to office by Tuthmosis III and Hatshepsut, has been discounted on the score that it was reported long after the event and is therefore suspect; but probably all contain a germ of truth, and are merely enhanced rather than totally fabricated. The report by Ramesses II in fact serves to show the various stages in the appointment of a co-regent – the presentation of the heir apparent to the people or the court, usually at his birth; his promotion to high military office, which would entail athletic exercises and weapon training; his elevation to a post in the administration, which would require the education of a scribe and priest; and on reaching manhood, his coronation as the co-regent of his father.

The existence of two courts each with its pharaoh ruling at the same time has proved a severe stumbling-block for most critics. 'The proponents of a co-regency (of Amenophis III and Akhenaten)', declares one objector, 'must explain how two separate bureaucracies could have managed the country . . . without conflicting with each other; or, what is more remarkable, without leaving some trace of the other's presence in contemporary inscriptions.' The same strictures could be levelled against all co-regencies, whether of a few months or several years, yet the system seems to have worked without visible signs of strain and we must assume that the two organizations operated as though each were self-contained and independent of the other. *The Story of Sinuhe*, a novel about Sesostris I, shows the institution of co-regency functioning in the Twelfth Dynasty without apparent difficulty. The junior partner was properly consecrated at his coronation with appropriate ritual, being granted a full titulary and regalia, a harim and the privileges of appointing his nominees to office in his court, and dating events to his own years of rule. From then on, he became the more important member of the duumvirate, although foreign potentates, whose ideas of kingship were quite different, held to what they understood and continued to correspond with the older pharaoh until death removed him from their ken. It may also be that this continuity was preferred by the pharaohs, since their younger partners might die and have to be replaced during their lifetimes. It is at least clear that *Pl. 13* Amenophis III received foreign letters up to his thirty-sixth regnal year.

On his crowning as co-regent, the new pharaoh would appoint his own men to office and these would usually be the young companions and followers who had been brought up with him as a kind of shadow court. They were nearly all sons of senior officials who duplicated their fathers' posts and would in due course succeed them, according to the Egyptian ideal of appointing the son to the place of his father. It is evident that whole families of officials existed side by side with the dynasties of kings whom they served, though it is seldom easy to trace lines of descent from the ambiguous and incomplete genealogies that have been vouchsafed us. The entourage of the elder pharaoh continued to serve him for as long as he lived, and ignored completely the establishment of the younger co-regent. The appointment of the son to a parallel post to that of his father, therefore, appears to be no more than the prudent taking of 'a staff of old age', as the Egyptian expression describes it, since on the death of the old king, the majority of his officials retire without trace.

It has often been maintained that the time-honoured custom of appointing a son to his father's post was abandoned in the reign of Akhenaten since he surrounded himself with upstarts or new men, free from the old prejudices and influences, in conformity with his revolutionary and heretical 'teaching'. It is true that a number of his henchmen, like those of some earlier kings, pay him extravagant compliments by describing themselves as mere nobodies whom the king made great and whose career he advanced, but for the most part these must be examples of gross flattery made to enhance the graciousness of their lord. It is extremely doubtful whether Akhenaten, in the absence of a system of universal education, could have formed any cadre of educated and trained officials outside the old scribal families to carry on the business of state. Nor is there anything to show that such men would have been any less loyal than the *novi homines*, since both equally would have owed their prosperity entirely to the favour of the reigning sovereign. There are a number of instances where the son under Akhenaten succeeded to an office held by his father under Amenophis III, and it is to be suspected that other close relationships lurked under non-committal names, and titles devoid of their affiliations.

On the face of it, therefore, a co-regency between Amenophis III and his son Akhenaten is only to be expected, especially as the former pharaoh had a long reign, and conditions during his later years when he celebrated no fewer than three jubilees in seven years, and when his health may have been precarious in a plague-ridden world, would have been conducive to the appointment of a junior partner.

Historians, nevertheless, have until recently taken the view that Akhenaten succeeded his father only on his death and ruled for his full term of seventeen years alone. In truth there is much that is attractive in this conclusion, which is held by an influential body of opinion and has been persuasively argued by Professor Redford. It avoids certain awkward problems, such as the existence of two courts ruling simultaneously for eleven or twelve years, which is the optimum period that has been assessed for such a co-regency. It also avoids the difficulty of the overlapping of powers, the division of responsibilities, and other perplexities which seem intractable, to our modern way of thinking, such as the existence of two rival cults which were presumably anathema to each other.

Yet the British archaeologists, particularly John Pendlebury and his epigraphist Herbert Fairman, gained the impression during their excavations at Amarna that Amenophis III had also lived there, and his sojourn lasted late into the reign of his son Akhenaten. They pointed to such clues as the presence of two fragments of pottery which they turned up on the site with dockets of Years 28 and 30 written upon them. Such dates must have referred to a longer reign than that of Akhenaten, who did not found Akhetaten before Year 5 and died in Year 17. The dockets in question must have been written in the reign of Amenophis III, who was the only king of the period to enjoy such a long rule. Their conclusion was that if the jars had reached Amarna full of wine and properly sealed, the contents must have been at least fourteen years old at the time of delivery; but as wine is presumed not to keep long in permeable pottery jars in a warm climate, they argue that it is most likely that Years 28 and 30 of Amenophis III were near to Year 6 of Akhenaten when Amarna began to be occupied by the official classes. It must be admitted that none of Fairman's reasoning is utterly conclusive, and has been largely demolished by Redford's critical scrutiny.

Pl. 26   Similarly, the stela found by Griffith in the ruins of a house of Pinhasy at Amarna, showing Amenophis III seated beside Queen Tiye under the rays of the Aten with its name in the later form that appeared about Regnal Year 9 of Akhenaten, has been cited as warrant for the belief that the elder king lived on well into the reign of his son. That Amenophis III resided at Amarna is to be inferred, so it is argued, from the references which have been found to his estate and mansion there, besides other texts which may indicate that he owned several other habitations in the city. An equipoise of the separate households of the co-regents is carved on a lintel in the tomb of Huya at Amarna, and each king is shown with his chief queen and their children as though living together beneath the rays of the Aten bearing the late form of its name. The appearance of two rulers and their families opposite each other in the same scene, however, can be ambiguous during this period because religious practice at Amarna avoided the epithet *maet kheru* ('justified') with its Osirian overtones of 'deceased', after the name of dead royalty, in favour of *ankh er neheh* ('living for ever') and similar benedictions. The problem then is to know whether one is confronted with a dead ancestor or living royalty. In the case of the stela and the lintel, Redford and others have argued that the juxtaposition of such names and scenes is due solely to filial piety, not to co-existence. The fact that several buildings at Amarna were associated with Amenophis III only serves to emphasise the importance there of the cult of dead ancestors, since houses of Tuthmosis I, Amenophis II and Tuthmosis IV are also mentioned at Amarna, and no one would claim that those kings ever lived there.

Ancestral piety of this nature is also ventured by Redford as the explanation of a scene in the tomb of Kheruef, where an erased figure of Amenophis IV (Akhenaten) is shown making an offering to his father and to his mother who stands beside her husband and clasps his wrist in an affectionate embrace. It is certainly bizarre to associate so intimately with a dead king a queen who is shown elsewhere in the tomb in company with her son making offerings to the gods, unless the scene is anticipatory, i.e. both parents existing together in a future state of blessedness. Fairman, however, believes that the sandals worn by the royal pair reveal that they are not immortals, but are in the costume of the living, and the unusual garb of the king indicates that he is not dead but deified. The most plausible explanation to which Redford seems to subscribe is that the royal pair are represented as a statue, despite the absence of any pedestal, and their son makes an offering to them in that guise. A statue could quite often act as a substitute for the living person when his presence in the flesh was not practicable or opportune.

Reliefs in the tombs at Amarna, and on the talatat from Hermopolis, show temple precincts in which standing statues of kings and queens are seen bearing offering-trays on their outstretched hands. Smaller versions of such statues have also been recovered from house-sites at Amarna. Fragments of trays supported by hands from life-size examples of such statuary were retrieved by Carter and others from the dumps of demolished sculptures outside the southern boundary wall of the Great Temple. One such fragment, inscribed with the name of Akhenaten, the prenomen of Amenophis III, and the names of the Aten in its later form, has also been cited by Fairman as evidence that Amenophis III lived late into the reign of his son. Indeed, on the face of it, the nature of the object, and its finding-place, suggest that an offering was to be made to the Aten by its means on behalf of one or both kings; but in the absence of the statue itself, it is impossible to say which of the donors was represented, or whether both of them were. Again, the problem is to decide whether Amenophis III is associated with his son as a living co-regent or as a dead ancestor, as a giver of offerings or a recipient of them.

This is another example of the doubt and ambiguity that have arisen through incomplete evidence, and the refusal of Akhenaten and his followers to accept that deceased royalties should be represented in the trappings of the dead and with the epithets of the Osirian elect. It is therefore not difficult for a sceptic to marshal arguments to show that a co-regency is not really in question, but that what we are seeing is mere filial piety. It seems obvious in the present climate of disputation that isolated fragments of monuments, however suggestive, are too ambiguous to overcome disbelief, and that if something decisive is to be achieved we must look in another direction.

For such evidence it will be necessary to revisit the tomb of the southern vizier Ramose, No. 55 in Western Thebes, at which we have already cast a cursory glance, and in particular to its main hall which is the only part to be decorated. The east wall, which upon entering is at our back, is carved with elegant low reliefs showing Ramose and his near-relatives and household servants making consecrated offerings to the solar deities and the gods of burial, and assisting at a funeral meal. The west wall, 13 metres away on the opposite side of the hall, is the one that shows the young king, Amenophis IV, newly enthroned on the left and accepting bouquets and temple staves with appropriate benedictions, from Ramose. In the corresponding scene on the *Fig. 11* other side of the central doorway in this same wall is the celebrated icon of the king and his queen, Nefertiti, on the balcony of their palace in the Gempaaten *Fig. 12* at Karnak, under the radiant Aten, presenting Ramose with collars of honour and other golden awards, all in the new revolutionary distorted style of art. Hardly had these scenes been partly sketched in ink, and the sculptors begun their task of cutting the reliefs, than work suddenly ceased. The absence of colour on the reliefs, the lack of funerary statues in the shrines cut in the chapel of the tomb, and the blank north wall of the main hall, all point to the conclusion that Ramose died suddenly while work was in progress, and his tomb was then hastily prepared as his last resting-place. That he was not disgraced is clear from the entire absence of any signs of deliberate desecration of his name and figure throughout the tomb, apart from the later Atenist erasures. The tomb, too, was not abandoned as a result of the move to Amarna, like the Theban tomb of Parennefer. No record of Ramose has been found at Amarna, where Nakht functioned in his stead, having a large mansion in the southern city and a tomb (No. 13) begun for him in the southern group.

The haste with which Tomb No. 55 was finally got ready for Ramose is evident in the way that the main hall was finished off. The reliefs on the east wall were denied their final coat of paint, but eyes and eyebrows were picked out in black, though with omissions. The west wall remained in its state of initial sketchiness, but more attention was paid to the south wall. This had been started probably a little before the west wall had been made available by the stone-masons and plasterers, and on it a relief of the essential funerary ritual was begun in the contemporary orthodox style. This had progressed for about a quarter of the length of the wall towards the burial vault when, in order to finish off the decoration in time, the entire wall was rendered in flat colour; but so well is this done that it is very difficult to see where the relief ends and the paint begins. This must have been the last part of the tomb to be decorated by the workmen before its owner was laid to rest.

The scene with which we are concerned is on this south wall, at the very end of the funeral procession where in the lower register the high officers of state, who are designated by their titles only, follow in the train of mourners behind the catafalque. Included in this cortège are the four high priests of Amun, three of whom are distinguished solely by their sacerdotal titles, First, Second and Third Prophets of Amun, with the Amun element erased by an Atenist hand. The last of them, however, the Fourth Prophet, is singled out from his colleagues not only by the peculiar gesture of his right hand (the staff on which it was resting has probably been omitted through haste), and the unobscured aspect of his entire person, but also by the peculiarity that of all the eminent officials, he is the only one to be named. He has not escaped the vandal's attention, however, and the first element in his name has been excised; but it is clear that it was that other Atenist proscription, the vulture of the goddess

18 Copy in line of a wall-painting showing the four senior prophets of Amun in a funeral procession, the last being named as Si-mut although the name of the goddess, like that of Amun, has been erased (cf. Fig. 20).

Mut. His name must therefore be read as Si-Mut, and he thus materializes as a well-known and busy official of Amenophis III.

Si-Mut is first mentioned as Fourth Prophet in Year 20 of Amenophis III; and ten years later he held the same office at the king's first jubilee, in which he took part together with Ramose and other high functionaries. He enjoyed the same title in Year 34 during the second jubilee, for which celebrations he built the temple of Amun in the king's palace at Malkata on the west of Thebes. Possibly just before this, or just after it, he was elevated to the position of Second Prophet, and was granted a fine painted tomb in the Theban necropolis which was still open to Wilkinson and other travellers in the early years of the last century, but is now lost to view. It would appear that Si-Mut was responsible for building projects at Western Thebes about this time and was probably charged with preparing the tomb of Ramose to receive the vizier's burial. He took the opportunity of earning a little immortality on his own account by distinguishing his fully-revealed figure on the south wall of the main hall by adding his name to it and the epithet 'justified' for good measure, just as he did on a door-jamb at the temple of Amun in the Malkata palace. Thus when he finished off the painting of the south wall, he had not reached the crown of his career, and the reign of Amenophis III still had some years to run. Yet at this juncture, he left the carving of the scenes on the west wall largely incomplete. The reliefs and sketches on this wall, the early names of the Aten, of the king and of the queen, the absence of even the first-born daughter from the group in the Window of Appearance, and the new revolutionary style of art on the northern half of the wall, all indicate that the scenes reflect events in the earliest years of the new reign. We must deduce, in fact, that Ramose died and his tomb was got ready for him soon after the advent of the young king Amenophis IV; and as the presence of the Fourth Prophet shows, this must have occurred while Amenophis III was still ruling. Apart from the scenes on the west wall, we have no inkling of Ramose's service as the southern vizier of Amenophis IV. All his other memorials concern his duties in that office under Amenophis III; and after his attendance at that king's first jubilee, we hear nothing more of him.

The evidence from the tomb of Ramose is therefore oblique, but decisively in favour of a co-regency between Amenophis III and his son. Its duration, however, will have to be determined from other sources.

The writer has several times drawn attention to the significance of a scene in the tombs of Huya and Meryrē II, which from their position among the northern tombs in the eastern hills, and the nature of their texts, were clearly among the last to be cut and decorated at Amarna. In both these tombs there are scenes which appear nowhere else during the reign, either at Amarna or Thebes, and show the royal family attending the great durbar which was held at Akhetaten late in the reign. Each of the two versions of the scene is different in the prominence it gives to certain events in the ceremony, but both are *Fig. 27* accompanied by a similar text which is the only example in the Amarna tombs to bear a precise date – Year 12, Month 6, Day 8. The fuller version in the tomb of Huya reads:

> The appearance of the King of Upper and Lower Egypt, Neferkheperurē-Wa'enrē, and the Chief Queen, Neferneferuaten-Nefertiti, may she live for ever and ever, upon the great golden state palanquin in order to receive the gifts of Syria and Kush, the West and the East, all lands united at the one time, and the Isles in the midst of the Great Green Sea [the Mediterranean], when they proffered gifts to the King upon the great throne of Akhetaten. Receiving the products of every land and granting them the breath of life.

This caption applies to a relief showing Akhenaten and Nefertiti with their retinue, the princesses, nurses, ladies-in-waiting and stewards, leaving the palace in the great state palanquins, accompanied by fan-bearers and a military escort, to proceed towards a pavilion set up in an open space, probably in the desert, where a vast concourse of peoples awaits them, including delegates from the nations who are in embassy with Egypt bringing precious gifts to lay before the throne. The version in the tomb of Meryrē II shows the same features but places emphasis upon different elements. The procession with palanquins is less important than the presentation of gifts. The reviewing dais with its two thrones beneath a double canopy is shown on a larger scale with the king and queen seated, holding hands, and flanked by all six of their daughters. The delegates and their gifts are also represented in some detail – the negroes and Nubians, Libyans, Aegeans, Asiatics of various tribes and races, and their soldiery, with contingents of foreign mercenaries. The two state carrying-chairs for the conveyance of the king and queen are seen resting near the royal chariots which may be the preferred means of return from the ceremony.

These reliefs and inscriptions present a picture which is not uncommon in the tombs of the grandees at Thebes during the Eighteenth Dynasty, when the tomb-owner took pride in showing himself as introducing the delegates to his king on an occasion of great splendour. Such scenes have generally been interpreted as the aftermath of some successful campaign, or the reception of annual tribute exacted from Egypt's vassals in Africa and Asia. The writer, however, has sought to show elsewhere that a different explanation is to be preferred for this ostentatious display of ornate and precious goods, which often includes young Asiatic slave-girls and the 'black ivory' of Africa, the latter heavily manacled. The Egyptians, according to the evidence, led no military expeditions to the Aegean islands, or the Hittite lands, or to distant Punt, and yet these nations are listed among those who presented themselves at such displays. *Pl. 44*

Plunder, too, as distinct from gifts freely presented, is of quite a different character and includes such items as armour and weapons gleaned from the field of battle, and severed hands and phalli of dead foemen used in the count of victory. Such trophies are sometimes represented on temple walls, but the subject does not belong to the decoration of private tomb-chapels.

While no Roman triumph is therefore in question, the gifts are different from annual taxes which the Egyptians occasionally imposed upon their imperial possessions in Asia, and regularly exacted from Nubia and Kush. The staples such as grain and timber are absent, and the objects presented are of great intrinsic value, such as elaborately worked gold and silver vessels carried by the Asiatic and Aegean delegates, or heavy gold rings made into ornate set-pieces proffered by the Nubians and Kushites. The Amarna Letters reveal that nearly every dispatch from the royal correspondents was accompanied by valuable gifts, which the pharaoh was generous in reciprocating. Such traffic has all the features of a primitive gift-giving economy; but however well regulated, it did not happen that the various messengers would arrive at the same time at the Egyptian court except by a concerted design.

The writer's study of these articles of prestige and luxury, which were brought by special delegations from the contiguous nations on an occasion of great pomp and ceremonial necessitating the use of the state palanquins, convinces him that they refer to an event when a new pharaoh came to the throne and received homage and gifts, not only from his own people who are occasionally seen among the delegates, but also principally from foreign nations. The pharaoh as a god incarnate ruling over a powerful and wealthy state, was also revered abroad by nations who worshipped divinity wherever it was found, and sent ambassadors on a Magi-like journey to the new king at his advent, with rich gifts, in order to receive his blessing ('the Breath of Life'). As a damaged text of Ramesses IV puts it, a century later:

> God caused the King to seat himself upon the throne . . . and mankind, the patricians and the ordinary folk, and all who are upon earth, brought gifts of homage, being loyal . . . and the princes of all foreign lands came to do obeisance.

The occasion was one of great joy and jubilation, and release from anxiety. The death of the old king was the triumph of Evil over Good, Seth over Osiris, but the advent of the new king saw the reappearance of Horus, the Champion, the Avenger-of-his-Father, on the throne of the Living. This victory was symbolized in the scenes in the two Amarna tombs where youths are shown wrestling, boxing, single-stick fencing, running, dancing and hand-clapping. Similar festal games are represented elsewhere at other functions, such as the jubilees of the pharaoh when a repetition of many of the coronation rites were enacted.

The co-regency of Amenophis III.with his son, according to our view of the evidence, thus lasted for over twelve years before Akhenaten was recognized by the Asiatic kings and vassals as their new correspondent upon the throne of Egypt; disturbing as this conclusion may be, we shall have no option but to accept it.

The event that brought ambassadors at this time to the great parade of gifts at Amarna is confirmed by a hieratic docket written on an Amarna Letter (Kn. No. 27) which the Egyptian filing-clerk wrote as an annotation on the edge of the tablet as follows:

Year 12 [?] 5th Month, 4th [?] day, when One [i.e. the King] was in the Southern City, in the palace [called] 'The Rejoicer on the Horizon': copy of the letter from Naharin delivered by the messengers Pirizzi and Pupri.

The date is damaged and the year number for long has been problematic, apart from the figure '2'. The question is whether a '10' stood before it, as Adolf Erman maintained from the first. Opinion has since vacillated between 2 and 12, though latterly the balance seems to have tilted decisively in favour of the higher year-number.

So it would appear that about a month before his attendance at the durbar in Amarna, Akhenaten was staying at Thebes ('the Southern City'), probably in his father's palace which he had renamed 'The Rejoicer on the Horizon' (a well-known title of the Aten), when Pirrizi and Pupri, the messengers of Tushratta, king of the Mitanni, arrived from Naharin with a dispatch to the pharaoh, of which a copy was made and sent on to Amarna. Why Akhenaten was visiting Thebes at this time is not disclosed, but he may have been attending his father's burial in the western branch of the Valley of the Kings after the prescriptive seventy days of embalming. This date incidentally confirms the view that Akhenaten did not receive dispatches from Asiatic rulers until late in his reign, after his father's death, and this will require to be taken into account when examining the significance of the Amarna Letters in the next chapter.

There exist further data which may act as a rough check upon the timetable of events outlined above. If the Alexandria-Michigan team is correct in identifying the royal mummy No. 61070 found in the tomb of Amenophis II as of Queen Tiye, her age at death could be a critical factor in deciding whether the reigns of her husband and son would have overlapped during her life-span.

The 'Cattle-Hunt Scarab' shows that by his Regnal Year 2, at the latest, Amenophis III had been married to Tiye, and the Amarna Letters from the Mitanni reveal that she had outlived him. Since a date near the end of his thirty-eighth regnal year is known from wine-jar dockets found in the ruins of the Malkata palace, we may confidently claim that he completed 37 full years on the throne before his reign ended with his death. She, on the other hand, is identifiable under the title of the 'King's Mother', found on dockets from Amarna, the latest of which is dated to Year 14 of Akhenaten. Thus she lived a minimum total of 50 years between her marriage and her death, if one accepts that the reigns of Amenophis III and Akhenaten did not overlap. Assuming that she was a babe in arms at her marriage, which is not impossible, she would have attained a minimum age of 51 at death.

The calculations of the Alexandria-Michigan team, however, assign to mummy No. 61070 an age of between 25 and 35 at death. This, like most of their estimates, is too low; but in view of Elliot Smith's report that her lustrous hair bore no trace of grey, she was certainly younger than 51, and probably little more than 40 at death, making it possible for her to be the mother of the child-princess, Beketaten, who is the little companion of her widowhood as represented in the tomb of Huya. Thus, if the medical experts have correctly identified the mummy of Tiye, her son's reign must have overlapped her husband's by a margin of ten years or more.

Fig. 29

While we have attempted to dispose of the problem of a co-regency between Amenophis III and his son, the ancillary question has been left suspended as to whether Akhenaten had a younger monarch ruling with him in his last years, as many scholars maintain, including Redford the arch-opponent of the idea of an earlier co-regency in the same reign. It will, however, be considered in a later chapter when we come to deal with the mystery of the deposit in Tomb No. 55 in the Valley of the Kings.

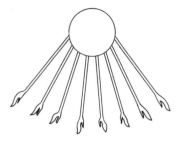

CHAPTER 17

The Amarna Letters

Despite the magic casements that they throw open on the world of the fourteenth century BC, the Amarna Letters show only interrupted glimpses of the shifting historical scene and the characters who played their parts in it. Scholars have from time to time attempted to fit bits of the puzzle together so as to produce a coherent picture; but no one solution has been generally accepted, and the suspicion remains that most of the important pieces are missing. The shadows these letters cast are unfortunately as numerous as the vistas they reveal. We have already referred to the finding of this part of the state archives; and we have given brief samples of their contents (see Chapters 5 and 11). In this chapter we shall touch upon some of the problems they raise for the historians of ancient Egypt.

The Amarna Letters consist of nearly 350 little pillow-shaped slabs of sun- *Pl. 13* dried clay impressed with cuneiform signs in a language which for the most part is Akkadian or Babylonian, the diplomatic *lingua franca* of the day, in use among the great kings and princelings of Western Asia. The majority of these documents are dispatches sent from the local prince or governor to the Egyptian court; but there are also one or two copies or drafts of the letters which the pharaoh sent to his correspondents.

The translation of these letters has proved very difficult, and is far from settled, since the scribes who wrote them were using a language which was not their own but derived from an earlier form of Old Babylonian, modified however by Canaanite innovations in its vocabulary, morphology and grammar, and fossilized by inaccurate teaching from one generation to the next into a diplomatic jargon, unintelligible except to its adepts. Professor Albright, a leading expert in this field, summed up the difficulties of translation in these words, '. . . it is not enough for the would-be interpreter to know Akkadian, he must also be a specialist in Hebrew and Ugaritic, and above all he must be so familiar with all the letters that he knows what to expect from their writers.' This is important because it reveals that very few specialists even in the ancient world could have been capable of translating these texts; and the existence of school exercises, vocabularies and literary works show that they had to employ some of their time teaching pupils to carry on their esoteric learning, doubtless perfecting their own knowledge in the process.

The difficulties of interpretation are just as great as the problems of translation; and the sorting of this archive into its proper sequence has not achieved universal agreement, though several solutions have been proposed. The obstacles in the way are formidable. In the first place, the tablets have survived in a generally poor condition, their edges in particular having crumbled away and taken with them many of the superscriptions containing the names of the sender and recipient. Moreover, the cuneiform scribes did not date their documents, probably because an international calendrical system did not exist; and not a single Amarna Letter has any indication to show in what order it should be read. It may be that at the time of their abandonment a number of them, the majority perhaps, did bear dates written in hieratic by the methodical Egyptian filing-clerks, in ink on the margins: some of them still carry dockets showing when and where they were received, but they are now in so fragmentary a condition that only one (Kn. No. 23) can be read for certain as 'Year 36, Month 8', and even that has its day omitted. Another (Kn. No. 27), as we have seen, was inscribed with the controversial date 'Year (1)2'.

A third obstacle is the fact that, with one or two exceptions, only the kings of the Mitanni, Babylon and Assyria name the pharaoh with whom they are corresponding by employing his prenomen, Nibmuaria (Neb-maet-rē) and other variants in the case of Amenophis III, or Naphuria (Neferkheperure) among other versions for Akhenaten. The king of Alashia addresses his letters to 'The King of Egypt' without specifying to which particular pharaoh he is writing. Except in two instances, the vassals address their correspondent as 'The King of Egypt', or by some such circumlocution as 'My God', 'The Sun', 'My Father', 'The Great King', 'My Lord', and so forth. Similarly, in the few copies that exist of dispatches sent by the pharaoh to his vassals, the sender refers to himself by his title of 'The King', and not by name. In general, therefore, with little more than two dozen exceptions, there is no indication of the pharaoh who sent or received the letter. When it is remembered that besides Amenophis III and Akhenaten, Smenkhkarē and Tutankhamun have left evidence of their sojourn at Amarna, opportunities for confusion are increased several-fold.

Another difficulty in attempting to put these letters in their chronological order is doubt about the exact circumstances in which they were found. The original report was that they were discovered by a peasant woman searching for *sebakh* among the ancient ruins at Amarna, and the area was then rummaged by other villagers who got wind of the find. It has been alleged that many of the tablets were broken during this illicit grubbing; but since they were small and readily portable, it is unlikely that much damage was done to them during their recovery, especially as it is most probable that they were found deposited together in one particular spot. It has also been surmised that the finders deliberately broke up many of the tablets, 'either for the purpose of easy carriage on their persons . . . or so that the number of men who were to share in the sale of the tablets might be increased'. It may be doubted, however, whether any were broken up for the purpose of easy carriage, since they were neither large nor heavy and were already in an eminently portable form. It is equally improbable that any were broken to increase the number of shareholders in the proceeds of a prospective sale. This was not a single papyrus, for instance, that had to be cut up into as many portions as there were shareholders, and sold piecemeal. Over 300 tablets had been found, and the number of diggers, one may be certain, was probably limited to not more than the members of the family of the original finder, and each would get a fair number of complete specimens anyway, assuming that they were all in sound condition when found. Moreover, it should be remembered that the vendors could have had no idea of what these lumps of clay covered with strange indentations really were, since nothing like them had been unearthed in Egypt before. With true peasant caution, it is more likely that the owners would have tried to find out the value of a single intact specimen before flooding the market with the entire mass of tablets, or resorting to division and the other tricks of their trade. In the event, they must have been disappointed by the responses they received, because no one in Egypt would at first accept them as genuine.

It is then that the tablets may have suffered some damage in being hawked from one dealer to the next. A story is related, for instance, of their being taken to Luxor in sacks thrown across the backs of asses and camels. This would have been an unusual, slow and costly method of transport when the river was at hand, and its truth may be doubted. The Revd A. H. Sayce, who travelled extensively in the Near East throughout most of his eighty-eight years, reported in 1917 that he had heard from those who made the find in 1887 that, in the process of recovery, nearly 200 tablets had been totally destroyed, and fully as many broken and otherwise seriously damaged. It would, however, have required considerable skill and experience of interrogating Orientals on the part of Sayce to have elicited the true answer from his informants and not the one that they thought he wanted to hear, assuming that they could divine his motives for questioning them. It is probable that here, too, the amount of destruction has been exaggerated. It is indeed remarkable, in the light of all these horrific tales, that of the 340 tablets that are dispatches, only some 35 are not substantially complete. Since the original find was made, other tablets have been unearthed at different times, as a result of careful excavation on the site of the Records Office at Amarna by Petrie, Borchardt and Pendlebury, and it is *Pl. 23* curious that of the 35 tablets so recovered, only 2 are intact; the rest are mere fragments, none of which fits on to incomplete letters found earlier. This suggests that the original finders may not have bothered to collect mere fragments, and reduces still further the probability that they deliberately broke up tablets in order to divide the spoils.

It might be justly claimed, therefore, that a substantial part of the original archive has survived, and if it is now damaged that is mainly because it was in such a dilapidated condition when it was abandoned. This conclusion, however, is not accepted by the majority of scholars: there are too few letters in the hoard, they argue, if one assumes that the records extend over the seventeen years of Akhenaten's reign, as well as a probable three years of Tutankhamun and, in addition, include a number of dispatches dating from the reign of Amenophis III and brought to Akhetaten for reference purposes. Thus some students have set a minimum of about thirty years for the scope of the correspondence, and a total of 340 dispatches for this period is remarkably small. Some of the correspondents are represented by 1 letter only, whereas Ribaddi, the Prince of Byblos, is represented by nearly 70. On the other hand, there is not a single draft letter to any of the Egyptian officials resident in Palestine and Syria at such centres as Gaza, Jaffa, Simyra, Beth-Shan and elsewhere.

The incompleteness of this dossier has not deterred scholars from attempting to put the tablets into some kind of order. The pioneer work was done by the Norwegian Knudtzon and his successors, during the years 1907–14, and in their publication the letters have been grouped according to their place of origin from north to south; within each group the arrangement is also chronological in so far as the editors could estimate the provenances and sequences from internal evidence. It is obvious, however, in the present state of our knowledge, and in the postulated incomplete condition of the archive, that any arrangements can only be arbitrary and subjective. The many letters of Ribaddi, for instance, have been used to tell a story of the progressive decline of Egyptian power in Asia, whereas the course of events, by a rearrangement of the sequence, could be shown to have been an ebb and flow rather than a constant retreat.

In recent years, valiant attempts have been made by scholars in America and Europe, taking advantage of improvements in the translation of the documents, to seek out internal clues that would help to put the group of letters from each correspondent into a chronological sequence and to relate the groups to each other. It is possible, for instance, by taking note of the mention of neighbouring rulers with whom the correspondent had dealings, to decide which princelings were near-contemporaries. Where letters have been received from these neighbouring states, it is possible to arrange groups to form 'clusters'. Thus Abimilki, the ruler of Tyre, wrote ten letters to the pharaoh, during the course of which he named Zimridi of Sidon, Etakkama of Kadesh, Aziru of Amurru, the King of Hazor, and others. Since letters also exist from these rulers, it is possible to bring them and the events which they recount into some kind of relationship, especially as the letters from Abimilki must, from their context, be spread over the short space of about four to five years. Similar 'clusters' can be built around other nuclei, but it is not possible to bring the whole archive into order in this way owing to lack of contacts between some of the groups, and complete ignorance of the length of reign of a particular prince. Moreover, it has proved very difficult to find data that would show during what particular period in a pharaoh's reign a contemporary princeling exercised power, and whether his tenure of office was spread over several reigns.

A useful peg, however, on which one group of letters can be hung, has been the demonstration by Albright that a certain Mayati, whose name appears in the Abimilki correspondence and in other letters, is a pet-name for Akhenaten's eldest daughter Meritaten, who played an important role in his later years and as the wife of his putative co-regent Smenkhkarē. This has resulted in the firm placing of a number of letters to the last four years or so of the reign of Akhenaten. Unfortunately, it has not been possible to find similar pegs for other batches of letters. In this impasse, Albright and his pupil E. F. Campbell have fastened upon the mention in a few letters from Palestinian rulers of a certain Maia, the deputy or high official of Pharaoh, and have equated him with the official May, who was granted a tomb at Amarna which was never completed. They have pointed out that the name of the Aten occurs in its early form in this tomb, where the depiction of three princesses only shows that it could not have been inscribed earlier than Year 7 of Akhenaten. Soon after this date, so they claim, May was disgraced and his name and figure erased from his tomb reliefs, apart from oversights. From the equation of the 'Maia' of the letters with the 'May' of the Amarna tomb, Albright and Campbell have made large deductions.

Unfortunately, they have overlooked a number of serious objections to their thesis. The name May is one of the commonest at this period and could apply to one of several men, not just to the owner of the Amarna tomb who held high administrative rank in the army and had several stewardships in Heliopolis. He was not, however, a King's Envoy, which would have been a necessary title if he had exercised power as the King's Deputy abroad. It is clear from the letters that Maia was on the spot in Palestine discharging his duties, and it is difficult to see how he could have carried out other responsibilities, including important court functions, *in absentia*. In any case the fact that the tomb of May was still incomplete before Year 9 at the latest is of no significance. Precisely the same criteria could be used to prove that Ay died before the pharaoh whom he served, whereas it is known that he survived Tutankhamun. Lastly, as we shall emphasize, the dating of Amarna monuments by the number of princesses represented in the train of the royal family is quite unreliable.

The imposing edifice erected by Albright thus largely crumbles; and it remains doubtful, in default of fresh evidence from elsewhere, whether the Amarna archive will ever be sorted into its proper chronological sequence, and whether a study of the letters from the vassal princes can ever produce any solid results, in view of the extremely flexible limits within which they can be dated on a relative basis. Those who have pursued such investigations have had to make a number of assumptions during the course of their studies in order to reach any firm conclusions. It may be time, therefore, to approach the problem from another direction.

All the investigators who have examined the problems of the Amarna correspondence have accepted without any question that it is a truly Egyptian archive, used as a serious tool by the pharaoh and his advisers. The name of the building where the letters were found, 'The House of the Correspondence of Pharaoh', more commonly rendered as 'The Records Office', has helped to drive the idea home that they were found in a repository of state documents, and the fact that such important records were left behind has been used as an illustration of the panic haste in which Akhetaten was abandoned, or else to show that there was some uncertainty in official quarters as to whether the city was being relinquished temporarily or for ever. Other scholars have argued that what was left behind was a collection of out-of-date letters belonging to previous reigns and of no significance to Tutankhamun who, when he moved from Amarna, took all the current correspondence with him. The existence of one certain and two possible letters dating to his reign they explain away as oversights.

Both these assumptions need very careful probing. The idea that these clumsy lumps of clay, impressed with outlandish signs expressing an esoteric diplomatic jargon, were part of the Egyptian state records, needs to be dismissed at once. It presupposes that whenever the king or an official required to refer to previous records, he had to call for a translator to search out the appropriate tablet and read it off. This is so unlikely as not to warrant much consideration. It must be emphasized that the pharaoh, unlike medieval European kings, was literate. His training included the education of a scribe, though he had secretaries to do much of his work for him. This tradition of the educated king was of great antiquity in Egypt, and the Pyramid Texts of $c.$ 2400 BC speak of the pharaoh acting after death as the scribe of the gods. It is, in fact, unthinkable that the god incarnate would not have been instructed in the magic arts of reading and writing presided over by Thoth, the god of wisdom: and it is almost certain that he would peruse all important state documents. After the cuneiform dispatch had been read and glossed by the appropriate messenger, it would then doubtless be translated for any subsequent reference and filed away in The House of the Correspondence of Pharaoh. It is the translation that would form part of the Egyptian records, composed in a more convenient and portable form than cuneiform tablets. It is virtually certain that copies of the foreign correspondence would have been kept on rolls of papyrus, all carefully dated in the meticulous manner of the Egyptian scribe. The Egyptians had had their own method of keeping records and their singular tradition of office procedure since the dawn of history and were not likely to change them to suit the cumbersome system employed by barbarians and vassals. Translations of the cuneiform dispatches would be accompanied by the replies that had been sent by the king or his officers. It is records of this kind that would have to be consulted by advisers of the king, such as the Chamberlain Tutu, or the Private Secretary Ay, whenever a reply was to be drafted, particularly as it is clear from the letters themselves that replies were sent a long time after their receipt. The process of turning the king's words into Akkadian would be left to the cuneiform clerks of The House of the Correspondence of Pharaoh who, after the bureaucratic manner of their kind, duly filed the incoming letters as soon as they had been translated. When the court moved from Amarna, a golden opportunity was presented for discarding this useless lumber, and it was left behind, though there is evidence for thinking that a hole had been dug below the foundations of the Records Office in which to bury it, since, unlike papyrus, it could not be destroyed by burning.

That the cuneiform tablets represented a system of communication which the Egyptians had to accept with resignation because of the Asiatic princes, whose use of the system had its own traditions, is shown by the circumstance that not a single draft dispatch has survived addressed to any of the Egyptian commissioners and garrison commanders in Palestine or Syria. These officers would have received their instructions written in Egyptian on papyrus; and model letters from Ramesside times exist to show the form they would have taken. That the cuneiform letters were not part of the Egyptian records is shown by the extreme paucity of any copies of the replies from the Egyptian court to the many letters it received. Apart from nine draft replies, we have no means of telling what the pharaoh said to his correspondents.

We can surely dismiss from consideration, therefore, that any cumbersome cuneiform letters were brought to Amarna from earlier reigns for reference purposes, or that such letters were removed when the court departed. The Egyptian Foreign Office must have come to Amarna and left it with its records on sheets and rolls of papyrus contained within light portfolios or cabinets. In other words, it is not unreasonable to suggest that the letters found at Amarna were those received when the king was in residence there from the time of its occupation to its relinquishment. As it was his chief seat after Year 5 of the reign, it is probable that the bulk of the foreign correspondence of this period has been found there. But it is also likely that similar dispatches were received at Memphis, Heliopolis and Medinet el Ghurab where there were royal palaces to which the court repaired on occasion. Whether tablets were sent for storage to a central depot at Amarna after being formally read and translated is doubtful. Copies (Kn. Nos. 23, 27) were made of at least two tablets received at Amarna before they were sent on to Thebes where the king was officiating at the time. But where the originals were kept is not known, presumably in the Malkata palace at Thebes. On the whole, it seems most likely that the dispatches were brought to wherever the court was residing, and after translation were stored in an office of the local palace. The central archive, kept on compact and portable papyrus, as we have suggested, would no doubt have been in the charge of officials in the king's retinue, for it is a mistake to believe that the court remained rooted to one spot, or that Akhenaten shut himself up in Amarna and never ventured beyond its confines.

Since Amarna was occupied about Year 6 of Akhenaten and abandoned probably soon after Year 1 of Tutankhamun, the correspondence received during that time must stretch over a period of some dozen years and not the wider extent that has been postulated by some scholars. It is true that the letters of Ribaddi of Byblos have been used as an argument for thinking that a considerable portion of the total archive is still lacking, since the dispatches from this prince far outnumber those of any other correspondent, suggesting that by chance his letters have survived practically intact, whereas those of his contemporaries must be represented by about one-fifth of their original number. It should be remembered, however, that some of Ribaddi's letters are duplicates sent off by different messengers when he was beleaguered, in the hope that one at least would get through. Byblos, too, was an important port of call and dispatches could be sent quickly and conveniently by ships on the Byblos run. Moreover, Ribaddi was an indefatigable letter-writer and the pharaoh had to complain about the volume of correspondence with which he was inundating the court.

This is but one example of the imponderables that result from considering the letters from the vassal princes, and in view of the meagre chronological rewards to be gleaned from them, and the uncertainty about the pharaohs to whom they were addressed in the absence of any name in the superscriptions, we shall ignore them in our examination in favour of the letters from foreign royalty.

This group consists of dispatches from Kadashman-Enlil I and Burnaburiash II of Babylonia, Ashuruballit I of Assyria, Tushratta of the Mitanni, Tarkhundaradu of Arzawa in western Asia Minor and Suppiluliumas of Hatti. We exclude the letters from Alashia (Cyprus?) in this group, since they are addressed to the pharaoh by title and not by name. It will be noted that no great power in the Near East is unrepresented in this dossier, a fact which encourages the belief that the 'royal' letters form a proper statistical sample; and this view is reinforced by the pharaohs who are named therein, including as they do Amenophis III, Akhenaten and Tutankhamun, all residents from time to time at Amarna, according to our opinion. Smenkhkarē's name is missing from the tally unless he is the *Khuri(a)* of Letter Kn. No. 41 to whom Suppiluliumas writes. This, however, is unlikely, especially as the context speaks of the pharaoh succeeding his father, or father-in-law. In view of the strong probability that if Smenkhkarē exercised any independent rule it could have lasted for a few months only, it is exceedingly doubtful whether he received the usual embassies from Asia before he died.

If we now examine the letters in this 'royal' group in which the pharaohs are unequivocally named, we shall find that ten (namely, Kn. Nos. 2–4, 17, 19–24) were received by Amenophis III, and an equal number by Akhenaten (namely, Kn. Nos. 7, 8, 10, 11, 15, 16, 25, 27–29). One letter (Kn. No. 9) was sent to Tutankhamun, and another (Kn. No. 26) to Queen Tiye. The drafts of letters sent by named pharaohs are few, but two (Kn. Nos. 1 and 5) were sent by Amenophis III and one (Kn. No. 14) by Akhenaten. The allocation of the royal letters almost equally between Amenophis III and Akhenaten suggests that the rest of the correspondence should be divided roughly in the same proportion.

If our contention is right, that no letters from an earlier period were brought to Akhetaten because the Egyptian records were not kept on cuneiform tablets written in a language obscure to all but a few initiates, it follows that the dispatches sent to Amenophis III must have been received at Amarna during his reign; and this reinforces the view that he was alive when Akhetaten was built and was ruling with his son as co-regent. Akhetaten began to be occupied by the official classes from Year 6 of Akhenaten's reign, which according to our reckoning corresponds with Regnal Year 33/4 of the older king. This means that letters were reaching Akhetaten for the first five years of its existence during the reign of Amenophis III and for its next five or six years during the reign of Akhenaten. If the volume of correspondence remained constant, one would expect a similar number of letters to have been received during these two periods, and this in fact is what we do find in respect of the ten dispatches received by each pharaoh in this particular 'royal' group.

It also means that the events mentioned in the correspondence which belongs to Akhenaten should refer only to the last years of his reign and not to his first twelve years of rule. An examination of the contents of the letters addressed to him reveals that this is also the case. There is no mention of Queen Nefertiti who played such an important part in affairs during the greater part of his reign, but the Crown Princess Meritaten is referred to under her pet-name of Mayati in several letters in the archive. She is named not only in the vassal letters by Abimilki of Tyre, whose city appears to have been dedicated to her though it almost certainly would have belonged to Nefertiti earlier, but also by Burnaburiash of Babylon (Kn. No. 10). There is some doubt, too, whether it is she or her sister Ankhesenpaaten who is the subject of a complaint by Burnaburiash in another letter (Kn. No. 11) that 'the mistress of Pharaoh's house' did not raise his head when he was distressed. In any case, the grumble must have been received late in the reign when Meritaten and Ankhesenpaaten were important figures at the Egyptian court.

Of the four letters by Burnaburiash definitely sent to Amarna during the reign of Akhenaten, two (Kn. Nos. 10 and 11) clearly refer to events of the pharaoh's last years; and the other two (Kn. Nos. 7 and 8) make no reference to any incident that can be recognized as belonging to the first twelve years of his reign. On the contrary, the Babylonian envoy, a caravan leader mentioned in letter Kn. No. 7, is the same merchant Salmu who acts as a messenger in Kn. No. 11, a circumstance which suggests that the two letters are separated from each other by a gap of a few years only. Of the total of six letters received from Burnaburiash, one (Kn. No. 6) seems to refer to his accession to power and may have been sent to Amenophis III, though the name of the recipient is missing; and another (Kn. No. 9) was sent to Tutankhamun, the successor to Akhenaten. The four or five relevant letters in this part of the archive, therefore, can hardly be spread over the seventeen years of Akhenaten's reign, but they might cover five years of it. In the last five years of his reign Amenophis III, too, received only four letters from the king of Babylon.

The correspondence from the Mitanni is no less significant. In this dossier, eight letters are addressed to Amenophis III, four to Akhenaten and one to Queen Tiye. The series begins with a letter (Kn. No. 17) from Tushratta to Amenophis III in which he recalls the circumstances which have brought him to the throne and seeks the pharaoh's friendship and support. This is apparently the first letter not only from Tushratta but also from Naharin to be received at Akhetaten and suggests, therefore, that Tushratta came to the throne about Regnal Year 33 of Amenophis III. The rest of the correspondence during the reign of the older pharaoh is largely concerned with negotiations for the marriage of Tadukhipa, the young daughter of Tushratta, to Amenophis III, and the fixing of a suitable bride-price. The princess was dispatched with a rich dowry; and had followed her aunt Gilukhipa into the pharaoh's harim by his Regnal Year 36. Tushratta, in letter Kn. No. 23, dated to this year by a hieratic docket, sends greetings to her as the wife of an Egyptian king.

Letter Kn. No. 27 is the first dispatch from Tushratta to Akhenaten; and the fact that there is no break in the sequence of events is shown by the sending with the letter of his special envoys Pirizzi and Pupri, presumably to proffer the customary gifts on the accession of a new pharaoh; and reminding Akhenaten that the presents which Amenophis III had promised, apparently as a further instalment of the dowry of Tadukhipa, had not been received. This is the letter which bears the controversial date which we prefer to read as Year 12, to which point in Akhenaten's reign it naturally belongs, according to the argument exposed above. The rest of the correspondence from the Mitanni is almost entirely concerned with Akhenaten's failure to honour his father's alleged promises. According to Tushratta, before his death Amenophis III had undertaken to send him additional presents, including two statues of solid gold; but when the gifts, reduced in number and value, arrived in Naharin during the first months of Akhenaten's reign, it was found that inferior statues of wood overlaid with gold had been substituted. Tushratta was exceedingly angry at what he regarded as despicable chicanery on the part of the pharaoh, and his indignation was repeated in all his subsequent correspondence with Akhenaten. But however mean the deception, the incident could surely not have rankled for the entire seventeen years of Akhenaten's reign and must have been confined to the last five. If it be objected that four letters from Tushratta are too few to cover even this shorter span, especially in view of the eight received by Amenophis III in a similar period, it should be remembered that Tushratta also complained of the length of time his messengers were detained at the Egyptian court; and it could be argued on the evidence that during the reign of Akhenaten there appears to have been a coolness between the Egyptian and the Mitannian courts, despite the marriage alliance, perhaps as a result of an armed excursion which the Mitanni made into Syria about this time in order to check the growing pretensions of Hatti.

Letter Kn. No. 26, addressed to Tiye, in which Tushratta replied to a communication from the dowager queen asking him to continue to send his embassies to her son, the new pharaoh, and his advice to Akhenaten in Letters Kn. Nos. 28 and 29 to consult his mother Tiye, are generally taken as an indication of the youth and immaturity of Akhenaten at his accession, since he still required the practised hand of his mother to guide him in statecraft. This apparent lack of experience is one of the arguments of those who deny that the new king can have been anything more than a mere youth at the time of his accession; and who therefore regard as out of the question a co-regency, especially one lasting as long as eleven or twelve years. It also seems to refute our contention above that the letters to Akhenaten are concerned entirely with events in the last five years of his reign.

A careful reading of the dispatches in question, however, does not support the view that Tiye was the adviser of her son. Tushratta was so vexed that he should have been cheated out of his gold statues and the other gifts promised by Amenophis III that he used every means in his power to make Akhenaten honour his father's word, including the enlistment of Tiye's support for his case. He also referred Akhenaten several times to Queen Tiye for the truth of his claim that her husband, before he died, promised to send massy, chased, gold statues and other gold to the Mitanni.

The argument that the mention of Tiye in the letters from the Mitanni must refer only to the early years of Akhenaten's rule thus falls to the ground; and nothing conflicts with the view that the dispatches addressed to Akhenaten belong to the last five years of his reign. The whole of the Amarna archive, in the writer's view, represents little more than a decade in the history of Egypt's foreign relations from the last regnal years of Amenophis III to the first regnal years of Tutankhamun.

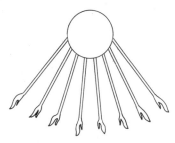

CHAPTER 18

Tomb No. 55 in the Valley of the Kings

Early in his season of 1907, Theodore M. Davis, an American lawyer and amateur of Egyptology (see Chapter 9) succeeded in uncovering a tomb a few yards west of the tomb of Ramesses IX in the Valley of the Kings. Now catalogued as Tomb No. 55, it lies on the other side of the path and almost opposite the spot where fifteen years later, when Davis's concession had passed to the Earl of Carnarvon, the tomb of Tutankhamun was discovered. Davis had some friends with him in 1907, including an American painter, Joseph Lindon Smith, and his wife Corinna, Edward Ayrton as his archaeologist and Arthur Weigall representing the Antiquities Service. They were later joined by an artist, Harold Jones.

After clearing a considerable mass of limestone chips thrown out by the ancient masons engaged in cutting Ramesside tombs in the vicinity, the excavators reached an earlier level and were eventually rewarded by striking a flight of twenty-one well-cut stone steps leading to a sealed entrance. This doorway was completely closed by a 'loosely-built wall of limestone fragments, resting not on the rock beneath, but on the loose rubbish which had filled the doorway'. This was unusual and should have made the party pause and reflect. Unfortunately, the evidence is all too clear that instead of proceeding with caution and skill, these men, two of them at least with specialized training and experience, somehow managed to conduct one of the worst pieces of excavation on record in the Valley. The word 'record' is used only loosely. The official publication is perfunctory in the extreme, no plans or dimensions are given, the descriptions are slipshod and incomplete, and the various accounts that the eyewitnesses subsequently gave, sometimes long after the event when their recollections were at fault, are often conflicting where they are not so vague as to be worthless. Where they do correspond, it is to be suspected that the authors have merely cribbed from each other's reports. When in doubt, the writer has chosen to follow the account that Emma B. Andrews confided to her unpublished diary, a copy of which he consulted in the Metropolitan Museum, New York. Mrs Andrews acted as hostess to her cousin Theodore Davis on his *dahabiyah*, and her careful daily jottings, unpretentious and private, inspire more confidence than some other memoirs of the occasion which can be shown to have flaws. Mrs Andrews, however, was not always present as an onlooker and recorder, and it is now extremely doubtful whether a totally reliable account can be elicited of what was originally discovered in the tomb and the state in which it was found. The problem is complicated by the imprecise English used by the different excavators, Davis, Weigall and Ayrton, in reporting what they saw during their operations. It now seems impossible to resolve the ambiguities of which they are all guilty, although Ayrton's account seems the most trustworthy, since he alone was in charge of the finding and excavation of the tomb. Davis and Weigall, for instance, can only repeat what he says with regard to the removal of the outermost blocking, since they were not present when he dismantled it. We shall follow Ayrton, therefore, in claiming that the tomb was completely sealed by a drystone wall which was intact at the moment of discovery and demolished by him as part of his preparatory clearance of the tomb approach.

Behind the drystone wall lay another obstruction that evidently formed the original blocking of the tomb. This consisted of rough blocks of limestone set in mortar and coated on the outside with very hard cement bearing impressions of an oval seal, the jackal couchant over nine pinioned captives. This device, which often appears on similar tomb-sealings in the Theban necropolis, was also found on an area of the walled-up doorway to the tomb of Tutankhamun. There it was used only on those areas of the blocking which had been replastered by the necropolis officials when they made good the damage caused by thieves who had tunnelled through the entrance to gain access to the interior of the tomb. The intact portion of the original doorway bore seals giving the name of the royal occupant. In the case of Tomb No. 55, the excavators report only the presence of the seal with the jackal over nine captives. Weigall however, four years later, claimed that the entrance was sealed with the seal of Tutankhamun, a fragment of which they found. We are dependent upon his *bona fides* for this report, though Mrs Andrews indirectly tends to confirm it.

According to Davis, the ingress to the tomb measured about 2.45 metres in height and 1.83 metres in width, but the blocking with its cemented face bearing the oval seals had been removed, except for a wall about a metre high. When the excavators had demolished this, they found themselves in a corridor about 1.83 metres wide and filled with clean limestone chips to within a metre or so of the ceiling at the proximal end, and to within 2 metres at the distal end which was about 10 metres away. Reposing on this filling near the entrance was the side of a gilded wooden shrine, and on it lay a door, also part of the same shrine, with its copper pivots still in place.

At the other end of the sloping approach corridor was a large oblong room 7 metres long, 5 metres wide, 4 metres high, and sunk 1 metre below the level of its ingress, from the sill of which a long broad ramp of stone debris extended into the room. On this second slope of chippings lay a counterpart to the door in the corridor, and a large alabaster vase-stand. Against the opposite wall of the tomb were leaning other parts of the shrine, and a second long side lay on the floor with its posts and beams scattered about it. All the woodwork in the tomb was in a very fragile condition, and of the large dismantled shrine strewn over the chamber and its corridors, two planks are all that is now exhibited in the Cairo Museum.

Pl. 55

The walls of the room had been plastered but not decorated. At its southern end, a start had been made on hewing a second chamber but this had not progressed beyond the stage of forming a deep recess, 1.8 metres high, 1.4 metres wide and about 1.5 metres deep. In it had been deposited four Canopic jars of polished calcite with beautifully wrought stoppers in the form of human heads wearing a short, military style of wig that in the late Eighteenth Dynasty was popular with high-ranking women as well as men.

On the floor, just outside the recess, lay a handsome coffin of a kind which had not been found up to that time, but which we can now see bore a distinct resemblance to the second coffin of Tutankhamun, except that the wig, which was of the same type as that represented on the Canopic jars, was quite different from the usual funerary royal headdress. It had been placed on a lion-headed bier, also similar to one which supported the nest of coffins within the stone sarcophagus of Tutankhamun, but this had collapsed through decay and brought the coffin crashing to the ground, jerking off the split lid and exposing its occupant.

Pl. 56

When the excavators came to clear the tomb of its contents, they found a number of small objects strewn among the chippings and rubbish in the corridor and main chamber, including four 'magic bricks' of a kind which were usually sealed at the four cardinal points in the walls of royal tombs of this period. Three of them, from the excavators' vague accounts, appear to have been more or less correctly orientated against appropriate walls except for one 'brick' which was found under the bier. In addition, a number of faience vessels, boxes and amulets were found, also the base of a wooden statue, statuettes and model boomerangs in faience, and the remains of ritual implements used in burial ceremonies. One stone toilet vase was inscribed with the name of Amenophis III; another with the names of Queen Tiye and Amenophis III, whose nomen had been erased; and a fragment of wood from a piece of furniture bore the names of the same king and his queen. A stone *pesesh-kef* amulet bore the name of Queen Tiye alone. In the rubbish under the bier and behind the wooden panels leaning against the east wall were found numerous fragments of small clay seals, some of which were impressed with the cartouche of Tutankhamun.

It was clear to the excavators that the tomb and its furnishings had suffered damage from two sources. A long crack in the ceiling of the corridor, ineffectually stopped with cement, had allowed rainwater, scouring down the valley floor in the occasional torrents that sweep the area, to seep into the tomb and wreak havoc with most of its contents, chiefly the woodwork and the mummy in the coffin. But, in addition, there were evident signs of deliberate destruction wrought by the hand of man. The names on the coffin had been cut out and the gold portrait mask ripped off the lid and removed. Inscribed gold banderoles inlaid with coloured glyphs, which bordered the upper edge of the shell and ran down the centre-line of the lid, had been damaged by the excision of names within cartouches; and certain figures and names had been hacked out of the reliefs on what was left of the gold-covered shrine. The uraei on the Canopic jars had been snapped off and were missing: inscribed panels on the belly of each jar had also been chiselled away until the merest traces of the deeper incised signs were all that remained. The amulets on the 'magic bricks' had also been removed. At the same time it was apparent that this selective destruction was hardly the work of thieves, who would not have left any gold-work behind them nor bothered to close up the tomb with a new drystone blocking. The tomb, in fact, bore all the signs of having been opened since its original sealing and its contents deliberately desecrated by removing all traces of the name and features of the owner, though this operation had not been quite complete and there were one or two oversights. Thereafter it had been sealed with a new blocking, care being taken to leave no stamp or inscription on it that would serve to identify the owner.

Pl. 53

Pl. 57

The burial posed a number of questions which the excavators and subsequent scholars over the years have attempted to answer, without however producing any finality, though a consensus of opinion is beginning to emerge on some aspects of the find, as we shall disclose presently. Controversy began early when Davis was convinced that he had indeed found the tomb of Queen Tiye, and, according to Weigall, rejected any other opinion with vehemence. While he may have stumbled across an incomplete or secondary burial, there was no doubt in his mind that it was the queen's, since the smaller inscribed pieces bore her name sometimes accompanied by those of her husband. He insisted that the heads of the Canopic jars were portraits of Queen Tiye: and a vulture made of sheet gold, which was found bent around the head of the mummy, was a queen's crown, the same vulture headdress shown so frequently in portraits of the royal consorts. Above all, the undamaged parts of the dismembered shrine were decorated in relief with figures of the queen and with her cartouche, and an inscription on it declared that it had been made for her by Akhenaten, whose name, however, was erased, though it was clear from the context that it could only be his.

Weigall on the other hand, took the view that the bones could not be those of Tiye, but must be of Akhenaten, and that his burial must have been hastily removed from Amarna when that city was abandoned, brought to Thebes for reinterment, and subsequently desecrated. In support of his theory, he could point to the fact that everywhere in the tomb Tiye's figure and name remained intact, whereas Akhenaten's had been hacked out except for some careless omissions. Every name had been excised from the coffin and from the gold mummy-bands which he maintained had encircled the body. The gold portrait-mask had also been ripped off the lid. Moreover, the 'magic bricks', which were designed to protect the tomb-owner from hostile intruders, were inscribed with the cartouche of Akhenaten on those two specimens which were substantially intact. The other pair were of a flimsier construction and were greatly decayed and damaged, and their ink inscriptions were illegible. The gold-sheet vulture amulet over the face was not a crown but the 'vulture collar' of pharaonic burials.

The argument became somewhat heated, and to settle the matter Davis invited the local European physician at Luxor, and a prominent American obstetrician who was visiting Thebes at the time, to examine the body while it was still *in situ* in its coffin and pronounce upon its sex. The mummy-wrappings had decayed through damp and could be lifted off in great pads, exposing the bones from end to end. The pelvis was admitted to be the criterion of sex. It is reported that both surgeons instantly agreed that it was the pelvis of a woman. This opinion seemed to vindicate Davis's beliefs and he published his account of the excavations of 1907 under the title of *The Tomb of Queen Tiyi*.

The two practitioners, however, were probably misled by post-mortem damage to the skeleton which had resulted in the separation of the hip bones from the sacrum, though the injury was doubtless disguised by the wrappings and debris within the coffin. The eminent experts who at different times have since examined the remains have been unanimous that the pelvis is that of a male. The bones, together with the decayed wrappings, gold mummy-bands and inlaid gold banderoles from the coffin, were sent to Elliot Smith, then Professor of Anatomy in the Cairo School of Medicine; but when Smith came to examine them in July 1907, he found to his intense surprise that instead of the body of an old woman that he had been led to expect, he had been sent the remains of a young man who had apparently died at the age of twenty-three or twenty-five since, among other features, certain epiphyses had not united with their bones. Elliot Smith soon found himself engaged in controversy not only with Davis and his supporters for denying that the bones were those of Tiye, but also with several Egyptologists for asserting that they were those of Akhenaten, since they found it impossible to crowd all the momentous events of the 'Heretic's' reign into so short a life-span. A way out of the difficulty was suggested by Norman de Garis Davies, who thought the bones might be those of Smenkhkarē, the putative co-regent of Akhenaten in his last years. His memory had also been persecuted in the same way as Akhenaten's. Elliot Smith considered this, but was obviously much influenced by tendentious reports that the coffin and gold bands had borne the names and titles of Akhenaten, even though they had been excised.

In after years, he attempted to reconcile the anatomical evidence of the bones with the demand for an age at death for them of at least thirty years if they were to be considered as the remains of Akhenaten. Nearly twenty years after his first examination he wrote:

> In considering this difficult problem I naturally turned to consider those pathological conditions which might cause delay in the union of the epiphyses. Of these, the most likely seemed to be the syndrome described by Fröhlich in 1900. . . . In patients presenting this condition cases have been recorded in which the bones at 36 years of age revealed the condition which in the normal individual they show at 22 or 23, so this suggested the possibility of bringing the anatomical evidence into harmony with the historical data. In support of this solution there are the very peculiar anatomical features of Akhenaten when alive, which have been made familiar to us by a large series of contemporary portraits. . . . In the light of our present knowledge, however, they seem to be quite distinctive of Fröhlich's syndrome and afford valuable support to the suggestion that this was the real cause for delay in the fusion of the epiphyses. In addition to this, the skull – both the brain-case and the face – reveals certain important peculiarities. There is a slight degree of hydrocephalus such as is often associated with Fröhlich's syndrome and also an overgrowth of the mandible, such as may result from interference with the pituitary.

In 1931, the uneasy acceptance of Elliot Smith's opinions was subverted by a *Pl. 53* new study of the coffin and its contents. Rex Engelbach of the Cairo Museum had the greatly damaged coffin-lid repaired and restored, during which time he was able to devote close attention to its texts and alterations that had been made to them. Previously, in 1916, the French scholar Georges Daressy had argued that the inscriptions showed that the coffin had first been made for a woman, whom he took to be Queen Tiye, and subsequently adapted for a king. Engelbach now tried to show that the coffin had been made for Smenkhkarē as a private person and modified for him when he became a king. There were thus strong reasons for regarding the bones found in the coffin as those of the young co-regent. At the same time, Professor D. E. Derry, Elliot Smith's successor at

Cairo, who had examined the mummy of Tutankhamun and written the official report on it, published a re-examination of the skeletal remains from Tomb No. 55. He denied that the skull showed signs of hydrocephalus, and claimed that while of unusual shape, it was not abnormal but closely resembled the platycephalic skull of Tutankhamun. His study of epiphyseal closure in modern Egyptians convinced him that the bones were those of a young man, not more than twenty-three years of age at death, and he accepted that the occupant of the coffin found in Tomb No. 55 must be Smenkhkarē.

In 1957, the distinguished scholar Alan Gardiner opened the whole case again by publishing a new study of the texts on the restored coffin, and reached the conclusion that there was no reason to believe that the coffin had ever belonged, or was ever intended to belong, to anyone other than Akhenaten. According to him, whatever the anatomical examination may have disclosed, the archaeological evidence suggested that the people who buried the mummy in Tomb No. 55 believed it was that of the 'Heretic King' himself.

This thesis provoked rejoinders from Professor H. W. Fairman and the writer who, arguing from different standpoints, independently reached the conclusion that the coffin had undoubtedly been designed for a woman of the royal family, most probably Meritaten, and subsequently adapted for the person who was found buried in it. On the identity of the occupant, however, their views diverged, Fairman believing it was Smenkhkarē, and the writer, Akhenaten. For the latter opinion there was the archaeological testimony of the 'magic bricks' as pointed out by Gardiner. Moreover, the several reports, both published and unpublished, on the human remains, gave grounds for believing that they showed abnormalities which could be reconciled with the peculiar anatomy of Akhenaten as revealed by his monuments.

It was clear that little further progress could be made in resolving this problem without a more extensive and up-to-date examination of the skeletal remains from Valley Tomb No. 55. Accordingly, in 1963 the late Professors R. G. Harrison of Liverpool and A. Batrawi of Cairo, with the assistance of M. S. Mahmoud, Professor of Radiology in the Qasr el Aini Hospital, Cairo, subjected the remains to a minute and fully documented investigation which set entirely new standards in the medical examination of the royal mummies. Evidence in certain parts of the skeleton of a trend towards feminity, consistent with a minimal effect of hypogonadism, was found, but it was not sufficiently marked to correspond with the features of eunuchoidism and the sort of physique displayed by Akhenaten on his monuments. The subject was undoubtedly male, and it was possible to be definite that he died in his twentieth year. The form of the facial skeleton and mandible was inconsistent with the appearance of the face and chin represented on the Akhenaten monuments, but closely resembled those of Tutankhamun.

The anatomical examination was complemented by a photographic reconstruction of the skull by Mr D. J. Kidd, the medical artist to the Faculty of Medicine at Liverpool University. Contours produced by maximum and minimum criteria were superimposed upon photographic prints of lateral and frontal views of the skull. The resulting features bore no resemblance to those of Akhenaten as depicted on the monuments, but were found to bear a striking likeness to the mask of Tutankhamun on his second anthropoid coffin. Recent serological tests have also shown that both these kings possessed blood-groups type A2 with the serum antigen MN, suggesting that they were closely related, either as brothers or father and son.

It might seem that with such a weight of evidence in its favour, the body in the coffin has been unquestionably shown to be the remains of the short-lived Smenkhkarē, a shadowy figure who played an ill-defined role as co-regent of Akhenaten, and husband of the heiress-princess Meritaten in the last two or three years of the reign. The age at death of the mummified body, now estimated to be twenty, apparently eliminates him from the possibility that he could be Akhenaten, who reigned for seventeen years. Yet there are scholars who are prepared to regard as unreliable all estimates of age at death based upon anatomical development. For them it is at least an even chance that the skeletal remains from Valley Tomb No. 55, despite their normality, are those of Akhenaten.

In the face of such doubt, recent attention has focused more upon the coffin than on its contents. As already mentioned, it had been found in a very damaged state, owing to the penetration of water into the tomb, and the excavators were not able to preserve more than the detached lid and fragments of the rotted shell. Despite its ruinous condition, at the time of its discovery it was the most opulent piece of royal funerary furniture that had then come to light, being made of fine woods, covered with thick gold leaf and inlaid with a feathered and imbricated pattern of coloured opaque glass imitating carnelian, turquoise and lapis lazuli.

While the anatomists may have proved to their satisfaction that the body which was found in the coffin was indubitably male, and apparently the young co-regent Smenkhkarē, some Egyptologists, such as Georges Daressy as long ago as 1916, had maintained that the coffin was originally made for a woman of the royal house, but had been altered to apply to the burial of a king, and had been desecrated. The inscribed gold bands, which Weigall described as passing down the front and back of the mummy outside the wrappings, and at right angles to them around the body, had had their cartouches cut out, leaving oval holes wherever they had occurred. None of the excavators made a copy of these inscriptions and we are now wholly dependent upon Weigall's vague report for knowledge of their existence. The gold bands were sent, together with the

Nearly everyone who has studied the deposit from Tomb No. 55 has remarked upon the resemblance between the wig on the stoppers of the Canopic jars and the coiffure on the coffin-lid. Both conform to a secular fashion worn by Nubian soldiers and their officers, and also affected by the court ladies during the Amarna period, giving a 'gamin' cut to their hairstyle. The Canopic jars were evidently made *en suite* with the coffin. If the latter were prepared originally for Kiya, so, argued Perepelkin, the effaced inscriptions on the jars must have borne the same standard text that was established for her. Since the time of their discovery, the stoppers have been identified by various authorities, on circumstantial grounds, as carrying portraits of Tiye, Akhenaten, Smenkhkarē, Meketaten and Meritaten. Now it would seem that the final verdict has to be that they were made for Kiya and must resemble her. The confirmation of this surmise has recently been made by the Berlin scholar Rolf Krauss, who from one or two almost obliterated signs has succeeded in showing that the standard Kiya titulary was initially inscribed in the rectangular panel on each jar. He has also argued, *contra* Geoffrey Martin, that the bodies of the uraei have been cut later into the striations of the wig, an alteration that had previously been noted by Guy Brunton and the present writer. Martin, from his study of the fourth specimen in New York, had observed that the 'heaven' sign which, as commonly is the case, formed a deeply cut upper border to each inscribed panel, had been partly filled in by a sliver of calcite cemented into position, and the area on the right side of the inscription, beneath this sliver, had been rubbed completely smooth. Krauss has shown, moreover, that this area of careful erasure eliminated three columns of the inscription within the panel, although part of the deeply cut 'heaven' sign could not be erased by such means and had to be filled in with a sliver of calcite cut to shape. The removal of the columns of text from the right side of the panel made the inscription apply exclusively to Akhenaten instead of Kiya.

It has been conjectured that the dismantled shrine of Tiye and some of her grave goods were originally stored in the tomb as surplus equipment no longer wanted after the move from Amarna, since she was probably transferred to the tomb of her husband Amenophis III in Thebes, where two suites of chambers opening off his sepulchral hall are believed by Hayes to have been provided for the burials of Tiye and her eldest daughter Sitamun. If that is so, the bulk of her equipment would already have been installed in it in expectation of her interment there. The storage of surplus furniture in Valley Tomb No. 55, however, is extremely unlikely. A large shrine made of imported fine woods and lavishly covered with gold leaf was an exceedingly costly item, and would not have been consigned to oblivion in another's tomb when its metal could have been stripped off and melted down and the carcass overlaid with fresh gesso and regilded for another member of royalty.

Pls. 53, 57, 59

Moreover, there is evidence that the shrine was once erected in the tomb and was in process of being moved out when the operation was abandoned. Two gilded copper disks, worked as marguerites, were found among the debris; and these were of a kind and size identical to roundels that in the tomb of Tutankhamun were sewn onto a black linen pall covering all the equipment within his outermost shrine. These suggest that a similar pall covered the deposit within the shrine where Tiye once rested.

The evidence left in the tomb also furnishes clues to another former occupant of this same chamber. Though the name of Akhenaten had been cut out of the equipment he provided for Tiye, there were one or two oversights and his name was also conspicuous on two of the 'magic bricks' that had been distributed at the cardinal points to protect the deceased from inimical forces, according to Egyptian belief. Such objects would not have been installed to store them, particularly as they were of little intrinsic value and had been positioned in their correct protective sites, or as near to them as made no difference. The presumption must be that Akhenaten also rested in the tomb, in equipment that had originally been made for Kiya but had been adapted to apply to him.

The history of the deposit in this tomb thus devolves into two phases, possibly three if the first episode be, in fact, two separate events. As the result of a decision, probably taken quite early in the reign of Tutankhamun, to abandon Akhetaten as the royal residence in favour of the old capital Memphis, it became imperative to remove the burials that had been made at Akhetaten during the fourteen years or so of its existence, in order to prevent them from being plundered by lawless elements as soon as the police garrison was withdrawn. The deceased were presumably transferred by their relatives to the family burying-grounds. In the case of royalty, however, it was some time later that they were removed to the necropolis on the west bank of Thebes (see Chapter 25). Valley Tomb No. 55, which was probably being prepared for a private person, was one of those that were hastily requisitioned at this later time to serve as 'a great place' for members of the royal family. The original deposit of Queen Tiye had almost certainly been made by Akhenaten in one of the larger tombs adjacent to his own in the Royal Wadi at Amarna; and in accordance with his eschatology he had provided a handsome shrine for his mother of a kind which has not been found in the burial of any other queen. He probably supplied other furniture of a similar standard, but the shrine must have been the most considerable part of her equipment. It was comparable in size and design with the third shrine of Tutankhamun, being made of fine timber, covered with gesso and gold foil and worked in relief with scenes and texts redolent of the Aten cult. The two longer sides each measured about 3.4 metres in length and 1.9 metres in height; and although it would have been quite feasible to take them into the tomb when it was completely free of obstructions, it would still have been a hazardous task, having regard to the steep staircase at the entrance.

The shrine evidently enclosed one or more coffins nesting within each other, and presumably similar in design to the coffin found in the tomb which is the only queen's coffin surviving from this period to serve as a comparison. There was also room within the shrine to accommodate a wooden frame supporting a black linen pall sewn with gilded copper marguerites to shroud the entire contents. What other major equipment was installed for Tiye is not known for sure, but doubtless there was a chest holding four Canopic jars similar to the examples provided for Kiya, but with uraei. Additional equipment, such as shawabtis in special boxes, statuettes, toilet vessels, oil-jars, jewel-chests and other articles hardly inferior to what her husband had supplied for her parents' burial were probably provided.

When all Tiye's funerary equipment had been installed with due rites, the corridor was filled with stone chippings and similar debris, and its outer doorway sealed with limestone blocks cemented together, the outer face being impressed with the necropolis stamp and the name of the reigning king, Tutankhamun. The question remains whether other burials were also moved into the main chamber of the tomb before the doorway was sealed, or whether they were subsequently intruded by partly removing the blocking, redistributing the debris in the corridor so as to effect an entry into the chamber lying at its lower level, and building an outer drystone wall without any mark or stamp upon it, as has recently been suggested. The nature of this outer blocking ensured that the drystone wall could have been built and dismantled a number of times without leaving evidence of different intrusions. Nevertheless, the writer believes that the deposit of any secondary burials was made at one and the same time; and that later they were all removed except for the body that Davis found in the tomb (see Chapter 25).

The second phase of the history of the deposit occurred at a subsequent date, but presumably not long after the initial sealing. Someone, who can only have been a pharaoh, evidently decided that Tiye's deposit should be moved to another resting-place, perhaps to the tomb of her husband in the western branch of the Valley of the Kings. At the same time all trace of 'that Rebel of Akhetaten' should be obliterated. The officials charged with these duties, of course, were no desperate robbers with nothing to lose: nevertheless they appear to have carried out their orders in a hurried and perfunctory manner. It is probable that the tomb and some of its contents were beginning to suffer from damp when they entered it, and falls of rock which occur when such sealed sepulchres are opened to the air may not have encouraged them to linger over their work. The light coming through the half-choked entrance may have been too dim to enable them to see some of the smaller items that they dropped or left behind in the rubbish strewn over the floor of the burial-chamber.

Their first task was to break down the walled-up entrance of the tomb, but only for about half its height, and to redistribute the filling so as to form a slope leading down the corridor into the burial-chamber at its lower level. The lighter articles, vessels, chests, shawabtis and the like, could then be easily man-handled up the ramp into the daylight beyond the entrance. But perhaps because they were already in a fragile condition some of them lost their clay seals which fell off among the rubbish. Of these, some bore the stamp of Amenophis III, evidently from Tiye's equipment dating to the days of her husband, or at any rate sealed with his name. The rest were impressed with the prenomen of Tutankhamun under whom the tomb was first brought into use.

As soon as a space around the entrance to the chamber had been cleared, more debris could be thrown down so as to extend the ramp up which the heavier equipment could be carried. This operation involved the dismantling of the shrine, the various parts of which were stacked against the eastern wall. The pall was then taken off its support, losing some of its roundels in the process. The coffin of Tiye could be taken out of the tomb and passed through the orifice at the ingress which measured about a metre high by nearly 2 metres wide. Such a size of opening would permit all but the larger items to be removed without any trouble. The shrine, however, even in its dismantled state, could not have been taken out without emptying more of the filling in the corridor to allow the long sides to pass. For some reason, perhaps because the shrine was already in poor condition, the officials in charge of the clearance decided not to demolish more of the blocking, but to leave the shrine in the tomb, and contented themselves with adzing out the figure and names of Akhenaten wherever they appeared in the decoration. In their haste, however, they overlooked a cartouche of Akhenaten on one of the long sides and forgot that, though they had neutralized the 'magic bricks' by removing their amulets, they had left the name of the original owner intact upon them.

The evacuation of most of Tiye's equipment left the way open for attention to be directed to any other burials remaining in the tomb. The 'magic bricks' inscribed for Akhenaten suggest that his deposit was also there, protected by such devices, and presumably he was resting in the coffin usurped from Kiya which had been adapted for him. But this had an internal measurement of 1.78 metres, and unless he was a short man like his father, his fully bandaged mummy would only just have fitted it, leaving no room for a funerary mask of the usual helmet type. It is clear, however, from Harrison's report upon the skeletal remains and Kidd's reconstruction of its cranio-facial appearance, that it was not his body that was left behind in the coffin; and the presumption is that Akhenaten was removed from it together with his other burial trappings.

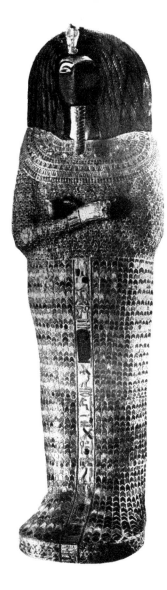

53 The restored coffin lid of Queen Kiya
from Valley of the Kings Tomb No. 55
(Pl. 56), made of gilded wood inlaid
with coloured glass in a feathered
pattern typical of the royal coffins of the
Eighteenth Dynasty. Modifications were
made to convert it from a woman's coffin
into a king's; namely the addition of a
beard and uraeus, and the replacement of
amulets held in the hands by regal
sceptres. The wig, however, which is still
a military coiffure, worn also by
princesses of the period, was not altered,
but the entire coffin has been left
nameless and dishonoured.

54 A coffinette of similar design, but
made completely of gold inlaid with
coloured glass, for holding each of the
four packets of embalmed entrails that
comprise the canopic contents. The four
coffinettes were the core of the elaborate
Canopic equipment of Tutankhamun, but
the interior inscriptions reveal that they
were originally made for Smenkhkarē.

55, 56 (left) Two views in Valley Tomb No. 55
photographed two days after its discovery on 11
January 1907. The back of the decayed gilded
wooden shrine that originally sheltered the burial of
Queen Tiye is shown (above) lying on the floor
where it had been left by the officials concerned
with moving it elsewhere. The figure of the queen
making an incense offering to the Aten is depicted
intact near the right-hand edge. The preceding
figure of Akhenaten has been adzed out of the
scene.

   Another view in the tomb (below) shows the
royal coffin (Pl. 53) lying on the floor near the
opposite side of the burial chamber. The lid lies
slightly athwart the shell which rests on a collapsed
lion-headed bier beneath it. The gold mask has

been torn off the face which is summarily carved.
The sceptres have been removed from the hands but
the uraeus has been left untouched.

57 (above) One of the four identical covers of the
Canopic jars made for the burial of Queen Kiya
and given by the Antiquities Service to Theodore
Davis in 1907. It is now in the Metropolitan
Museum, New York. Jars and covers are made of
calcite, with details in coloured glass, and show the
queen wearing the short Nubian wig and a broad
collar. The uraei had been added later, probably in
polychrome glass, and subsequently broken off,
though the bodies of the snakes have been cut into
the striations of the wigs, but somewhat crudely.

58, 60 *Details from a house-stela in Berlin carved in sunk relief with Akhenaten, Nefertiti and their three eldest daughters in a light pavilion beneath the rays of the Aten. Left, the king sits on a cushioned stool, and lifts Meritaten to kiss her, while she fondles his cheek and childishly points her finger to the group opposite. Right, the queen sits on a more substantial stool. Meketaten sits in her lap and points to the pair opposite, while Ankhesenpaaten plays with her mother's ear-ornament. The stela is carved in the grotesque style of the earlier half of the reign, but no more charming and complete an expression of family affection has survived from the antique world (cf. Fig. 26).*

59 *(below) A limestone talatat showing a party of court ladies in festal attire lifting bowls of drink to their lips. The scene, which is difficult to interpret, is unique but appears to be part of an occasion of ceremonial feasting. The ability of the Egyptian craftsman to represent a mass of heads in slightly differing poses and patterns is not in doubt, however, in this skilfully contrived composition.*

61 (below) Limestone talatat carved in sunk relief with part of a group of escorts holding their great flabella aloft as they run beside the royal chariot. The two pairs of reins by which the king directs the span of horses that draw the chariot cut into the base-line of the composition (cf. Fig. 10). The faces of the 'foreign legion' are ethnically differentiated as two Asiatics followed by two Nubians. All have suffered from the attentions of an iconoclast who has struck out their eyes (cf. Pl. 37).

62 (above) *Limestone talatat with another unusual scene of the king in the act of sacrificing a pin-tail duck upon an offering-table under the rays of the Aten. The down-turned mouth of the king as he wrings the bird's neck well expresses his wry grimace at a moment of tension.*

63 (left) *A 'block' statue in white calcite of Yii, the First Prophet of Mut and the Second Prophet of Amun under King Ay. Yii was a nephew of Queen Tey, and Steward of her temple in the domain of Amun on the west of Thebes. His sacerdotal offices suggest that he must have been influential in the return to orthodoxy after the death of Akhenaten, as is evident in the design of this statue, a kind of ex voto particularly associated with the cult of Osiris which had been suppressed in the reign of Akhenaten.*

65, 66 *Although architectural elevations were pictured in some of the Amarna reliefs, and have been used as guides in the restoration of ground-plans on excavated sites, none is fully reliable and does little more than give an impression of individual features assembled into a* capriccio *on the part of the artist. The* talatat *above shows an altar as the focal point of a sanctuary beyond a baffle wall with standing statues of the king presenting offerings on trays held waist high. Other altars are also shown heaped with food and flowers in chapels behind open doors. The other* talatat *(below) shows similar features, including an ambulatory with a triple row of columns. Such elements have been excavated in the Great Temple but cannot be exactly reconciled with the layouts composed by the pictorial artists.*

64 *(left) Statuette in white calcite, originally painted and doubtless inscribed, carved in the early style of Akhenaten's reign, showing him holding a tablet before him. This statuette is probably a miniature version of the three-quarter life-size sculptures which were smashed and discarded on a dump to the southeast of the Great Temple at Amarna (cf. Pl. 7). As such it would be kept in a small house shrine or similar reliquary which has preserved it from total destruction.*

67 Fragment of a large food jar excavated on the site of the Malkata palace of Amenophis III and inscribed with a docket giving the date as the 38th Regnal Year of the king, 'the birthday of Osiris' (i.e. the 361st day), and describing the contents as, 'dripping from breast meat of cattle from the stockyard . . . a gift to His Majesty from the King's Scribe Ahmose, prepared by the clarifier Iu-Amun . . .'

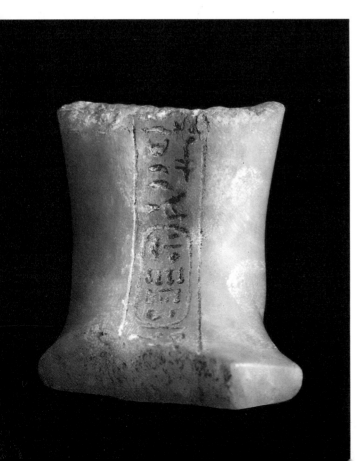

68 Lower part of the legs and feet of a calcite shawabti, incised with the end of an inscription reading, 'The Chief Wife of the King, (Neferneferuaten-Nefertiti), may she live for ever (and ever!).' It was acquired in 1933, probably as a result of illicit operations in the Royal Wadi at Amarna. The upper part of the figurine was acquired probably from the same source and is now in the Louvre. It gives the beginning of the inscription and enough information to enable it to be completed as, 'The Heiress, High and Mighty in the Palace, One trusted (of the King of Upper and Lower Egypt, (Neferkheperurē, Wa'enrē), the Son of Rē, (Akhenaten), Great in his Lifetime) . . .'

Like the coffin, the associated Canopic jars were allowed to remain in the tomb, but were desecrated by snapping off the uraei and chiselling away what remained of their inscriptions. A similar anonymity was imposed upon the coffin by cutting out the names in the cartouches wherever they appeared in its exterior banderoles and in its gold lining, and by wrenching off the gold mask from the face but leaving the summarily carved support unmutilated.

Despite the attempt to remove all physical traces of Akhenaten, it is doubtful whether the contents of the Canopic jars were tampered with by the desecrators. In 1931, Alfred Lucas, the chief chemist of the Antiquities Service who examined the three jars in Cairo, reported that each contained a black, stony-hard mass, resembling wood-pitch, surrounding a core of coarse woven fabric which enclosed nitrogenous material containing a small proportion of fatty matter, evidently the remains of wrapped viscera. Although Lucas made a careful examination he could find no evidence that the filling of the jars had ever been disturbed, and was of the opinion that the contents of the vases were original. But it is now impossible to hazard a guess as to whose entrails they were – whether Kiya's, Akhenaten's, or the anonymous male left in the tomb.

For the recognition of this latter body we are almost totally dependent upon a process of elimination. It was neither Kiya nor Akhenaten, but a young male aged about twenty at the time of death. He had been thrust into a coffin with a uraeus upon it; therefore he was ostensibly royal, but all other marks of identification had been excised, including the gold coffin-mask which may not have resembled him in any case, like the heads on the Canopic jars. A clue did survive, however, which might have revealed his identity. Weigall is insistent that the usual gold straps encircled the outer wrappings of his mummy at the time of discovery, though he is equally positive that these bore the titles and excised cartouches of Akhenaten. But he made no copy of the inscriptions, and may have been deceived by a confusion between the titulary of Akhenaten and that of Smenkhkarē. It might have required careful study before one could be categorical about the true owner of such bands when the names had been cut out. The theft of these bands by Elliot Smith's laboratory assistant has thus deprived us of the possibility of establishing the identity of the occupant of the coffin for certain.

In these straits we shall have to depend largely upon the close resemblance in his physical characteristics to Tutankhamun in recognizing him as a member of the same ruling house. Such a person fits the co-regent Smenkhkarē better than anyone else. He must have died before Tutankhamun who apparently usurped much of his burial equipment. In support of such a solution, a further slender clue has by chance survived. A piece of gold sheet, different in thickness and quality from the prosthetics that were used to convert the inscriptions on the coffin of Kiya into those referring to Akhenaten, was found among the debris, and reads, 'beloved of Wa'enrē'. This could be a part of the equipment of Smenkhkarē, and is peculiar to the earlier forms of both his names. What it was doing in this tomb is difficult to suggest, unless it had been cut out of his gold-covered furniture and had not been retrieved in the haste and gloom.

The party that desecrated his burial probably found that the two kings had been deposited together with Queen Tiye, who was certainly the mother of one of them, and probably of the other also, thus turning Tomb No. 55 into a family vault. They removed two of the occupants elsewhere, deprived the third of his burial equipment, though leaving him anonymous in the tomb, and built a drystone wall beyond the earlier blocking to seal the place in, without any stamp or mark upon it to betray what lay behind.

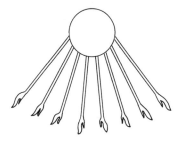

CHAPTER 19

The Amarna Queens

The doyenne of the senior queens who have left evidence of their sojourn at Amarna was Tiye, the chief wife of Amenophis III and the mother of Akhenaten. Her exalted position has already been touched upon above. References to her 'house' or estate have been found at Amarna, and her name has appeared on the jambs of a doorway to a mansion in the palace precincts to the north of the city; but in the absence of further details it is impossible to say if this was her residence. At least she paid a visit to Amarna after Year 9 of her *Fig. 29* son's reign, where there was certainly one limestone quarry bearing her name among the northern hills. The visit, however, was in connection with the consecration of a sunshade temple which Akhenaten had built for her in the town; and a relief in the tomb of her High Steward Huya at Amarna (No. 3) shows the king taking her by the hand to lead her and her daughter, Beketaten, into the new building. It may well have been that she ended her days at Amarna, for it seems likely that she was buried in a tomb in the Royal Wadi, although no definite evidence has come to light.

Tiye was probably born near Akhmim, where her father Yuya was the Chief *Pl. 39* Prophet of the local god Min, and Superintendent of his Cattle: but this was doubtless in his later years when he had retired from his main duties as the King's Lieutenant of the Chariotry and Master of the Horse, posts that he held under Tuthmosis IV and perhaps also in the last years of Amenophis II. He was probably related to these kings, and as an influential member of the royal entourage had been given in marriage to an important court lady Tuyu who was the Superintendent of the Harim of Min of Akhmim and of Amun of Thebes. As such she was high in the hierarchy of the cult of Queen Ahmose-Nefertari and from whom she may well have descended. Her daughter Tiye was, therefore, no less important, perhaps being regarded as the heiress whom the pharaoh was destined to marry according to a tradition established at the beginning of the dynasty. It is true that she did not bear the title of God's Wife of Amun, but she may not have filled that office before she was married to the young king Amenophis III at his advent.

On the Accession Scarab, and the Gilukhipa Scarab of Year 10 of Amenophis III's reign, she is referred to as the daughter of Yuya and Tuyu who are given no titles, a brevity that has encouraged the view that her parents were people of humble origin: and a love affair has been concocted by some susceptible scholars to account for her rise to sudden eminence. But we have seen that her position as the child-bride of the infant Amenophis III owed more to her position as a putative descendant of Ahmose-Nefertari than to romantic sentiment. So far from being people of humble position, Tuyu, as Superintendent of the Harim of Amun, would have been the deputy in her sacerdotal office to Queen Mutemwiya, the mother of Amenophis III, who may have been a sister of Yuya. The latter had risen to the command of the king's chariotry, but he may also have inherited this post from Yey, an earlier Master of the Horse and a Father of the God, a title which is borne by Yuya in preference to any other distinction, and almost certainly indicates at this period that his daughter had entered the harim of the pharaoh.

Tiye was not the only child of Yuya and Tuyu. She also had a brother Anen, who held a high position in the priesthood of Amun at Thebes, being the Second of the Four Prophets of Amun and the Greatest of Seers, or High Priest, in the temple of Rē-Atum. He held office during most of the reign of Amenophis III, being present in his official capacity at many of the ceremonies attended by his royal brother-in-law, though not apparently at the jubilee of Year 30, by which time he was evidently dead. It was doubtless Amenophis III who honoured him with the gift of a tomb (No. 120) in the hill of the Sheikh Abd el Qurna in Western Thebes. Despite Anen's prominence, with the reticence characteristic of all officials in a similar position, he made no admission of his kinship with the royal family. His relationship with Tiye, in fact, would not be known were it not that an inscription on Tuyu's coffin names him as the latter's son.

It is extremely unlikely that this important family, so closely connected with royalty for several generations at least, did not have another son to carry on the tradition of arms that they professed, since Anen had evidently deserted a military calling for sacerdotal office. We do not have to look far for such a successor. In the next generation at the court of Akhenaten, we find a Divisional Commander, Ay, holding most of the titles and offices claimed by Yuya under Amenophis III. Both men were Fathers of the God and Masters of the Horse. Both referred to themselves as 'One Trusted by the Good God [the king] in the Entire Land'; as 'Foremost among the Companions of the King'; and as 'Praised of the Good God'. These titles are generally taken to be honorific: on the other hand they may convey some degree of kinship with the ruler. Ay was a 'Fan-bearer on the Right of the King', and 'King's Own Scribe', or personal secretary. It is also noteworthy that Ay bears a name that approximates to Yuya which could be rendered in one of its many variants as Ay. As has already been mentioned, this family had a predilection for one or two similar sounding pet-names and Yey, Yuya, Ay and Yii are certainly suggestive of some relationship between the various courtiers of the time.

There is also another connection between these men. Yuya held important offices in Akhmim near where his daughter Tiye had extensive estates. Ay also built a chapel there to its local god Min, presumably because it was his birth-place or family seat. It is noteworthy that references to Min and names compounded with Min and the goddess Mut become common in court circles at the time of the ascendancy of this family. It is surely no coincidence that two near-contemporaries whose titles and careers offer such close parallels as those of Yuya and Ay, and who both have connections with a small provincial town, should have been related. The evidence that Ay was a son of Yuya, appointed in his father's place in the time-honoured Egyptian tradition, is thus strongly circumstantial.

There is, moreover, a close physical resemblance between these two men. It is true that we lack the body of Ay from which to draw comparisons, but the distinctive profile of Ay has been represented in various reliefs from Amarna *Pl. 4* and shows that he had the same beaky nose, thick lips and jaw-line as Yuya's, as revealed by the latter's mummy. This, according to Elliot Smith, had a pecu-liar and individualized physiognomy, not commonly encountered in Egypt. *Pl. 39*

The title that Ay uses in preference to any others is 'Father of the God', which he even incorporated into his nomen when he became king on the death of Tutankhamun. The title usually denotes the holder of a priestly office and *Pl. 76* historians in the past have referred to Ay as the 'Priest Ay', accrediting him with some of the religious thinking behind the Aten heresy, largely because the much quoted Great Hymn to the Aten appears in its fullest form in his tomb at Amarna. But Ay was primarily a soldier and held no priestly offices at Amarna where Pinhasy, Pentu and Tutu officiated as Chief Servitors, and Meryrē I as High Priest. Moreover, Ay is the only dignitary at Amarna to bear the title of 'Father of the God'. Many years ago the German scholar Ludwig Borchardt argued that in some circumstances this ambiguous title could mean 'The Father-in-law of Pharaoh', and this is particularly the case with Yuya, who is stated on two of the commemorative scarabs of Amenophis III to be the father of Tiye, the distinction, 'Father of the God', being used when there was no space for other titles. It would appear, therefore, that Ay too must have been the father-in-law of a king, though Akhenaten was the monarch he served. In that case, Ay's daughter must have been a wife of the pharaoh, and presumably his chief wife. Such a person can only have been Nefertiti.

Queen Nefertiti's parentage has been a subject of much speculation. As the chief wife of Akhenaten she should have been the Heiress, and that indeed is the position she is declared to hold wherever her full titulary is displayed, as it is in the Boundary Stelae and the encomiums addressed to her in the tombs of Huya and Tutu. There she is proclaimed:

> The Heiress, Great of Favour, Lady of Graciousness, Worthy of Love, Mistress of Upper and Lower Egypt, Great Wife of the King, whom he loves, Lady of the Two Lands, Neferneferuaten-Nefertiti, may she live for ever and ever!

As the Heiress she is presumably a descendant of Ahmose-Nefertari, though she is never described as God's Wife of Amun, for the good reason, if no other, that Amun was proscribed in court circles almost from the beginning of the reign.

She nowhere lays claim to the title of King's Daughter, which she certainly would have done if her mother had been Queen Tiye, so she cannot have been an heiress in the direct line of descent. That privilege was held by Sitamun, the eldest daughter of Amenophis III and Tiye. Probably Nefertiti was a daughter of a cognate branch, a niece of Tiye. While her putative father was Ay, his wife *Pl. 4* Tey should have been her mother, but here we encounter a difficulty. Tey is not called, as Tuyu was, 'Royal mother of the chief wife of the king', but only 'Nurse' and 'Governess' of the king's chief wife. It may therefore be that Nefertiti's mother died shortly after giving birth to her daughter, an inference surely not too adventurous in the case of the ancient world where infant and maternal mortality rates, even among royalty, were very high. The orphaned Nefertiti would then have been brought up by the next wife of Ay, and it is perhaps as 'Step-mother', rather than 'Wet-nurse' and 'Governess' that Tey's titles would best be rendered. There may be another explanation, however, which will be offered below.

In some of the earlier tomb reliefs at Amarna there appears the figure of a lady-in-waiting who is given rather more prominence than the other women in the queen's retinue, and is often accompanied by two dwarfs who appear to be attendant on the daughters of Nefertiti. She is described as the queen's sister Mutnodjme, and the fact that she lays no claim to the title of King's Daughter is another indication of the non-royal parentage of Nefertiti. Her father is presumably Ay, particularly as it is in his tomb that she figures most prominently, as well as in others whose decoration was influenced by it. She is shown in those reliefs where the detail has survived as wearing her hair arranged with a side-lock in the fashion of the earlier half of the reign, and appears to be a little older than her eldest niece Meritaten. She was probably therefore a younger sister of Nefertiti, but we do not know whether she was a full sister or, as a daughter of Tey, only a half-sister. Mutnodjme disappears

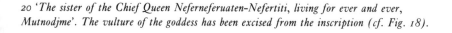

20 'The sister of the Chief Queen Neferneferuaten-Nefertiti, living for ever and ever, Mutnodjme'. The vulture of the goddess has been excised from the inscription (cf. Fig. 18).

from view as the reign wears on, and is not distinguished by name or title in the groups of attendants appearing in the later reliefs at Amarna. It is a significant fact, however, that the chief wife of King Haremhab was called Mutnodjme – a *Pl. 77* somewhat rare name at this period. She appears on his coronation statue at Turin sitting beside him, equal in size and importance. From the days of the German scholar Heinrich Brugsch, therefore, historians have been disposed to recognize the chief wife of Haremhab as the sister of Nefertiti; and the identity of the two has recently returned to favour as philological objections to the equation have been convincingly refuted. Elsewhere Mutnodjme bears the title of Heiress and it was presumably through her claim to this distinction that her husband was able to consolidate his uncertain right to the throne on the death of King Ay. On a fragmentary statue of her unearthed at Dendera, she supplements her title of 'Chief Queen' with 'God's Wife [of Amun]', which puts her in the line of those other great consorts who traced their descent from Ahmose-Nefertari.

If Mutnodjme was thus one of those royal heiresses whom kings made their chief queens on their accession, Nefertiti, too, must have had a similar familial claim to eminence and both sisters must have belonged to the family of Yuya and Tuyu, to trace their descent no further back. Their connection with the cult of Amun could not, however, have been openly proclaimed at Amarna – the *mut*-vulture for instance was excised from the name of Mutnodjme in the tomb of Parennefer. Nevertheless, if Nefertiti did not bear the title of God's Wife of Amun, she may well have acted a cognate part in the sun-cult, particularly of Rē-Atum, as we have seen the Adorer of the God, Huy, did in the reign of Tuthmosis III.

While Nefertiti could not enact the ritual proper to the God's Wife of Amun, in other respects she followed the forms fairly closely. She was equivalent in her sacerdotal position, being virtually paramount. Unlike other chief queens, she is shown taking part in the daily worship, repeating the same gestures and making similar offerings as the king: in fact the divine service is a reciprocation between the god and the royal pair. She is one of the triple powers, with the Aten and the king, that were invoked by the courtiers for funerary favours. She may appear wearing a king's crown like that other Great Heiress of the *Fig. 21* dynasty, Queen Hatshepsut. She may undertake the duty of exorcising the state enemies or the forces of Evil, if only in effigy, by the icon of the massacre of foe-women, in the posture of a pharaoh. *Pl. 41*

She also affects the same costume as a God's Wife. From her first appearance in the Karnak talatat, she wears the same clinging robe tied with a red sash with the ends hanging in front, and the short rounded hairstyle, in her *Pl. 36* case as exemplified by the Nubian wig, the coiffure of her earlier years, *Fig. 12* alternating with a queen's tripartite wig, both secured by a diadem bearing

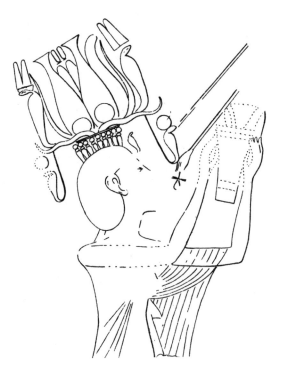

21 *Nefertiti wearing a kingly crown, a slightly less elaborate version of the triple Atef-crown usually worn only by kings.*

double uraei. Sometimes she varies this with double plumes and a disk, like Tiye and her later Kushite counterparts. Her sacerdotal duties of maintaining the god in a state of perpetual arousal is emphasized by the erotic nature of her Pls. 69, 70 allure. As the Aten is intangible and abstract, the appeal must be to his son the king. The epithets applied to her, 'sweet of love', 'in the sound of whose voice the king takes delight', refer to the affection between the royal pair, but also inevitably recall the relationship between the deity and the God's Wife in Kushite times, when the act of propitiation is described as 'her fair hands holding the sistrums'. This phraseology is anticipated by Ay, who praises Nefertiti for 'joining with her beauty in propitiating the Aten with her sweet voice and her fair hands holding the sistrums'. She is rarely shown, however, Fig. 22 playing the sistrums, soon delegating that rite to her elder daughters.

In this aspect of her function Nefertiti seems to have undertaken the duties, if not the office, of God's Wife, who had charge of 'the recluses of Amun', or 'the harim of the God', a foundation of Ahmose-Nefertari on Western Thebes, a college of temple-singers and musicians who took part in religious ceremonies. In the case of Nefertiti, 'the Mansion of the Ben-ben' served this liturgical purpose. Her pre-eminence in the Mansion of the Ben-ben is illustrated in the scenes from the Karnak talatat which show the chief officiant to be the queen accompanied by her eldest daughter, both playing sistrums, on the numerous piers so far recovered from this structure, in which the king is nowhere in evidence. A similar choir of singers and musicians appears among the servants of the Great Temple of the Aten at Amarna.

In the case of a solar deity like the Aten, however, which did not exist in an iconic form, much of the cult of Amun was irrelevant, and the queen assumed the identity of Tefnut, daughter and wife of Atum the primordial sun-god. The blue mortar-shaped cap she wore after the fourth regnal year was the headgear of Tefnut in her leonine aspect of a sphinx. In Kushite times the Wife of the God is sometimes referred to as the daughter of Atum or Rē, as well as Amun. She is also referred to as 'Tefnut herself'. Tefnut, at once the daughter and the wife of the sun-god, reflects that incestuous ambiguity that exists in the pharaonate in the New Kingdom, when several kings, including Amenophis III and Akhenaten, marry their own daughters who are designated 'wives' from a very early age.

The importance of Nefertiti in the cult thus owes everything to her position as the wife and daughter of the sun-god, an incarnation of Tefnut. Presumably as such no mortal could claim to be her mother, and that may be the reason why Tey has to content herself with the titles of 'Wet-nurse' and 'Governess' instead of progenitrix. Nefertiti, however, was everywhere proclaimed as the mother of the king's daughters whose upbringing was entrusted to her divine hands. In turn, each inherited her offices from the start; and not only became the wife of the king, but also the means by which their husbands, Smenkhkarē, Tutankhamun and Ay, inherited the throne after the death of Akhenaten.

News of Nefertiti during the later years of her husband's reign is sparse and the few records that have survived are not as explicit as one would wish. She is present with all her six daughters at the great durbar held at Akhetaten in the middle of Regnal Year 12, as reported in scenes in the tombs of Huya and *Fig. 27* Meryrē II. So it must be after that event that she is shown in chambers alpha and gamma of the Royal Tomb mourning over the biers of her second daughter Meketaten and of another royal personage, both evidently dead in child-birth. *Fig. 5* Dockets from wine-jars reveal that wine from Meketaten's estate imported into Akhetaten ceases after Year 11, and the presumption is that although the princess appears in the durbar in Year 12, it was shortly after that date that she

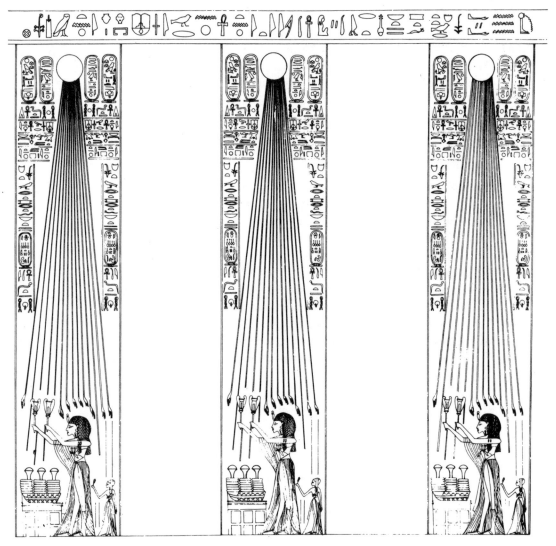

22 *Pillars, c. 9½m high, from a colonnade in the Mansion of the Ben-ben at Karnak, a temple in which Nefertiti officiated as the chief celebrant together with her daughter, Meritaten, who also shakes the sistrum in the worship of the god.*

died and was entombed. As the second of the six daughters, Meketaten could not have been born at the earliest before Year 2 of the reign, and could not normally have reached child-bearing age before Regnal Year 12 or 13. Although the scene of the burial of Meketaten in chamber gamma of the Royal Tomb is not dated, it cannot be earlier than Year 13 that Nefertiti was still alive to mourn her passing: but that is the last we see of the great queen.

The course of events at Amarna has henceforth to be gleaned from the ink dockets written in hieratic script on the shoulders of wine-jars recovered in fragments from various sites at Amarna, a somewhat uncertain source of information since, apart from difficulties in reading some of these damaged and ill-written labels, doubt can be cast upon the completeness of the archive. Interruptions to the wine supply from a particular source in certain years could also occur for reasons which are now unknown. Nor are the dates to be accepted as absolute, since wine might have been bottled for a time after the owner of an estate had died. Nevertheless, the information revealed from the random collection of wine-jar dockets will have to be accepted in default of anything better.

Delivery of wine from the estate of Nefertiti, identified as 'the House of Neferneferuaten', ceased at Akhetaten after Year 11, which is a year before the durbar at which Nefertiti was present and about two years before the burial of Meketaten. In Year 14, however, dockets appear upon jar-fragments referring to wine of 'the House of the King's Wife', and similar labels dated to Years 15 and 17 also survive. The estate in question does not appear to be Nefertiti's under a change of designation, but presumably is that of Meritaten, who about Year 14 had become the consort of Akhenaten, and 'the mistress of [his] house', as the Babylonian king mentions about this time in a letter to the pharaoh. Nor can the reference be to that other great queen of the reign, Tiye, whose estate is designated on wine-jar labels as 'the House of the King's Mother'. In her case, such dockets are not found after Year 14.

Another queen who can be excluded from this count of dockets at Amarna is Kiya. Her estate is known as, 'the House of the Favourite', but without her name, and has contributed very little to the corpus of information. Only two dockets have so far come to light, one dated to Year 11 and another to Year 6. The latter date, however, is damaged and the numeral has probably to be amended to 16, especially as the orthography of the word 'vintner' mentioned in the docket is in a form which is not generally employed until Year 13. That Kiya was living as late as Year 16 in the reign of Akhenaten has astonished some scholars, but should not really come as a surprise since she appears in company with the king himself and his two eldest surviving daughters, but not Nefertiti, in talatat from Hermopolis that belong to his last years.

The evidence of the wine-jar dockets, therefore, is in favour of accepting that Nefertiti died after Year 11, and probably in Year 14. But there has been a reluctance among historians to believe that Nefertiti should thus have left the scene so quietly and completely. The British excavators in the 1920s formed the impression that she had retired in disgrace to the Northern Palace area in the later years of the reign. The name and figure of the eldest daughter replaced hers on temple reliefs particularly in the *Maru*-aten. These alterations and excisions, however, would have been much more widespread and radical in such a proceeding: it is doubtful, for instance, whether so many intact sculptures of her would have been found in the studio of Djhutmose. In any case, the researches of Perepelkin have now shown that the queen whose monuments suffered such iconoclasm was Kiya, not Nefertiti. The idea that the latter did not die at this time, but underwent some kind of transmogrification, still persists and takes the form of two different scenarios. The first contends that after Year 14 she clung to power and formed a kind of government in exile, with the infant prince Tutankhaten (later Tutankhamun) as her protégé, until her death about three years after that of Akhenaten. The other idea, much canvassed in recent years, is a change of sex-role, similar to that of Hatshepsut earlier in the dynasty. This thesis claims that Nefertiti assumed the names, styles and habit of a pharaoh and ruled as the co-regent of her husband, adapting her epithet, Neferneferuaten, as a nomen, adding the qualification, 'beloved of Akhenaten', and taking as her prenomen the name of Ankhkheperurē, also with the addition of 'beloved of Akhenaten'. This latter prenomen has been generally recognized since the days of Petrie's discoveries at Amarna as that of the young king whose nomen was Smenkhkarē. Now, according to this new theory, he must be eliminated entirely from the family, the presence of a male body in the Kings' Valley Tomb No. 55 notwithstanding. Despite the ingenious arguments of its sponsor, Professor J. R. Harris, this hypothesis has won few adherents and will here be shown to be unacceptable.

Queen Nefertiti's fate for some theorists has been bound up with the history of Egypt's relations with North Syria at this particular period. We have earlier touched upon the appearance of a new protagonist in the struggle between the Hittites and the Mitanni that developed in the last decade of the reign of Amenophis III and the sole reign of Akhenaten. Suppiluliumas I, the new Hittite ruler, proved to be a dynamic warrior king of great skill and resilience, who decisively defeated his opponent Tushratta, Egypt's ally, in the closing stages of his campaigns against the Mitanni, and took their Syrian dependencies into vassalage. According to a memoir in the cuneiform archives found at Hattusas, the Hittite capital in Anatolia, while Suppiluliumas was besieging Carchemish during his second foray into the Amqa region of the Beqa Valley, word was brought to him that the pharaoh 'Nibhururiya' had just died, to the consternation of the Egyptians. Soon afterwards Suppiluliumas received a letter from the widowed queen saying, 'My husband has died and I have no son. They say about you that you have many sons. You might give me one of your sons to become my husband. I would not wish to take one of my subjects as a husband.' This offer was so extraordinary, and so much outside the tradition of diplomacy between Egypt and the great powers of Asia, that

Suppiluliumas thought it advisable to send a chamberlain to Egypt to investigate whether the request was genuine. By the time the emissary had returned, the opportunity for action had passed; and although the king dispatched his son Zennanza, the prince was murdered on the way to Egypt.

The problems that have vexed scholars in interpreting this memoir concern the identity of the queen in question who is not mentioned by a name but only by a title, 'Dahamansu', which is now generally accepted as a rendering of the Egyptian phrase *ta hmt nesu*, 'the wife of the king'. The second problem has proved rather more intractable. The name of the pharaoh Nibhururiya has been equated by some scholars with the prenomen Neferkheperurē, i.e. Akhenaten, and by others as Nebkheperurē, the prenomen of Tutankhamun. In the first case the queen would be Nefertiti; in the second, Ankhesenamun (formerly Ankhesenpaaten). The chronology of the period is sufficiently flexible to admit either possibility; but the situation outlined by the widowed queen fits conditions better for Ankhesenamun than for Nefertiti, since there were no royal sons surviving on the death of the former's husband, whereas there was certainly one (Tutankhaten), and possibly another (Smenkhkarē), still living at the death of Akhenaten.

The final choice between the two candidates resolves itself into a philological wrangle between two sets of experts, with arguments almost balanced, although there has lately developed a distinct tilt in favour of Ankhesenamun.

A new factor, however, has now entered the equation, by the discovery in the Louvre of another fragment of the shawabti of Nefertiti, the lower part of *Pl. 68* which has been in the Brooklyn Museum since 1933. This has enabled its discoverer, the young German scholar Christian Loeben, to reconstruct all the inscription on the figure as referring to, 'The Heiress, high and mighty in the palace, one trusted [of the King of Upper and Lower Egypt (Neferkheperurē, Wa'enrē)|, the Son of Rē (Akhenaten)|, Great in] his Lifetime, the Chief Wife of the King (Neferneferuaten-Nefertiti)|, Living for Ever and Ever.' The *Fig. 23* significance of this titulary is that it confirms that the shawabti was indeed made exclusively for Nefertiti, and was not for donation by her in Akhenaten's burial, as has been suggested on the strength of the greater prominence of his names in the inscription. This object was presumably made after the queen's death. The usual practice in the case of royal shawabtis was to make and inscribe them during the days of embalment. Many, apart from special presentation pieces donated by friends, show signs of hasty and crude workmanship. A workshop found by Petrie in the Great Palace at Amarna rendered up broken fragments of shawabtis in process of manufacture, and heaps of stone dust, showing that the figurines had been among the last objects to be made for the king's funeral, and the debris had been left behind still untouched when the place was abandoned. There is another feature of these

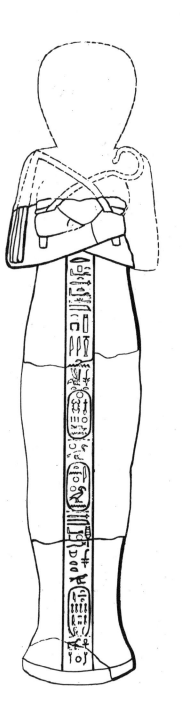

royal shawabtis which is significant in showing the late date of th
manufacture. We have already mentioned that in the anathe
against Osirian practices during his reign, Akhenaten dispens
with the orthodox funerary benediction, *maet kheru* ('justifie
after the name of the deceased. It is also missing from
inscription on Nefertiti's shawabti; but it should be noted t
already immediately after Akhenaten's death it returns to favo
At least two of his shawabtis have *maet kheru* added to his titula
as had his 'magic bricks' deposited in Valley Tomb No. 55. It see
improbable therefore that Nefertiti could have died aft
Akhenaten and had her funerary equipment inscribed long aft
his.

The inscription on her shawabti also makes it clear that desp
the holding of kingly sceptres, the crook and the flail, the shawa
represented her as a queen regnant and not as a co-regent in m
attire. The theory that Nefertiti after Year 14 acted as h
husband's co-regent thus withers and falls, for it is inconceivab
that an anointed and consecrated ruler with a distinctive prenom
and nomen, and a king's titles, would not have retained su
honours after death and burial.

Thus the evidence strongly supports the view that Nefertiti di
about Year 14 of her husband's reign and was buried by him a
mourned as a great queen, loyal to his teachings.

*23 Calcite shawabti of Nefertiti restored from two fragments in the Louvre and Brooklyn
Museums, the head conjecturally added. Like the king's examples it carries the sceptres and
emblems of regal power and not the implements of labour in the Osirian fields (cf. Pls. 11, 12).*

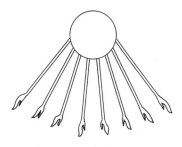

CHAPTER 20

The Pathology

The early travellers who found their way to Amarna and its rock tombs may well have been forgiven for thinking that the figure of the king in the reliefs was that of a woman, and two queens were depicted acting together. Akhenaten is represented with the same elongated neck, broad hips, swelling breasts and *Fig. 6* plump thighs as Nefertiti. Since he occasionally wears a long clinging robe similar to a woman's gown, figures of the king have often been confused with those of the queen, and vice versa, especially when his distinctive headgear has been destroyed, or when Nefertiti wears a crown similar to a pharaoh's. The feminine nature of Akhenaten's physique is well illustrated in the torsos from the broken statues which Carter found in the dump near the Great Temple at *Pl. 7* Amarna. It is quite impossible to decide on anatomical grounds alone whether they represent the king or the queen.

The French scholar Eugène Lefébure, for instance, nearly a century ago surmised that Akhenaten was really a woman masquerading as a man; and he pointed to a notable precedent in Hatshepsut, the queen who had usurped pharaonic power earlier in the dynasty, and who had herself represented in male attire, even wearing the fictive beard of a pharaoh attached to her chin. In *cf. Pl. 33* support of his argument, he drew attention to a tradition which had been briefly mentioned by Manetho, and quoted by Josephus, to the effect that a certain Akencheres who ruled after Orus was the latter's daughter. Lefébure equated Orus with Amenophis III, and Akencheres with his successor Akhenaten. These theories have generally been dismissed or ignored by subsequent scholars, though they require to be weighed as symptomatic of a malaise in the minds of Egyptologists when confronted with the epicene monuments of Akhenaten.

It is not simply that Akhenaten had himself represented as effeminate or androgynous, he specified certain distortions that belong neither to normal men nor normal women. In an exaggerated form these are the abnormalities that have enabled a number of pathologists independently to diagnose that the subject depicted in this way may have suffered from a disorder of the endocrine system, more specifically from a malfunctioning of the pituitary gland. Elliot

Smith identified it in 1907 as Fröhlich's Syndrome, a complaint in which male patients exhibit a corpulence similar to Akhenaten's. Adiposity may vary in degrees but there is a typical feminine distribution of fat in the regions of the breast, abdomen, pubis, thighs and buttocks. The lower limbs, however, are *cf. Fig. 24, Pl. 8* slender, and the legs, for instance, resemble 'plus fours'.

Fröhlich's Syndrome may arise from a variety of causes, but among the commoner is a tumour of the pituitary gland which controls the gonadial characteristics of animals, including human beings. Lesions in the area of the pituitary often interfere with the adjacent hypothalamus and vice versa, and this may affect the adiposity of the patient. At an early stage of the complaint there may be a fugitive over-activity of the pituitary which can lead to such distortions in the skull as an excessive growth of the jaw, but this is followed by a sub-normal functioning of the gland and by hypogonadism. The diagnosis of Fröhlich's Syndrome may only be made when the patient, having reached the age of puberty, fails to develop normally, his voice stays shrill, body hair does not appear and the sexual organs remain infantile. Moreover, as tumours in this gland are rare before puberty, the onset of the disorder may occur at the same time as adolescence. A later stage of the complaint is the plumping-out of breasts, abdomen, buttocks and thighs. An occasional concomitant is hydrocephalus, which, because it has arisen when the bones of the skull have hardened and closed, does not distort the cranium to the usual globular shape, but results in a bulging of the thinner parietal areas.

Figs. 2, 26 The pathological condition in which Akhenaten chose to have himself represented is shared to a lesser extent by all his family and entourage. The skull of the vizier Ramose, for instance, in the drawings in his tomb, shows a sudden and violent change from the normality of his appearance at the advent of the king, to the chronic distortion visible at his presentation at one of the first investitures of the reign. This sudden alteration cannot be attributed to an abrupt attack of the disease. It is rather to be suspected that the peculiar Amarna physiognomy was the ideal shape that the artists were instructed to follow, and it became fashionable for the king's followers and relatives to adopt the same peculiarities. It is probable that Akhenaten had an unusual platycephalic skull, like those of Tutankhamun and Smenkhkarē; but if the representation of the princesses' skulls, as shown in some of their statue heads and reliefs, is but a reflection of the ideal which Akhenaten sanctioned as the proper portrayal of the royal cranium, it goes far beyond the unusual. The *Pl. 18* exaggerated shape of the skulls of these princesses is such that it is legitimate to wonder whether they, or the pattern after which they were modelled, did not suffer from a form of hydrocephalus.

Such a violent departure from the wholly idealistic, even heroic, nature of Egyptian portraiture in the New Kingdom could have been made only at the pharaoh's insistence, since no artist would have dared to produce such an unflattering likeness of the god-king, even if it had occurred to him to flout all the traditions of his hereditary craft. Bek, the chief sculptor of Akhenaten in the early revolutionary phase of the new art, makes this clear in the relief he carved on the rocks at Aswan, and in his funerary stela from Heliopolis, where he describes himself as 'the apprentice whom His Majesty taught'. From the days of Petrie it has been maintained that the peculiar art of the reign is naturalistic, embodying the same revolutionary ideas which the king promoted in the spheres of religion and society. But actually Akhenaten did not alter a single convention of Egyptian drawing. The human figure continued to be rendered by the artist in the same visual terms as had persisted from archaic times when Egyptian art crystallized out at a conceptual stage of its development in the service of the divine king, and adhered to the same conventions for as long as kingship lasted. Akhenaten's innovations were mostly in the choice of subject-matter: style remained unchanged in its fundamentals, though the proportions of the human figure were adjusted to suit a canon which departed from the traditional, and, though varying, tended mostly to elongate the upper part of the body, particularly in the earlier part of the reign. These innovations are limited to representations of the royal family. The king's followers also hastened to have themselves depicted in the same fashionable mode as their 'god who had made them', though mostly to a lesser extent. Soldiers, servants, the common folk and foreigners are shown without these stigmata of the elect, albeit their often clumsy and careless drawing by lesser craftsmen is in the manner of the period.

It is strange that the 'expressionism', as it has sometimes been defined, introduced by Akhenaten into Egyptian art should take the form of showing the human figure as though it were exhibiting, to an exaggerated degree, the abnormalities of an endocrine disorder. As it is the figure of the king which shows these traits to the most marked extent, there is warrant for thinking that he suffered from Fröhlich's Syndrome, and wished to have himself represented with all those deformities which differentiated him from the rest of humanity. The earliest reliefs of his reign, those that were carved at Karnak on *Pl. 27* the portal at the Tenth Pylon which was erected but not decorated by Amenophis III, show the transition from the mature style of his father's reign to the innovations of his own. They may indicate that at his advent the young co-regent did not depart from the artistic and iconographic traditions of his father, which promoted the pharaoh as the ideal king: normal, heroic and perfect. On the other hand, they may indicate that during his first months on the throne he did not exhibit to a gross extent those outward signs of his disorder, just as a similar reticence is shown by his appearance under the royal baldachin in the tomb of Ramose at Thebes. A relief in the Louvre, however,

Pl. 28 from a later block from the same gateway at Karnak, representing the Aten in the fully fledged form of the radiant disk, shows Akhenaten with a heavy jaw, and pronounced paunch and buttocks. These are clear, if somewhat timid, signs of those physical peculiarities which shortly were to be paraded in a blatant manner on the colossi of the Gempaaten and the reliefs on the Boundary Stelae at Amarna.

There is, however, a serious obstacle in the way of attributing to Akhenaten such a disorder as Fröhlich's Syndrome, which has deterred pathologists from being more categorical in their diagnosis. Akhenaten is unique among the pharaohs in having himself represented as the family man. He seldom appears except in the company of his chief wife and some or all of her six daughters, *Pl. 15* embracing them, taking them on his knee and dangling trinkets for them to snatch. How could so uxorious a husband and so philoprogenitive a parent possibly have suffered from Fröhlich's Syndrome, which would necessarily have rendered him sterile and lacking in libido? The six princesses are entitled in each case, 'The daughter of the King, of his loins, born of the Chief Wife Nefertiti', leaving it to be understood that their father is Akhenaten, though other candidates have been suggested, such as Amenophis III, who, however, cannot be implicated unless he had a long co-regency with his son. There is, on the other hand, evidence that towards the end of the reign of Akhenaten, when each of his elder daughters had reached nubility, he sired children by them who were called after their mothers with the addition of *ta-sherit* ('junior'), such as Meritaten-ta-sherit and Ankhesenpaaten-ta-sherit. Although the co-regent Smenkhkarē has alternatively been credited with fathering them, considerations of timing render this highly improbable. The second generation daughters were born when their mothers were still princesses like Meketaten, who died in child-birth not long after Year 13.

Such incestuous relationships are not unknown elsewhere in the families of divine kings, but the paternity of Akhenaten, though it has been denied by some scholars, seems evident enough. Moreover, the existence of texts on the Hermopolite talatat referring to 'The Favourite' and 'greatly beloved' Kiya has revealed that this other queen also had a daughter by Akhenaten, though her name has been expunged wherever it appears. This sexual vigour on the part of the king does not suggest that he lacked virility. Despite the exaggeration with which he encouraged his artists to represent his person, he cannot have suffered from an abnormality which was chronic enough to impair seriously his procreative powers.

Pls. 17, 21 That the grotesque aspect of his appearance on the monuments owes more to the artistic expression than to a pathological condition is suggested by the art style of the later years of his reign. Models and sketches found in the sculptors' studios at Amarna, where their work was brought to an abrupt halt by the abandoning of the city, lack the exaggeration of the earlier style as exemplified in the reliefs on the Boundary Stelae, and the statuary recovered by Carter from the dumps at the Great Temple. According to the reports of Geoffrey Martin on the reliefs in room alpha in the Royal Tomb, some scenes have been later modified to mitigate the extreme style of the earlier carvings. Model reliefs, too, furnished for the guidance of workmen, and recovered from buildings under construction during the last years of the reign, show a more orthodox portraiture of the royal family.

Pls. 1, 25

The colossi uncovered in the 1930s by Chevrier at the site of the Gempaaten in Eastern Karnak have been largely responsible for this 'expressionistic' interpretation of the art of the reign, just as the fragment of indurated limestone balustrade, found by Petrie in the ruins of the Great Temple at Amarna in 1891, has spawned a plethora of fake reliefs, more or less successfully copying the mannerisms of the style sufficiently well to deceive some museum curators. It is now clear that this group of colossi must have sprung fully devised right at the beginning of the reign, and their appearance seems to have encouraged defacement and vandalism by shocked opinion in Thebes until their final demolition in the reign of Haremhab. One specimen, which has become the most notorious in the group, apparently represents the king as nude and without genitals. A theory to account for this epicene form has suggested that this colossus, and other more fragmentary examples in the series, are manifestations of the bi-sexual aspect of the sun-god, the demiurge, 'the father and mother of mankind', who impregnated himself in Chaos in order to create the diversity of the universe from the oneness of his self. The most plausible explanation, however, has been offered by J. R. Harris, who takes the view that some at least of the colossi represent not Akhenaten but Nefertiti wearing a close-clinging garment. The holding of kingly sceptres, and the wearing of a heavy beard in each case does not vitiate this argument, since there are other instances where such masculine adjuncts are occasionally arrogated by heiress-queens, particularly by Hatshepsut. Unfortunately, no complete range of stylistic details has survived on these statues which would clinch his argument. There are no feet to show evidence of a lower hem of the garment: and the upper part of the crown is also missing, thus thwarting any attempt to decide whether the queen's double uraeus was worn, and what the exact design of the headgear should be.

Pls. 33–5

cf. Pl. 6

Pl. 33

Harris obliquely suggests that the colossi may be intended to represent Rē-Herakhte (Aten) in different hypostases, or symbolic personifications, such as Shu and Atum. To complete the primal Heliopolitan trinity, Nefertiti should then be assimilated to the female element Tefnut. The reconstruction of the south colonnade of the Gempaaten, proposed by Redford as a result of his excavations at East Karnak, restores the colossi as gaily painted figures of Shu

Fig. 24

alternating with Atum(?), the latter as a king wearing the Double Crown. The colossi of Nefertiti as Tefnut, if she is indeed represented in that guise, must come from the same complex, though not necessarily from the same colonnade, and may be part of the Mansion of the Ben-ben which was in the Gempaaten. Future investigations in this area may be fortunate in settling such problems.

Contemporary with these colossi would be Akhenaten's diatribe against the representation of gods in iconic form (see Chapter 21), which makes it almost certain that these images are meant to be of the royal pair rather than of any solar gods to whom they are assimilated. While, therefore, explanations of a theological rather than a pathological nature seem to underlie the bizarre aspects that Akhenaten adopted for representing the members of the royal family in the early sculptures of his reign, why they should also be almost exact illustrations of subjects suffering from Fröhlich's Syndrome remains not the least of the enigmas which his reign has bequeathed us.

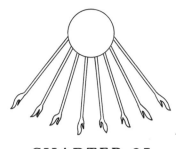

CHAPTER 21

The Heresy

The culture of Upper Egypt, which had coloured the outlook of the princes of Thebes, declined in its influence after the reigns of the first two pharaohs of the Eighteenth Dynasty; and the dominance of Lower Egypt, and particularly of its ancient capital, began to reassert itself during the reign of Tuthmosis I. As has already been mentioned, this king founded a great palace complex at Memphis, which was still flourishing at the end of the dynasty, and continued to be important under the Ramessides, despite the rise of the Delta residence of Pi-Ramesse. It became the custom for the eldest son of the pharaoh to assume the governorship of Memphis, as did Amenophis II before he became king, or Tuthmosis the son of Amenophis III who was also appointed High Priest of Ptah in the reign of his father.

The dominance of Lower Egypt is seen particularly in the revived sun-cult of Heliopolis which under the Hyksos kings maintained its supremacy during the Second Intermediate Period. Heliopolis, 13 kilometres to the northeast of Memphis, had always influenced the dynastic cult of Ptah and may have experienced a reinvigoration from ideas introduced from Asiatic sun-cults. Officials of Lower Egyptian origin had risen to high position by the middle of the Eighteenth Dynasty. Intervention at the highest level is seen in the undertaking of Tuthmosis IV to uncover the giant image of Rē-Herakhte, the god of Lower Egypt, from the sands that engulfed his great sphinx at Giza. The sun-religion had in fact been closely identified with the kingship from the days of Djoser at the inception of the Third Dynasty, by which time the sky-god Horus, incarnate in a falcon and the king, had become assimilated to the sun-god Rē. The myth had already developed that Rē, the first king to rule Egypt, wearying of mankind and its affairs, retired to the heavens leaving his son the pharaoh to rule on earth in his stead. The strength of these beliefs owed much to the intellectual vigour of the priesthood of the sun-cult in Heliopolis, the traditional wise men, or intelligentsia of Egypt, whose reputation was celebrated far beyond the borders of the land. Theological speculation has ever been the peculiar character of the Egyptian genius, whether in pagan or Christian times, or under Islam. It has maintained its vitality even in periods of political decline. The solar destiny, which had been exclusive to the king and his entourage in the Old Kingdom, extended its scope in the Middle Kingdom. This increased influence can be seen in the arrogation of royal privileges, particularly in the items of royal dress pictured on the interior of 'palace' coffins of private burials of the period, such as kilts, jewels, sceptres, amulets, and even the kingly uraeus. However lowly their position on earth, all the dead who could afford such coffins expected to become as kings in the other world.

These ideas continued to expand after the Middle Kingdom. The exhortation of the dead king in the Pyramid Texts, calling upon Nut, the universal sky-mother of the sun-cult, to descend and embrace him as the imperishable stars which were in her, now became an essential prayer inscribed upon the sarcophagus, just as the coffin was decorated with her enfolding wings
Pls. 53, 54   in a feather pattern which was still in fashion for royalty in the case of Queen Kiya. Thus the intervention of the solar gods was the best hope of eternal life in Egypt during the Eighteenth Dynasty, and by the reign of Tuthmosis III was well established in the Theban necropolis, when the private tomb emerged in its developed form, the superstructure crowned with a pyramidion representing the solar symbol of rebirth, from the primaeval mound in Heliopolis. Hymns to the rising and setting sun were inscribed at the entrance to the chapel, or on stelae held by kneeling statues of the tomb-owner. All such ritual was to ensure a destiny that was royal and dynamic, enabling the deceased, like the king, to enter the bark of the sun-god and take part in the transformations that would occur during its triumphal passage across the sky, following the daily birth of the god at sunrise, and his inert gestation during the hours of night, to a resurrection at the next dawn. The eternal return of the sun-god is the motive force that activates the universe, as is expressed in the later name of Akhenaten's deity.

This idea is given substance in the new religious texts that decorate the walls of the tombs of the kings at Thebes from the time of Tuthmosis I, when the first known version of the *Imy Det* (*The Book of What is in the Underworld*) makes its appearance. Another work, *The Litany of the Sun*, is written on a winding sheet of Tuthmosis III, while *The Book of Gates* is found in the tomb of King Haremhab soon after the Amarna period. In this the sun-god Rē is called 'The Lord of the Aten', which the gods of the morning lift up at every dawn in the eastern horizon of heaven, a theme which is illustrated most enigmatically on the second shrine of Tutankhamun, and in the burial chamber of Ramesses VI. *The Book of What is in the Underworld* is largely concerned with the progressive nightly transformation of a chrysalid divine power, called 'Flesh of Rē', into the new sun, the scarab Khepri, at the break of day. This metamorphosis took place during the twelve-hour journey of the 'Flesh of Rē' through the cavernous regions of the underworld, bringing light for each hour to its denizens and awakening them from death or sleep. During this transit, which was also through the star-studded body of the sky-goddess Nut, the dead king like the sun-god would be born again at the dawn. The constant element in this ever-changing transfiguration is the Aten, the disk of the sun, as carried by 'Flesh' through the regions of the night. During the Amarna period, the invisible source of energy of the solar divinity was identified as Rē-Herakhte; while the visible manifestation of such power appeared under the name of Aten, the Great, the Living.

The Aten had been known by the beginning of the Twelfth Dynasty at least, when Ammenemes I is referred to in *The Story of Sinuhe* as dying and flying to heaven to unite with Aten, the divine flesh mingling with him who had begot him. The same poetic expression is revived to announce the death of Amenophis I; while his successor, Tuthmosis I, chose as one of his titles the phrase, 'Horus-Rē, Mighty Bull with sharp horns, who comes from the Aten'; Rekhmirē, the vizier of Tuthmosis III, refers to the closeness of his relations with his king as, 'I saw his person in his true form, Rē, the Lord of Heaven, the Lord of Upper and Lower Egypt when he rises, the Aten when he reveals himself.' In the reign of Amenophis II, the symbol of the sun-disk appears with a pair of enveloping arms. Under Tuthmosis IV, the Aten is referred to on a large scarab as a god of battles who makes the pharaoh mighty in his domains and brings all his subjects under the sway of the sun-disk.

In the reign of Amenophis III references to the Aten as a solar divinity become more numerous. The name 'Radiance of the Aten' is applied to his state barge on the commemorative scarabs of his Regnal Year 11, and to the Malkata palace complex before his first jubilee, perhaps even to the king himself. A name compounded with the Aten was conferred upon at least one of his children. *Fig. 29*

There was thus a progressive increase in the mention and importance of the Aten as a separate divinity throughout the period. This is but one aspect of the rising ferment in the theology of the solar cult, in conjunction with such manifestations of the same beliefs evident in the religious texts that appear in the tombs of the kings and their more intimate officials. The new concept of Rē is that he is more than a sun-god. He is the Universe who has assimilated all the other gods in his being. He is 'the sole god who has made himself for eternity'. In the *Litany* he is invoked under his seventy-five names which are his bodies (or aspects), and these bodies are the gods. Thus Rē is the bodies of Atum, Shu, Tefnut, Geb and Nut, the entire first and second generation of the solar deities. He is hailed as, 'Rē of the Disk, supreme power whose forms are his transformations when he makes successively his appearance as the Aten or solar disk'. This dogma is already close to that proclaimed by the titles and didactic name of Akhenaten's god, the Aten, if not identical with it.

Thus a syncretism of religious beliefs in the Eighteenth Dynasty was already embracing a monotheistic conception of a supreme solar divinity. Furthermore, such a deity takes on the aspect of king in conformity with the ideas of the time at the level of the control of human affairs. While the sun-god from his inception in Egypt had been such a ruler, he was most triumphantly proclaimed in the heavenly king that Akhenaten affirmed, enclosing his name in double-bordered cartouches, and giving him titles and epithets like a pharaoh *par excellence*. It is true that other gods like Amun or Osiris had been conceived of as kings and given titles, 'Lord of the Thrones of Upper and Lower Egypt', 'Ruler of Eternity', and so on, yet their names were not enclosed in cartouches. The god that Akhenaten adjured in the Boundary Stelae at Amarna is a heavenly pharaoh, a 'Good God', 'Divine and Regal', whose reign began with that of the king. Indeed, the durbar of Year 12 is dated to the reign of the Aten in the tomb of Huya, and to the reign of Akhenaten in the tomb of Meryrē II, as though god and king were regarded as co-regents. Like a king, the Aten can also celebrate jubilees after a period of rule. As a pharaoh, like the king whom Rekhmirē salutes, he is the mother and father of mankind, alone by himself without an equal. The monotheism that Akhenaten proclaims is not the henotheism of earlier times, the belief in one supreme god without any assertion of his unique nature, but the worship of an omnipotent and singular divinity. The full development of the king's thought is seen in the careful suppression later in the reign of the plural form of 'god' wherever it appears in earlier texts. There was now but one god, and the king was his prophet.

This intimate relationship was expressed in a familial form. The king is still called by a title that the pharaoh had borne since the days of the early Old Kingdom, 'Son of the Sun-god', but now with the addition of 'The beautiful child of the Aten'. In the tomb of Parennefer, the courtier addresses his lord as 'the radiant child of the Aten who has vouchsafed a sight of thyself to us(?)'. To Ay, the king's relationship to the Aten is, 'Thy son who issued from thy rays. Thou transferrest to him thy duration and thy years. Thou listenest to him and what is in his heart.' A feature of the religious development that had evolved during the New Kingdom was the widespread worship of a group of gods who were represented as a Father and Mother figure, together with their male offspring, a trinity which appealed strongly to the love of family among the Egyptians. Thus Amun of Karnak had a consort Mut, and their son Khons the moon-child: other triads were Ptah, Sekhmet and Nefertem of Memphis; and Osiris, Isis and Horus the Child of Abydos. The Aten, however, was a sole god who created himself daily, having no female counterpart. Although he is sometimes addressed, in the tombs of Ipy and Meryrē I for instance, as 'the father and mother of all that thou hast made', he is predominantly 'Father Aten'. Nevertheless, one gains the impression that Akhenaten, in publicizing his domestic life as the family man with Nefertiti and one or more of their children, is consciously or otherwise creating a significant icon of a holy family as a focus of daily worship, particularly in the chapels attached to the private houses at Amarna. And while the Aten shares his divinity with no female principal, one suspects that the erotic extravagance given to Nefertiti, both in her appearance and in the epithets lavished upon her, have the effect of elevating her into a love-goddess, a Venus figure like Hathor or Astarte. The door-jambs at the entrance to the tombs at Amarna, where they are complete, contain prayers, addressed to this trinity of powers, the Aten, the king and the queen.

Pl. 24

At least the courtiers addressed their king as an incarnation of the sole god the Aten. Ay refers to him as 'my god who fashioned me'; for Pentu he is 'the god who fashions mankind, and makes the Two Lands live'; Tutu hails him as his 'god who fashioned and fostered him'. Their invocations to the Aten are also addressed to the king. The prayers that now appear in the tomb inscriptions expressing the quintessential tenets of the new creed quote from a longer composition which is generally taken to be the work of the king himself. The longest extract is found in the tomb of Ay, who as one of the king's private secretaries must have found a good copy for his scribe to follow, though it is not entirely free from corruptions. The doctrine enshrined in the psalm, to which the name of the 'Great Hymn' has been given in modern times, is that the universe has been fashioned by the sun-god immanent in the Aten, and he alone cares for his creation. His mysterious hand is upon all that he has made, although he is afar off in the remote heavens. When the living Aten goes to rest the world becomes dark and hostile, and sleeps after the manner of death until the next day dawns, when all creation by the power of the Aten awakens and rejoices. It runs as follows:

Thou arisest fair in the horizon of Heaven, O Living Aten, Beginner of Life. When thou dawnest in the East, thou fillest every land with thy beauty. Thou art indeed comely, great, radiant and high over every land. Thy rays embrace the lands to the full extent of all that thou hast made, for thou art Rē and thou attainest their limits and subduest them for thy beloved son [Akhenaten]. Thou art remote yet thy rays are upon the earth. Thou art in the sight of men, yet thy ways are not known.

When thou settest in the Western horizon, the earth is in darkness after the manner of death. Men spend the night indoors with the head covered, the eye not seeing its fellow. Their possessions might be stolen, even when under their heads, and they would be unaware of it. Every lion comes forth from its lair and all snakes bite. Darkness lurks, and the earth is silent when their Creator rests in his habitation.

The earth brightens when thou arisest in the Eastern horizon and shinest forth as Aten in the daytime. Thou drivest away the night when thou givest forth thy beams. The Two Lands are in festival. They awake and stand upon their feet for thou hast raised them up. They wash their limbs, they put on raiment and raise their arms in adoration at thy appearance. The entire earth performs its labours. All cattle are at peace in their pastures. The trees and herbage grow green. The birds fly from their nests, their wings [raised] in praise of thy spirit. All animals gambol on their feet, all the winged creation live when thou hast risen for them. The boats sail upstream, and likewise downstream. All ways open at thy dawning. The fish in the river leap in thy presence. Thy rays are in the midst of the sea.

Thou it is who causest women to conceive and makest seed into man, who givest life to the child in the womb of its mother, who comfortest him so that he cries not therein, nurse that thou art, even in the womb, who givest breath to quicken all that he hath made. When the child comes forth from the body on the day of his birth, then thou openest his mouth completely and thou furnishest his sustenance. When the chick in the egg chirps within the shell, thou givest him the breath within it to sustain him. Thou createst for him his proper term within the egg, so that he shall break it and come forth from it to testify to his completion as he runs about on his two feet when he emergeth.

How manifold are thy works! They are hidden from the sight of men, O Sole God, like unto whom there is no other! Thou didst fashion the earth according to thy desire when thou wast alone – all men, all cattle great and small, all that are upon the earth that run upon their feet or rise up on high flying with their wings. And the lands of Syria and Kush and Egypt – thou appointest every man to his place and satisfiest his needs. Everyone receives his sustenance and his days are numbered. Their tongues are diverse in speech and their qualities likewise, and their colour is differentiated for thou hast distinguished the nations.

Thou makest the waters under the earth and thou bringest them forth [as the Nile] at thy pleasure to sustain the people of Egypt even as thou hast made them live for thee, O Divine Lord of them all, toiling for them, the Lord of every land, shining forth for them, the Aten Disk of the day time, great in majesty!

All distant foreign lands also, thou createst their life. Thou hast placed a Nile in heaven to come forth for them and make a flood upon the mountains like the sea in order to water the fields of their villages. How excellent are thy plans, O Lord of Eternity! – a Nile in the sky is thy gift to foreigners and to beasts of their lands; but the true Nile flows from under the earth for Egypt.

Thy beams nourish every field and when thou shinest they live and grow for thee. Thou makest the seasons in order to sustain all that thou hast made, the winter to cool them, the summer heat that they may taste [of thy quality]. Thou hast made heaven afar off that thou mayest behold all that thou hast made when thou wast alone, appearing in thy aspect of the Living Aten, rising and shining forth. Thou makest millions of forms out of thyself, towns, villages, fields, roads, the river. All eyes behold thee before them, for thou art the Aten of the daytime, above all that thou has created.

Thou art in my heart, but there is none other who knows thee save thy son Akhenaten. Thou hast made him wise in thy plans and thy power.

All the sentiments expressed in the above hymn have little that is revolutionary about them, and would have been approved by most worshippers in the world of ancient Egypt. The sun-god is regarded as the demiurge who created the Universe 'when he was alone' (in Chaos), a concept which is of great antiquity. Many of the other ideas expressed in the hymn had appeared in similar compositions addressed to other gods during this same dynasty. A hymn to Amun which dates to the reign of Amenophis II, but which has elements of greater antiquity, reveals the same joy in nature, and speaks of the god almost exclusively in his solar aspect which had resulted from his identification with Rē-Atum. He is referred to as:

Father of the Gods, who fashioned mankind, and made the beasts, and the herbage which sustains cattle . . . Lord of the sunbeams who createst light . . . Thou art the Sole One who made all that there is: the Unique One who made what exists . . . He it is who has made pasturage for cattle, and the fruit tree for mankind. He it is who has made that whereon the fish live in the river, and the birds in the heavens. It is he who gives breath to him in the egg, and sustains the son of the worm.

He is also identified with Atum 'who fashioned men of different natures and created their life. He made them differ in colour, each from the other'. This universalist sentiment, that all the nations, barbaric as well as Egyptian, are God's creatures, is proper to a kingdom at the height of its imperial greatness, but it is expressed more powerfully in the hymn to the Aten. An epithet of Thoth, the god of writing and learning, referring to him as he 'who made different the tongue of one land from another', belongs to the very end of the Amarna period. Yet it appears to have been already of some antiquity. It is thus clear that even from the haphazard body of texts that has survived from an earlier time, the Great Hymn to the Aten contained ideas and phrases which had long been familiar in the religious literature. Its novelty lay not in what it expressed but in what it left out. Nowhere is there the slightest mention of other gods. An earlier hymn to the Theban Amun, which echoes many of its ideas, speaks of Amun as the Sole God yet equates him with Ptah, Min, Rē, Khepri and Atum. It apostrophizes him as the One and Only Creator from whose tears men originated and from whose mouth the gods came into existence, thus identifying him with Atum and Ptah in the same breath. There is no such pantheism evident in the hymns to the Aten, but, on the contrary, an austere monotheism which is quite unprecedented in the world of the Late Bronze Age.

The remarkable feature of this revolution in religious thought is that it apparently springs into life from the moment of the king's advent. The curtain falls on the old drama of the sun-god's progress across the heavens with his divine retinue defeating the ever-resurgent forces of evil by day, and bringing a brief hour of light and life to the dead in the various regions of the Underworld by night. In its place was presented a far less tumultuous monodrama enacted in the presence of worshipping mankind with its joyous offerings. The Aten rose and set in solitary majesty in a heaven devoid of other gods. In this respect Professor Redford is justified in speaking of Akhenaten as a literal atheist.

This is emphasized by a fragment of woefully damaged text found inscribed on two blocks from the interior of the Tenth Pylon at Karnak, and brought to notice by Redford. It gives the only hint of the king's new 'teaching', to which he often refers on his monuments, but all other examples of which must have been diligently suppressed after his death as utter heresy. Only disjointed phrases can be extracted from this inscription which is evidently from a homily which the king addressed to his followers very early in his reign when he still sanctioned the representation of Rē-Herakhte in the traditional form of a

Pl. 27   falcon-headed man bearing the disk of the sun on his vertex, and spelt his name in its first didactic form though not yet enclosed in double cartouches. The drift of his discourse seems to be that the original forms of the gods were known from the catalogues and specifications which were preserved in temple libraries and consulted only perhaps by wise men or scholars. But though these gods might have been made of gold and precious stones they had somehow died or ceased to function and were now ineffective. The mysterious god which the king proclaimed was self-created, unique, eternal, universal and omnipresent in the daylight.

The truths that the king expounded were to a large extent self-evident, though they took no account of sympathetic magic which could transform symbols into actuality. Since prehistoric times the gods of Egypt had existed as graven images, their forms defined in the manuals preserved in temple libraries. Thus when King Neferhotep I of the Thirteenth Dynasty wished to make a statue of Osiris for his monument in Abydos, he searched among ancient archives in a temple at Heliopolis to ensure that the image should be fashioned in its proper and correct form. Such images lived in 'great mansions' (temples), and were protected and tended by 'servants' (priests) who daily awakened them, cleaned, anointed, clothed, fed and put them to rest as though they were living grandees. All this ritual was condemned as a vanity by Akhenaten, who dismissed the gods, banished their images, abandoned their habitations and soon represented his sole divinity by a symbol, an elaborate form of the hieroglyph for sunlight – the many-armed disk of the sun. Thus on the Boundary Stelae, Akhenaten apostrophizes the Aten as one who fashions himself with his two hands, whom no craftsman has devised.

All this is new, or rather expressed for the first time; for it is to be suspected that not all the ideas were entirely of the king's invention. Such sentiments must have been abroad at this time, but it would have required the initiative and authority of the pharaoh to promote them. The 'Teaching' which he promulgated was dutifully followed by his friends and favourites, such as his old childhood servant Parennefer, his father-in-law Ay, and the chief servitors of the Aten cult, Meryrē I and Tutu; but it is doubtful whether whole-hearted support was secured outside court circles. The artisans, labourers and ordinary folk appear to have clung to their old gods and superstitions. Even among the king's entourage there were those who appear to have been no more than luke-warm to some of his ideas, for later he had to rally them to his views by declaring that it would be 'evil' if they listened to rumours concerning burial arrangements at Akhetaten. The proof of the shallow rooting of his reforms is seen in the almost complete withering that occurred as soon as his immediate successors achieved power. The images of the proscribed gods were fashioned anew, their shrines were refurbished, their priesthoods restored, the old worship re-established, and the traditional eschatology fervently embraced.

But for little more than a decade the elevation of an abstract and intangible god to the position of a lone supremacy wrought important changes in religious practices at Amarna and in Egypt beyond. The worship of a god in aniconic form simplified temple architecture which no longer had to consist of a 'mansion' but reverted to the court, open to the sunlight, and to the colonnades of the ancient sun-temples. The suppression of other gods made innovations necessary in beliefs concerning life after death, particularly in the influential cult of the resurrected god Osiris, despite the nature of the destiny that he promised all believers: an eternity at once blessed and agrarian, such as the deceased had enjoyed in life among the fields of Egypt, but more glorious. Osiris and his chthonic realms were opposed to the idea of an after-life among the stars, or its later development as a following of the sun-god in the regions of light. This dichotomy existed in Egyptian religion until paganism was replaced by Christianity in the third century BC; but as early as the Fifth Dynasty the Pyramid Texts had made it evident that the funerary cult of Osiris had penetrated the solar beliefs concerning the pharaonic destiny, and that the dead king had become assimilated to Osiris, while his successor stood as Horus, the champion of his murdered father and the ruler of the living. The gods of the Osirian cycle have in fact become the third generation of the solar gods in the great ennead of Heliopolis.

From the earliest Dynastic period, kings had built shrines and cenotaphs at Abydos, an Upper Egyptian focus of the cult of Osiris and the royal ancestors, to legitimize their claims to the long tradition of sovereignty. In the reign of Amenophis III this activity reached a climax with the clearing up of the royal necropolis at Abydos, and an antiquarian search for the tomb of Osiris which the pundits of the day identified in the cenotaph of King Djer, the third king of the First Dynasty. But this pious duty ceased abruptly under Akhenaten, when all mention of Osiris, together with the gods of his cycle, was suppressed in the funerary texts, and the Osirian epithet of 'justified' with the force of 'deceased' was dropped from the titles of the defunct. The votive block-statue in the form of a pilgrim to Abydos, or other holy places, squatting in his cloak, disappeared from the repertoire of funerary sculpture, and is not revived until the reign of King Ay. The shawabti figure, a substitute for the deceased in the corvée of the Osirian Underworld, however, was not discarded, but the texts inscribed upon it were considerably modified and lacked the magic spell that would activate it.

Pl. 63

Pls. 11, 12

In the reaction that followed the death of Akhenaten, not only were the temples and statues of Amun, Mut and other important gods restored on a lavish scale, but the cult of Osiris at Abydos received an unstinted rehabilitation, especially under the early Ramessides. Sethos I, for instance, entered the names of kings whom he considered his legitimate predecessors, commencing with Menes, the first pharaoh, in the Table of Ancestors carved on the wall of a corridor in the great temple associated with his cenotaph, the so-called Osireion, and so reconsecrated their memorials anew. Ramesses II did likewise in his temple on the neighbouring site.

Pl. 51

The proscription of Osiris by Akhenaten ensured that the gods of burial were banished together with the pantheon, and a new eschatology had to be invented, though much of the old funeral practice was retained, such as mummification, burial in an anthropoid coffin and Canopic jars, and the deposit of grave goods with the deceased. In place of the old funerary deities, Akhenaten undertook the care of his subjects in the afterlife, and it is to him that they pray for patronage and succour after death. Parennefer hails him as 'Lord of Burial, Giver of Longevity, Lord of the Life-span, at the sight of whom there is life'. Ay addresses him as 'this cool North wind, the breath by which I live, an infinity of Niles pouring forth its water daily'. 'Grant me,' he prays, 'a life prolonged by thy favours; award me a goodly burial . . . in my tomb which thou hast ordained for me . . . Grant me pure food which has been placed before thee from the surplus of thy Father Aten every day.'

Such petitions are commonplace in the inscriptions that the courtiers have left in their tombs at Amarna. Requests for 'a gift of loaves in the temple of the Aten', 'a sight of the Aten in the necropolis', 'departure in the morning from the Underworld to [see] the Aten as he rises every day' alternate with simpler appeals for 'unguent', 'water from the swirl of the river', and similar supplications addressed to the king. The prayer on the footboard of Kiya's coffin makes virtually the same requests by the queen to Akhenaten, but in a more poetic form:

> May I breathe the sweet air that issues from thy mouth. May I behold thy beauty every day – that is my prayer. May I hear thy sweet voice in the North Wind. May my body grow vigorous with life through thy love. Mayest thou give me thy two hands bearing thy sustenance, and I receive it and live by it. Mayest thou ever call upon my name and it shall not fail on thy lips.

In this address the deceased asks for mortuary favours from the king who is now the only donor of such privileges. The wandering soul could no longer pass through dangers and hazards to reach the Hall of the Two Truths where his deeds on earth would be weighed in the balance and his fate decided at a Last Judgment before Osiris. In the Royal Tomb at Amarna the drama of the sun's daily circuit as represented in the *Book of What is in the Underworld* is replaced by the scene on the eastern wall of chamber alpha of the rising of the Aten and the awakening of the temple and its royal worshippers to life and joy. On the western wall is the counterpoise, the relief of the setting of the Aten and the putting of its creation to rest. The part that the Great Temple of the Aten at Akhetaten plays in this daily cycle is paramount, and supersedes the apparatus of gods and demons that belongs to the old eschatology. The immense extent of the temple with its forest of offering-tables, two for each day of the year, heaped with consecrated food for the benefit of the dead as well as the living, is an indication of its importance in the cult.

There was in this a return to an earlier concept of immortality which was revived by the Aten-religion and opposed to the agricultural eternity of the Osirian beliefs. Fairman, following Etienne Drioton, has pointed out that the Aten-worshippers held that the souls (*bai*) of the dead came forth by day at sunrise to enjoy a full life in some immaterial world, returning to the tomb at nightfall, an imagery suggested from the habits of sand-martins in Egypt that nest in holes in the sandy river-banks and cliffs. Both the dead and the living were believed to lapse into sleep when the Aten sank beneath the western horizon, and were all awakened by its rays in the morning. The dead left their tombs, and the living their habitations, and all accompanied the Aten to his temple, and by his grace were permitted to share in the services and the food offerings. Thereafter they were to be imagined as continuing near their homes and 'houses of eternity' until sunset. 'Life after death for the worshipper of the Aten was to live near his god and his king in the temple on earth, and near his former home and tomb. The prayers for long life and for benefits after death are addressed by the dead man to the Aten, often to the king himself and occasionally to the queen.'

Such a creed reveals an attempt to rationalize beliefs that had developed accretions from prehistoric times. It sought to establish the relationship of the dead with the living, and mankind and all the natural world with a unique, invisible and self-created god. Its cult was simple, its worship enhanced by the enchantment of the arts and the excitement of a daily pageantry. But it seems to have satisfied no deep need in the mass of the people. Outside of Akhetaten life was no better than before and may, indeed, have been more burdensome and ominous. Plague and sickness were becoming endemic; rumours of military reverses percolated from abroad; and exactions by a new rapacious breed of tax-collectors in place of the old tithe-gatherers caused resentment at home.

There must have been among Akhenaten's courtiers sincere men who shared his convictions and were whole-hearted in following a charismatic leader. Others may have found it convenient to pay him lip-service. Such disciples were rewarded not only with lucrative office and the king's favour, but *Fig. 2* with more tangible rewards, the gold of honour, food and drink from the royal table, splendid tombs and burial equipment. Some of these followers, such as Tutu, Parennefer and Meryrē I, are not heard of again after the king's death; others, like Pentu and Ay, were prominent in the return of the *ancien régime*. The novel ideas of the king won no wide acceptance even among his privileged entourage and were quickly abandoned as an unfortunate aberration soon after his disappearance from the scene.

69, 70 *Dark red quartzite torso from a statue of Nefertiti showing an exaggeration of the erogenous zones in giving her the appeal of a love goddess such as Hathor or Astarte, which her titulary also expresses, 'Fair of Face, Mistress of Joy, Endowed with Favour, Great of Love.'*

71 *Newberry's suggestion, first advanced in 1928, that the two royalties represented on this carved and painted slab are Smenkhkarē and his first consort Meritaten, has been generally accepted ever since. The drawing lacks the characteristic portraiture of Akhenaten – the serpentine neck is absent; so are the thick lips and overgrown jaw. The features of the man are plump and juvenile and only the pronounced paunch resembles Akhenaten's. The queen wears a cap crown with double uraei, and the loose ends of her long red girdle clearly mark her as an heiress queen. The symbolism of the mandrake flowers and lotus blooms which she offers her husband alludes to the love between the royal pair.*

72 *(right) Panel in the lid of a casket, mainly veneered in ivory, stained and carved in low relief, found in the tomb of Tutankhamun. The king, standing before a pavilion in a garden, receives from Ankhesenamun two bouquets of flowers and mandrake fruits that the maidens are gathering in arbours. The queen, elaborately attired and perfumed, wears the double uraei and flowing girdle of a royal heiress (cf. Pl. 75). The composition, with the king resting upon his staff and the queen holding out significant flowers expressing the love between them, is similar to that of the carved slab in the illustration opposite (Pl. 71); but the panel from a piece of the palace furniture is technically more brilliant, if less impressionistic, than the private stone relief with its dashing line and less careful execution.*

73 *Fragment from an indurated limestone statue of a young king being crowned by a god, probably Amun of Thebes. The juvenile features are those of Tutankhamun, under whom an intensive and widespread programme of rehabilitation was inaugurated, as the king's innovative decree promises, particularly the fashioning anew of* images *of the persecuted gods. He wears the Blue Crown which in the Eighteenth Dynasty became popular as a crown of victory replacing some of the more traditional headgear used at the coronation of pharaohs. The hand of the god who performs the ceremony is seen touching the crown as he places it upon the head of the monarch (cf. Pl. 51).*

74 *(right) Opinion is divided over whether this quartzite head of a composite statue from the studio of Djhutmose represents Nefertiti or her daughter Queen Meritaten. The head, which lacks the final polish, has indications in paint as a guide to the sculptor for the final modelling of such details as lips, eyes, nostrils and ear-lobes. The neck is slightly shorter in proportion to Nefertiti's and the features seem to be less mature. The work may therefore be of the younger queen, and despite its lack of the final polish is a supreme masterpiece.*

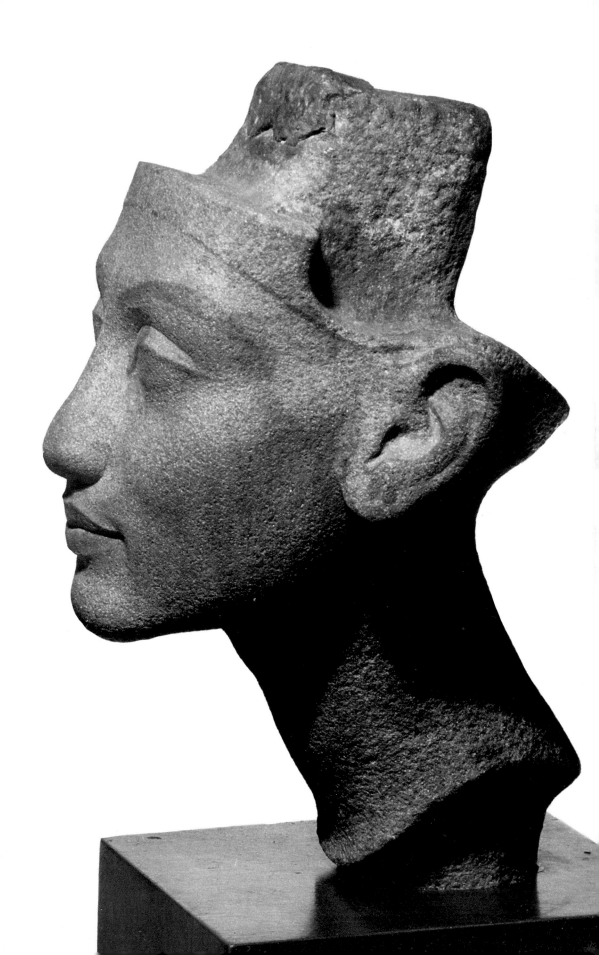

75 *Back panel of a throne, part of the 'lion' furniture which was provided for each king at his coronation and buried with him after death. The panel between two flanking formal bouquets, a common decorative motive of Amarna art, shows the 'Heiress' Ankhesenamun wearing the crown of a chief queen and anointing Tutankhamun from an unguent pot as he wears the triple Atef crown of Rē and sits on a chair of state at his advent. A collar and counterpoise, similar to the ones worn by the royal pair, rests on a stand. The Aten shines on both and brings life to their nostrils, but their names are now given in their Amun versions.*

76 *A unique scene, painted on the north wall of the burial chamber in the tomb of Tutankhamun in the Valley of the Kings, shows King Ay, the successor of the dead king, performing the ceremony of Opening the Mouth with an adze and other amulets on the mummy of his predecessor, Tutankhamun, who is now in the guise of the resurrected god Osiris. Such a rite was supposed to restore all his faculties to the dead man, and originally was peculiar to the burials of kings and performed by the eldest son. King Ay, who wears the leopard skin of a setem priest, here performs the prescribed rites, though he was not the son of his predecessor but probably his uncle.*

77 Granite dyad of King Haremhab and his queen, 'The Chief Wife of the King, the Mistress of the Two Lands, Mutnodjme', seated beside him on the great throne. The stela on the back of the statue gives a somewhat florid account of Haremhab's elevation to the kingship and its sanction by the oracle of Amun in Thebes during his Festival of Opet in the second month of the year. The winged sphinx on the side of the throne (cf. Pl. 52) doubtless symbolizes Tefnut upholding the name of the new king, and also signifies the importance of Mutnodjme in the event, since she was the 'Wife of the God', acting the part of 'Tefnut Herself'.

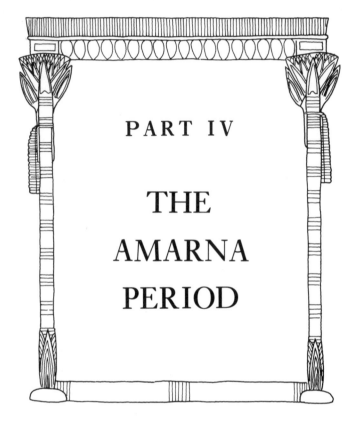

PART IV

THE
AMARNA
PERIOD

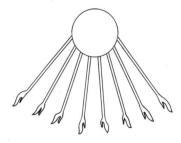

CHAPTER 22

The Reign of Amenophis IV

In infancy Prince Amenophis (Amenhotep), like his grandfather Tuthmosis IV, could have entertained little hope that he would ever mount the throne of his ancestors: yet like him, he succeeded by a similar stroke of fate – the death of an elder brother, Prince Tuthmosis. The latter had enjoyed splendid prospects: he was recognized as the heir of Amenophis III, and as such filled the office of Governor of Memphis and High Priest of its god Ptah. Amenophis III was responsible for the burial of the sacred Apis bull in which Ptah was incarnate, and which died during his reign. Tuthmosis is shown in a fragmentary relief, officiating with his father at this state funeral, a grandiose rehearsal for no less a poignant ceremony for the young prince than when he buried his pet cat 'Puss' (*miu*) in a miniature version of a stone sarcophagus. Apart from a handsome ivory whip which he apparently used as a commander of the king's chariot forces and which was found among the heirlooms inherited by Tutankhamun, nothing more is heard of him, probably because, despite the responsible positions which he held at Memphis, he was but a few years old at his death, when his younger brother Amenophis stepped into his empty sandals.

If Amenophis inherited the offices held by Prince Tuthmosis, he would have learnt statecraft in settling the affairs of Memphis and Lower Egypt with the help of their high officials. But it is probable that he was more deeply committed to the pursuit of the arts, particularly during a period when they flourished as never before. As High Priest of Ptah who held the additional title of 'Greatest of Craftsmen', he would be responsible for the design of art-works of all kinds. It may be these aspects of his duties that are referred to by his Chief Architect Ma'nakhtuf, and his Chief Sculptor Bek, when each describes himself as 'the apprentice whom His Majesty taught'. It is doubtful, however, how far the learning of the young prince was influenced by the theology of Ptah the Creator who had brought the universe into being by uttering a word at the beginning of time. In the light of what follows during the reign of Amenophis as king, it was the teaching of Heliopolis (On of the Bible), that more profoundly influenced the young prince. On had been a centre of intellectual activity from very early times, and its wise men continued to be celebrated.

Heliopolis was the city of the sun-god whose doctrines deeply influenced the rest of the pantheon. Unfortunately, through the destruction of the ancient city, and the difficulties in excavating its remains, very little evidence has been recovered of the character and institutions of the sun-religion in the New Kingdom. It would seem, however, that Amenophis had a palace in the town whose steward May, though later disgraced, was in his earlier years a high functionary holding important posts in the administration, including the offices of Scribe of the Elite Troops, which gave him charge of the entire labour corps, and the Superintendent of the Cattle of the Temple of Rē, which, fattened for sacrifice and drawn on huge wheeled drays, were to figure large in the talatat from Karnak. Later the Sacred Mnevis bull of Heliopolis was promised burial in Akhetaten in preference to the Apis bull of Memphis. May was but one example of the Heliopolitan officials who were to appear among the young prince's entourage. Others like Bek, and Pawah the High Priest in On, and their wives, were also destined to play influential roles, but the fact remains that we know practically nothing about the careers of kings' sons, apart from a few exceptional cases. Their claims to distinction usually depended upon the reputations of their fathers. If they succeeded to the throne, their renown was that of the pharaoh. If they did not, they tended to dissolve from the scene, leaving nothing behind them.

Prince Amenophis burst upon the stage as the Pharaoh Amenophis IV at a date in the reign of Amenophis III which has been variously calculated, but which to the proponents of a long co-regency between the two kings must fall in the twenty-eighth regnal year of his father. What little evidence has survived of the event comes from Thebes and Gebel es Silsila and is exclusively concerned with the young co-regent's advent. Presumably he acceded to the throne on reaching manhood at the age of sixteen, in a way that has been described by the later King Ramesses II in a memoir referring to his own accession. The installation of Amenophis is illustrated in the tomb of his vizier

Fig. 11 Ramose, when the new king is shown as a normal young man, with a somewhat heavy jowl, seated upon the archaic block throne of Upper Egypt with his mother or wife seated beside him in the guise of Maet, the daughter of the sun-god. He is described as 'the image of Rē who loves him more than any other king'. Wearing the *khepresh*, or Blue Crown of coronation during this dynasty, and holding the sceptres of kingly power, he receives his high officials represented by the sole figure of the vizier who proffers bouquets and temple-staves in the names of the gods of Thebes. At this time, like Ramesses II, he would have been espoused to a chief wife and have had a harim.

To recapitulate, the chief wife was an heiress called Nefertiti whose parentage is never disclosed, though her 'Nurse' and 'Governess' is named as

Pl. 4 Tey, a court lady of importance, the wife of the Commander of the Chariotry,

Ay. This pair may have been her corporeal parents masquerading under unassuming designations for reasons which are obscure, perhaps to conceal the fact that the progenitors of this high and mighty princess were not also equally divine. There seems little doubt, however, that she was descended from Queen Ahmose-Nefertari, the virtual female ancestress of the dynasty whose cult as a Theban divinity had been greatly expanded by one of her descendants, Queen Tiye. Nefertiti was doubtless of the same family as Tiye, who was perhaps her aunt.

Pl. 46

As the wife of the new divine king, Nefertiti appeared in the traditional garb of a clinging gown tied by a girdle with ends falling in front, and a short, close-fitting wig with a fillet carrying double uraei, showing her identification with Tefnut the daughter and wife of the sun-god. As such she played an equal role with the king, the son of the sun-god and the image of Rē, in making offerings to the gods and assisting at the ceremonial sacrifices. The god whom Amenophis IV proclaimed was a new version of the solar deity which had been gaining steadily in favour throughout the dynasty, particularly in court circles. In the reign of his father, the name of the Aten had been attached to the king's barge, to a temple in Memphis and to another in Thebes. But under Amenophis IV there was little doubt as to the *bona fides* of the new state god; this deity was grandiloquently proclaimed at the king's accession as, 'Rē-Herakhte rejoicing on the horizon in his aspect of the light which is in the sun's disk [the Aten]', although at the same ceremony it was Amun-rē of Karnak who took precedence. Officialdom, however, was quick to learn and this pre-eminence was short-lived. In the companion picture in the tomb of Ramose, Rē-Herakhte shines in lonely splendour, his unwieldy name now enclosed in two double-bordered cartouches, and the shortened version accompanied by titles, 'Aten the Living, the Great, Who is in Jubilee, Lord of Heaven and Earth'.

Pl. 6

Fig. 12

As no monument built by the young king was yet in existence, the opportunity was taken to decorate with reliefs the gateway that had just been raised but not finished at the southern entrance to the precincts of the temple of Amun at Karnak. The scenes carved in low relief on the reveals show Amenophis IV worshipping Rē-Herakhte in his traditional form as an heroic god, with the head of a falcon, bearing the uraeus-encircled disk of the sun on his vertex, and accompanied by his name in its expanded version as a declaration of faith. But by the time the faces of the gateway came to be carved in sunk relief, the rayed disk of the Aten had emerged and the name had been enclosed in cartouches. At this moment in the king's career it is probable that he made the pronouncement to his entourage concerning the new doctrine that he was henceforward to promulgate and expand. This proclaimed that, from the time of the first pharaoh, the gods had existed as graven images, their forms

Pl. 27

Pl. 28

defined by descriptions in books kept in temple archives. But the god whom he announced was not of this kind, made by the speculations of theologians and the hands of craftsmen, but was a self-created god who renewed himself every day and was gloriously alive. He was, moreover, an abstract entity not known to man but designated only by a symbol of the daylight that radiated from the disk of the sun by which his power was manifest. This sole god was henceforth to be supreme, a heavenly king whose reign had commenced with that of the king himself, his son and evident co-regent.

The woefully damaged text does not describe his auditors' reaction; but no doubt it was as enthusiastic as their reception of a later pronouncement on the founding of Akhetaten. The courtiers and the great and mighty leaders of the entire land prostrated themselves before the king and queen, averring that it was the Aten which had put such thoughts into the king's mind: whereat the whole concourse rejoiced and was festive. No doubt the sentiments expressed by the young monarch found an echo in the hearts of many of his followers, though few would perhaps realize to what extremes the king's ideas would be carried by the autocratic exercise of divine regal power.

The great innovative decree of the reign followed immediately – to erect a temple to this god, a structure which was to be given the name of Gempaaten, 'The Aten is Found in the Estate of the Aten'. Such a temple would have a palace attached to it, and this part of the complex would be constructed of mudbrick and was doubtless the first section to be completed. It was designed on an ambitious scale with a Window of Appearance, a new aspect of the worship of the solar deity, that would achieve a wide significance when the *Frontispiece* royal family used it to show themselves to their followers, and bestow their favours upon the deserving among them. New sandstone quarries were opened at Gebel es Silsila and granite was also hewn at Aswan. The quarrymen and the labour force were conscripted by organizing a corvée from one end of the country to the other, and the court officials were instructed to direct them. Included in the project were such men as May, the Scribe of the Elite Troops, *Fig. 13* and Bek, the Chief Sculptor. This great undertaking was set in train almost as a national enterprise, with an energy that had hitherto been devoted to foreign campaigns, 'to extend the borders of Egypt'.

The choice of East Karnak for the site of the new temple in the capital of Upper Egypt was certainly bold, if not challenging. The works of another sun-god, Amun of Karnak, were all around. The mighty pylon built by Amenophis III was dominant in all its pristine rawness, merely requiring the king to put his finishing touches to the portico. And while such a stylized symbol as the two hill-like towers, between which the sun-god arose each morning and set each night, would not be uncongenial to the Aten cult, the large representation of the river bark of Amun could only be an unwelcome reminder of the power and ubiquity of the original denizen of Karnak. The gold-capped obelisks, too, of previous kings from Tuthmosis I to Amenophis III, as symbols of the sun-god Rē-Herakhte and his holy city On, would also be acceptable to an Aten worshipper, save that in most examples their pyramidions would show an image of enthroned Amun crowning the pharaoh who knelt before him. *Pl. 51* Everywhere one looked, the name of Amun was writ large; and his couchant ram-headed sphinxes guarded the precincts.

During this phase, however, the king did not actively repress the cult of Amun-rē. The name of the god was heard whenever the name of the king was pronounced, not to mention a dozen or so names of his officials. Two anonymous 'chamberlains of Amun' appear among the officials of the king at the jubilee scenes. The High Priest of Amun was still active in Year 4 of the reign, superintending the cutting of stone for a royal statue. A red granite torso of Amun, now battered and nameless, with the pot-belly, protruding clavicles and other distortions of the royal physique, has also survived and seems to belong to this phase of the reign. It has been suggested by some scholars that *Pl. 26* the presence of his co-regent Amenophis III, 'the Son of Amun who loves him more than any other King', doubtless exercised a restraining influence on the iconoclasm of his young partner.

In the meantime, however, the building operations that had been put into effect by the decree recorded on the rocks of the eastern sandstone quarries of Gebel es Silsila were proceeding apace at East Karnak. The architects had devised a system of building and decorating the walls which was rapid and effective. The sandstone was selected from strata that allowed blocks measuring about a cubit in length (0.5 metres) to be easily prised out of their beds and readily handled by an untrained labour force. When such blocks were trimmed, they could be speedily built into walls of alternate headers and stretchers, with a generous application of gypsum plaster between the joints, to fill in blemishes and make all smooth. Such walls could be carved in sunk relief, *Pls. 29, 32* a method of decoration which was less laborious and time-consuming than the more usual and elegant low relief, but well suited to a more dynamic drawing and a more animated management of light and shade. The finished appearance was achieved by strong colour applied to a rendering of thick whitewash, but some of the detail, particularly of the royal family, was executed in fine brush-strokes.

The vestigial remains have been skilfully excavated by the Akhenaten Temple Project under their director, Donald Redford, to whom we are indebted for particulars. The temple was basically a rectangular court about 130 metres wide by perhaps 200 metres deep, orientated eastwards and surrounded at an interval of about 5 metres by a mudbrick temenos wall. This vast open court was probably divided by internal walls and gateways into

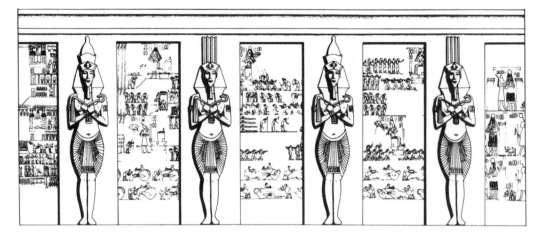

24 Façade of the south colonnade of the Gempaaten at Karnak as restored by the Akhenaten Temple Project, with colossal figures of the king as Atum and Shu (cf. Pls. 33–35), their backs against piers supporting the architrave and roof of the ambulatory, the rear wall of which is decorated internally with painted reliefs of scenes from the jubilee.

various smaller enclaves. An ambulatory ran around the perimeter and consisted of a roofed colonnade of square piers facing inwards rising to a height of more than 7 metres, including an architrave. Against each pier was stationed a painted sandstone colossus of the king holding the crook and flail sceptres and wearing a short kilt with cod-piece, his characteristic fashion of dress. His headgear, however, alternates the Double Crown of Upper and Lower Egypt with a double plume upon a *nemes* wig cover. These are the famous colossi which, on their discovery in the twenties and thirties of this century, astonished the archaeological world with their 'expressionist' distortions of the pharaonic form. We are perhaps to infer that these images are of the king as Atum and Shu, primordial aspects of the sun-god whose child he was.

The rear wall of the colonnade was built of sandstone talatat and decorated internally with long vertical borders of the epithets and cartouches of the Aten inscribed between long runs of relief showing principally the jubilee ceremonies which the king seems to have observed in this early phase of his reign. Various stages in the festival are shown in the procession of the king and queen with their retinue, leaving the palace, installing themselves in the great ceremonial palanquins carried by bearers and accompanied by the state fan-bearers. The progress is followed to the temple, where they are met by the temple staff. The return to the palace repeats all the incidents in reverse order, and constitutes a conspectus of the jubilee procession, though it does not depict every aspect of the ritual.

The Gempaaten appears to have been more than an isolated temple out of sight behind a massive mudbrick wall. It was a complex of buildings, including presumably on the southern side a palace area with a new feature, already alluded to, that figures prominently in the new iconography, a Window of

Appearance, at which the king and queen and the senior princesses could receive in audience high officials and foreign emissaries. The first representation of such a ceremony appears on the west wall of the tomb of Ramose when the young couple, unaccompanied by any daughter, bestow *shebu*-collars and other golden rewards upon the vizier.   *Fig. 12*

Another division of the Gempaaten was the Mansion of the Ben-ben, a temple devoted principally to the use of Nefertiti, who is seen in the reliefs of its talatat as dominating the ritual, as we have mentioned above. The Ben-ben   *Fig. 22* stone was originally the sacred fetish of the sun-cult in Heliopolis, probably a conical stone of meteoric origin, fallen from the sky-realms. At Karnak and elsewhere, however, it is represented as a stela or obelisk, rather than the pyramidion that surmounted the latter. Another enigma which may be connected with the Mansion of the Ben-ben is the fragmentary colossus wearing a large artificial beard and holding kingly sceptres, the most complete of a series of such statues. Doubt exists as to whether it is a representation of an epicene hypostasis of the sun-god, or Queen Nefertiti in a close-fitting gown   *Pl. 33* and in a pharaonic guise, since her shawabti-figure also shows her carrying such sceptres. The latter deduction seems more plausible in view of the king's anathema against gods depicted as graven images. Further excavation may succeed in resolving this particular problem, and determining its exact station in the Gempaaten.

The talatat from the other Aten temples at Karnak, the Rud-menu and the Teni-menu, believed to have been built in the vicinity of the Ninth Pylon, are still being assembled and studied. The purpose of these temples is obscure at present, but a feature of their decoration is the predominance of the soldiery of Asia and Africa, a veritable foreign legion in attendance upon the king, besides the native police, leaving some observers with an impression that the royal family lived in an armed camp, or amid a praetorian guard. There is also an immense display of viands heaped on altars and brought by phalanxes of servants to the palace or temple. The liberality of the king in dispensing food, the bounty of the Aten, is seen at Karnak, and to a lesser extent at Amarna. The tithes that were levied upon royal estates, temple domains, towns and other institutions, as well as on high officials and priests, amounted to an immense quantity of bread beer, flesh, fowl, cattle, vegetables, cloth, oils, honey and commodities of all kinds, used not only for the daily upkeep of all the new temples and their staffs, but also as beneficent donations which the king gave to the local populace on feast days. This was particularly the case at the jubilee festival when enormous supplies of food and drink contributed by individuals and institutions all over the country were consumed at public feasts. We have already referred to the largesse of Amenophis III at his three jubilees, and the same prodigality was shown by Amenophis IV in a jubilee held early in his reign, probably in Year 3, which receives its commemoration in extensive reliefs on the rear walls of the ambulatories of the Gempaaten, without however providing much more than a conjectural outline of the different ceremonies.

The jubilees of Amenophis III were important national functions, carried out with full ceremonial as a result of antiquarian research into aspects of the rites in the remote Archaic period. The first was celebrated as was normal in the king's thirtieth regnal year: but in the case of Amenophis IV no such length of interval could have supervened between his accession and the jubilee he held at Karnak. For this reason, scholars have been inclined to argue that the jubilee in question was that of the Aten himself, or of the Aten with whom the king was associated. In a study of the Karnak talatat, however, Dr Jocelyn Gohary points out that a scene of soldiers and courtiers saluting the king carries the inscription, 'admitting the magistrates, companions and standard-bearers of the army to stand in the King's presence at the First Jubilee of His Majesty which [the Aten] granted to him'. The missing word has been restored in brackets, but seems certain, and disposes of the idea that the function can have been a joint celebration by god and king. The Aten was simply performing an office previously fulfilled by other deities.

There are other features of the representation of the jubilee on the Karnak talatat which reveal that Amenophis IV was faithfully following the pattern that had been set by the festival in Regnal Year 30 of Amenophis III. The king _Pl. 31_ wore the traditional short jubilee cloak, and carried the 'flail' and a particular long-handled version of the crook sceptre. He assumed the crown of Lower Egypt for ceremonies on certain 'days of the Red Crown' and the crown of Upper Egypt for the 'days of the White Crown'. He was accompanied by special priests, a foot-washer and sandal-bearer, and a lector to read the prescribed liturgy, all wearing their fillets confining their wigs. All this and much else was traditional, but there were other ceremonies which were doubtless of archaic or very ancient origin, redolent of that antiquarian research which was undertaken to enact the first jubilee of Amenophis III. _cf. Pl. 50_ Thus the daughters of Asiatic rulers were present to pour libations from gold and silver ewers before the royal dais, purifying it four times in the king's presence. There was also a mysterious rite of acrobatic dancing performed by women who sang the words of an utterly obscure chant before the dais, while a band of musicians sang in turn a hymn to Hathor which in its polytheistic sentiments must have been anathema to a monotheist. These are evidently close imitations of ritual observed at the first jubilee of Amenophis III, and one wonders, in fact, whether the two jubilees did not coincide. There were, however, certain other rites which Amenophis IV must have rejected or considerably modified, such as the procession of gods and their emblems to their shrines in the 'Court of the Great Ones'. The various shrines are shown, but they are not of traditional design, and are indeed roofless kiosks into which the same Aten alone darts his rays.

The position of any co-regent during the jubilee of his senior partner must have been equivocal, and the ambiguity is apparent in the decoration of the Amada temple where Tuthmosis IV usurps scenes that, in view of his short tenure of the throne, evidently belonged to the second jubilee of his father Amenophis II. The paucity of monuments commemorating historic jubilees, as distinct from symbolic versions, doubtless prevents us from drawing other parallels. But the immense éclat with which Amenophis III celebrated his first jubilee must surely have had its effect upon his co-regent, who seems thereafter not only to have followed suit but also to have awarded his god, his heavenly father, the same honour. But apart from adding the distinction of celebrating jubilees to the titles of the Aten, there is no evidence that Amenophis IV held any further festivals coinciding with his father's second and third festivals at Karnak. The assigning of the jubilee to the Aten as a daily event absolved the king from commemorating a periodic festival which was indissolubly linked with ancient ritual and ancient gods: and with these his increasingly perfervid monotheism could have no commerce. We shall see later, however, that he spoke of holding a jubilee at Akhetaten.

While the Gempaaten from its decoration seems to have been the venue for the celebration of the jubilee feast, the purpose of the other temples of the Aten at Karnak is less certain. References in the texts to such unlocated structures connected with the worship of the Aten as a 'Broad Hall', and a 'House of Rejoicing', may apply to other buildings at Thebes, erected in the reign of Amenophis III or even earlier. There is, however, on the characteristic talatat from the Ninth Pylon, mention of the Rud-menu and the Teni-menu which *Pl. 32* can date only to the reign of Amenophis IV and which are briefly referred to above. The last building in this group to be completed appears to be the Mansion of the Ben-ben, a temple which from its decoration was exclusively devoted to the activities of Queen Nefertiti, particularly, as we have suggested above, in her role as the Superior of the recluses of the god and the temple *Fig. 22* choir.

During his sojourn in Thebes at the commencement of his reign, Amenophis IV evidently occupied a mansion in the Malkata palace complex, for the Americans found a potsherd dated to his first regnal year in the Middle Palace area. But he presumably moved his quarters across the river to the residence in the Gempaaten as soon as it was ready for occupation in Karnak. It was probably here that he lived with his family during each winter season. The first-born daughter makes her entry into the world apparently near the end of the first year, to be followed in succession by five sisters. Her figure is seen following behind that of her mother Nefertiti on the early talatat, and a certain amount of time must have elapsed before she could play a responsible part in the religious ceremonies. Redford has calculated, from representations in the Karnak talatat and in the Amarna tomb reliefs, that the three eldest daughters, Meritaten, Meketaten and Ankhesenpaaten, were all alive by Year 5 at the end of this phase. He places the birth of Nefertiti's younger daughters, Neferneferuaten-ta-sherit, Neferneferurē and Sotepenrē, in the ninth, tenth and eleventh years of the reign respectively. We shall examine later how far this opinion conforms to other data.

The first five years of the king's reign are mostly reported from Karnak, though at least one limestone talatat may well have come from a Memphite source with details of the jubilee, and bears no evidence from its style, and despite its material, that it originated from Amarna at a later period. The activity at the greatly ravaged and little-explored sites of Heliopolis and Memphis, however, is mostly a closed book to us at present. A little more information has come from Miwer, where the palace and harim complex had been in use as a recreation pleasance since the reign of Tuthmosis III. It was here that the letter from Ipy, the King's Steward in Memphis, was found, which gives the latest date by which the king's name appears in its Amenophis form. In the same locality, at the end of the last century, a group of wooden statuettes of ladies attached to the royal harim was brought to light by clandestine rummagers. The tomb in which they were discovered was dated by the royal toilet objects found with them to the reigns of Amenophis III and IV, but the haphazard and brutal looting of the deposit by local peasants destroyed any possibility of making proper deductions from what little evidence remained.

The erection of the Mansion of the Ben-ben was the last building enterprise that Amenophis IV would undertake in Thebes. A new dynamic was about to enter the insubstantial pageant of the time. The modern inquirer will still have to consult the fragmented and tangled vestiges of the past, but it will all be uniform and from the centre of the scene. Inspiration had come to the king to seek the place in Egypt where the Aten had manifested himself at the First Time when the world had come into existence. The Aten vouchsafed this holy ground to the king alone, and in the fifth regnal year the latter disclosed it to his faithful retinue of courtiers, high officials, and the priesthood of the Aten in a spectacular foundation ceremony. The career of Amenophis IV was over, and the reign of Akhenaten had begun.

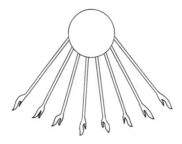

CHAPTER 23

The Reign of Akhenaten

The reason for the king's choice of a location in Middle Egypt for the siting of his new residence-city in preference to any other has not been disclosed, apart from his declaration that it was the Aten alone who brought him to this spot. Some years ago, when sailing downstream past modern El Amarna, the writer observed that the uniform band of distant cliffs on the east bank is interrupted at this point by a prominent gap which is formed by the Royal Wadi in the centre of the encircling hills, so forming a gigantic representation of the hieroglyph *akhet* $\square$, 'horizon', as the sun rises. This may have been the sign for which the king was searching, and indeed it is clearly visible from a long way off, and may also have suggested the name which the king gave to the place, Akhetaten 'the Horizon [or habitation] of the Aten'. If so it was a most happy discovery.

Akhetaten was well situated on the east bank of the Nile within a semicircle of cliffs that made policing of the region simple, especially with a narrow approach on the north and south extremities. The strip of alluvium on the river bank may not have been considered worth cultivating, for the area between the river and the hills is largely stony waste thinly covered with desert scrub. As such, it was an ideal spot in which to build a city without encroaching on the productive land required for cultivation. The western bank, by contrast, lying between the Nile and its aberrant branch the Bahr Yusef, was well watered and productive, a thriving district with the towns of Hermopolis and Cusae as large centres of population and reservoirs of labour. The king, too, found that the chosen site belonged to no other foundation, not to a divinity, prince, princess, private person, or anyone who had a claim to it: therefore it had belonged solely to the Aten from the beginning of time.

In his fifth regnal year, on the thirteenth day of the eighth month, the king, who had changed his name a month earlier to Akhenaten, reached the site with his retinue, probably by boat, on the eastern bank, and made his way by chariot to an altar set up under an open sky where a great oblation was to be offered to the Aten, and his approval for the project secured. The natural place for this sacrifice at a time when the city was not yet demarcated would have been what subsequently became the innermost shrine of the Great Temple or Seat of the

Pl. 65

Aten in the central area. Here presumably an offering-place had been erected, and parts of it may still exist in the fragmented balustrade that Carter recovered in 1892 from the adjacent dump, and which is now in New York

Pl. 6

divided between the Brooklyn and Metropolitan Museums. It is made of indurated limestone carved with reliefs in the style of the Karnak talatat, the name of the queen being in that simple form that she relinquished for ever soon afterwards.

It may have been from the elevated platform of this altar that the king addressed his followers, pointing out to them the full extent of the new township and recounting how the Aten had revealed his place of origin to him on this virgin site.

The king was clearly in a state of high excitement at the foundation ceremony. His words poured forth in a passionate elaboration, emphasizing how Akhetaten had been revealed to him alone by his Father, the Aten, as his chosen Seat. The king stressed that he would build the town in this place and nowhere else; and if anyone tried to persuade him to build it elsewhere, he would not listen, even if it should be the queen herself.

He then enumerated the buildings which he proposed to erect there: and it may be that at this point the actual positions of the various plots in the central city were reserved by means of 'name-stones' or markers. He further disclosed that he would excavate the Royal Tomb in the eastern hills, in which the burial of himself, his chief wife, Nefertiti, and their daughter Meritaten would be made in the fullness of time. If they should happen to die elsewhere in Egypt they should be brought back for burial in Akhetaten. This was a bold decision to announce, since it proclaimed that he was making a complete break with the dynastic tradition of cutting the Royal Tomb in the western hills on the territory of Amun at Thebes, where doubtless a sepulchre was already being prepared for him. His tomb would now be made in the Royal Wadi at Akhetaten where the rising sun each day would bring the world of the dead and the merely sleeping to new life. The tombs of the priests of the Aten and the high state officials would also be made in the eastern hills. A rumour, perhaps expressing a general hope that the courtiers' tombs would not be made there, away from the family burying grounds elsewhere, was vehemently dismissed by the king as a wicked invention more vile than anything which he or his immediate predecessors had heard; and he emphasized what a grievous matter it would be if his followers were not buried after death near their king in whom their hope of eternity reposed.

The rest of the king's harangue was concerned with edicts stating that the worship of the Aten was to be promoted in the new city, and outlining the offerings that would be made, the dues that would be levied for the cult, the festivals that would be held and the jubilees that would be celebrated. Lastly, he gave instructions as to the marking of the bounds by means of a tablet at the southern and northern extremities of the site, which together with its produce would be dedicated to the Father, the Aten. The ceremony may have ended with the setting up of some provisional marker, perhaps the tablet L as a sort of bench-mark, pending the carving of a great stela (M) from which the site might be laid out.

Despite the mention of jubilees in damaged passages in the stelae, there is no evidence that such festivals were held following the first jubilee of the king at Karnak. No great caches of debris have been unearthed at Amarna similar to the huge deposits of potsherds at the Malkata palace of Amenophis III; nor are there any scenes carved in the royal and private tombs, nor on temple talatat, that illustrate any of the traditional rites of the jubilee, leading us to conclude that no other jubilees were held according to time-honoured precedent at Akhetaten. Nevertheless, there is a preliminary cartoon for a relief drawn on a wall of the tomb of Parennefer at Amarna which shows Akhenaten at a public appearance beneath the state baldachin, seated on a royal stool and wearing the triple Atef crown of Rē, with musicians in attendance, at a great spread of viands which does not look like a modest daily repast, but rather a state banquet, perhaps in the Hall of Eating. Such a feast was part of the rite of the traditional jubilee ceremony, though it is not to the writer's knowledge ever represented.

Exactly a year later in his Regnal Year 6, the king paid another visit to Akhetaten. Work was proceeding with feverish haste, but the building operations were by no means complete nor the official residences ready for occupation. The king therefore had to lodge in a great rushwork tent made locally and named 'The Aten is Content'. It was from this temporary abode that he emerged on the festal day, mounted once more his ornate state chariot, and with his retinue took the wide road that had been made through the site, the present-day Sikket es Sultan, to the southernmost marker on the east bank. On this occasion he was largely concerned with confirming the boundaries of Akhetaten and dedicating the entire site to the Aten. The limits had been defined the previous year by Stelae X and M hewn into the cliffs at the northern and southern extremities. Stela M, however, was probably found to be already breaking up and Akhenaten may have given orders at this point to replace it with a copy (Stela K), according to his vow. A new southern point at Stela J was chosen and from here he indicated where the southern boundary of the town was to be sited on the opposite bank (Stela F). The corresponding northern boundary was fixed by another pair (Stelae X and A) so that Akhetaten extended on both sides of the river for a precisely measured length, about 15 kilometres. The oath that he swore on this occasion, that he would not pass beyond the stelae he had set up, was once interpreted that he would never leave this earthly paradise once it was built; but this interpretation is now generally dismissed, as it is contradicted by the statement in the earlier stelae that if he or members of his family were to die in any other place in Egypt, they were to be brought back for burial in Akhetaten. In fact, it is probable that the oath was no more than part of a conventional formula that was proclaimed when all boundary markers were set up or re-established as, for instance, when fields were re-surveyed after the annual inundation. At Amarna, the area delimited even to its exact length on both banks of the river was defined so precisely in order that its taxes could be properly assessed, and the revenue paid into the treasury of the Aten. In this way the new town would enter into the fiscal system of Egypt, and the income by which it would live would be fixed for all time.

Pl. 14   The new stelae were to be flanked by statues of the king and queen standing holding tablets carved with the names of the Aten, and with their own cartouches. Their two eldest daughters were represented by a pair statue standing beside their mother. The hewing of these monuments continued for another two years, the work increased by additional stelae erected at every entrance to tracks and roads into Akhetaten, so that it was not until Year 8 that the king was able to pay another visit to inspect progress and renew his oath to dedicate the town to the Aten. This vow was added as a codicil to at least two of the tablets on the west bank (A and B). Regnal Years 6 to 8 were in fact a feverishly busy time for workmen engaged upon the building of Akhetaten. Not only had the fourteen great stelae to be designed and finished, but the statuary, reliefs and architectural stonework had to be prepared for the Great Temple, the Mansion of the Aten, and the Great Official Palace. The private houses, which were also rising in the city as the large estates and office buildings were laid out, were of course constructed of mudbrick, and the local pebbly marl was eminently suitable for this, as it dried hard almost like concrete. A start was made on the Royal Tomb probably a little before Year 6. The heavier funerary furniture such as the alabaster Canopic chest, and the granite sarcophagus with the protective figures of the queen at each of its four corners, had been prepared from the first months of the reign, according to custom, and was then got ready for its transfer from Thebes to Akhetaten and the long haul to the Royal Wadi. Work continued on the sarcophagus for some two or three years after its arrival at the tomb, with inscriptions to take account of changes in the name of the Aten, but it was never completely finished, and the remaining fragments show no signs of a final polish.

About Year 6 a start was made on cutting some of the more important private tombs such as the large hypogeum of the Father of the God Ay and his Wife Tey; but generally work on the tombs, both royal and private, progressed only sporadically, and during intervals when more urgent commissions allowed. Building operations at Akhetaten appear to have absorbed much of the king's time and resources. Work on the Aten temples at Thebes began to decline after Year 5, and part of the labour corps in the Place of Truth on the west of Thebes, which was concerned with the cutting, decorating and furnishing of the royal and private tombs, was transferred to Akhetaten, where they occupied a walled village built for their accommodation on the far eastern verges of the site. But a certain amount of construction was still undertaken in Thebes by officials of Amenophis III. The temple of Amun was built in the Malkata palace complex by Si-Mut for the second jubilee of the old king in Year 7 of his son. Si-Mut also probably finished the tomb of the vizier Ramose in Year 4. Other high officials such as Kheruef and Surero were left with their large tombs incompletely decorated. The construction of the great Temple of Luxor was also abandoned with many of its statues lying on the site merely blocked out, or awaiting the master sculptors' final touches. The general impression remains that work on the monuments of the senior co-regent was falling into abeyance during the last years of his life.

While building in Thebes was running down, activity elsewhere was still being vigorously maintained, especially in the old centres of importance such as Memphis, where there was a temple to the Aten, and in Heliopolis where there was another, as well as a palace. It seems clear that the army was being used as a labour-force for much of the constructional work, since soldiers are shown prominently in some talatat, hauling the stone blocks into position. The size of the talatat in the limestone of Middle Egypt may have been decided by *Pl. 61* the dimensions of the sandstone archetypes from Gebel es Silsila, which had proved ideal for handling by an unskilled building corps working at full stretch.

By the end of the eighth regnal year a decisive stage had been reached in the king's projects and designs. Most of the township of Akhetaten had been established with the central administrative core largely built. This consisted on the north side of the enormous enclosure of the Great Temple, the House of the Aten, running west and east for a distance of 760 metres and a width of 290 metres. Within the mudbrick perimeter wall, the buildings were laid out on a processional plan: a colonnaded House of Rejoicing near the western entrance that gave access through a great pylon with five pairs of flag-poles, their penons aflutter, thence into a large court with foot basins for lustration and a balustraded offering-place, and the whole opening out through chicanes into six other courts, one after the other. These courts, open to the sky like most sun-temples in Egypt, had other altars and magazines for storing sacred equipment used in the cult. The last court on this processional way was the Gem-aten, 'The Aten is Found', having a great altar as its focal point. On each side of this complex was a forest of mudbrick altars, 365 in each, presumably

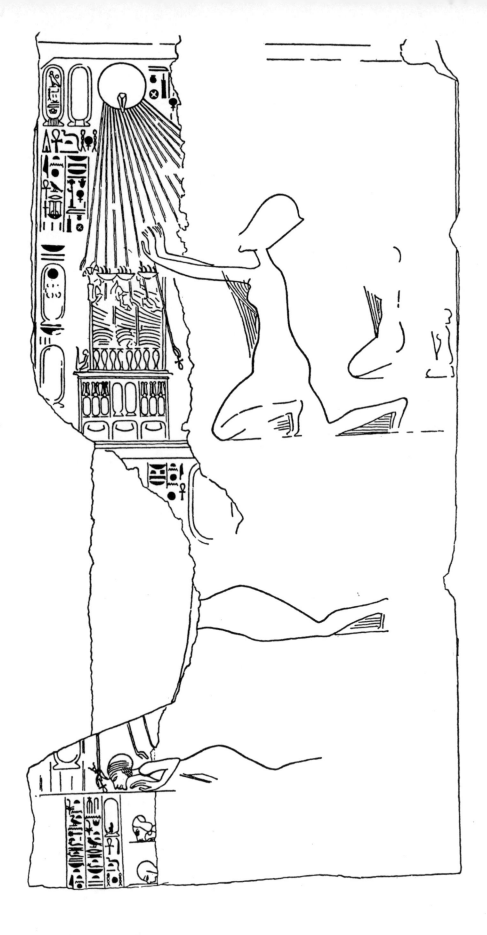

one for every day of the year, and separated to represent Lower and Upper Egypt. The considerable bounty of the Aten in the form of meat, pond-fowl, vegetables, loaves, wine, beer, incense and flower-offerings heaped on these altars, fed not only the officiating priests and temple staff but the local populace. No wonder a devotee should refer to Akhetaten as 'this perfect place' where such largesse was lavished upon them by the king's agency.

The Gem-aten in the House of Rejoicing was not the only temple in the House of the Aten. Separated from it by a gap of some 350 metres was the Mansion of the Ben-ben, at the end of an avenue of sphinxes that protected it from inimical influences. This building, with its choir of singers and musicians, was the holy of holies of the Aten cult. Its offering-place, another elevated podium with a ramp and balustrade, was in front of a great quartzite stela and beside a colossal seated statue of the king. Small fragments of the stela were found by Carter in his clearance in 1892, but its design is problematic. It is quite likely that it followed the design of another huge stela found substantially intact at Heliopolis which shows Akhenaten, Nefertiti and Meritaten kneeling before an altar, loaded with offerings and raising their hands in adoration of the radiant sun-disk. Below, in a lower register, the three royal officiants and a high priest(?) prostrate themselves to continue the service in another station of *Fig. 25* worship. This pose is an unusual one for kings to be represented in, but a statuette is known of Amenophis III in a similar posture of abject submission, and we shall find later the royal daughters in a comparable abasement.

Between the House of Rejoicing and the western entrance stood a series of hypaethral chapels which towards the end of the reign were taken over by the elder princesses. They were, however, originally erected for Queen Kiya, and we shall have occasion to refer to them again in the next chapter.

This, then, was the Great House of the Aten in Akhetaten, the sanctum and arcanum of the king's deity, and the centre of the Aten cult, the ultimate destination not only of the king and his family, but also of all worshippers living and dead who would be joined together there forever.

The other temple in this central section of the town lay about half a kilometre south of the Great Temple. This was the Mansion of the Aten, standing within its bastioned enclosure wall. The exact purpose of the building has long been doubtful, but recently the recognition of the building next door to it as the King's House, with a Window of Appearance on its south side, and giving access to a courtyard within the precincts of the Mansion, relates it to those similar temples with palaces attached that the Ramessides built at Gurna and Medinet Habu on the west of Thebes. It has therefore been plausibly suggested that the Mansion of the Aten is the king's mortuary temple, an argument that is reinforced by its orientation to the Royal Wadi and the king's tomb there. Its interior, however, has been almost completely denuded of its

25 Copy in line of a greatly eroded granite stela from Heliopolis showing the royal family first kneeling, then prostrating themselves in the worship of the Aten.

stonework and those reliefs that might have provided some clue as to the building's use and purpose.

The King's House is the only other important official building on this eastern side of the Sikket es Sultan. As mentioned above, it contained a small chamber on the eastern side decorated with a remarkable wall-painting *Fig. 26* showing the king and queen seated on stools opposite each other, and conversing with their six daughters between them. The three eldest stand before their parents' knees, the youngest, Sotepenrē, is a babe in her mother's lap, while the other pair fondle each other at the feet of Nefertiti.

The writer has pointed out that a fragment from the same wall-painting gives the name of the Aten in a form that is changed after Year 8, suggesting that all six daughters had been born to Nefertiti before Year 9. This view has been challenged by some, notably by Professor Redford (see above) who puts a later date on each of the princesses' debuts on the monuments. It must be the case, however, that the daughters would not have been able to take part in the religious rites until they had attained a certain age of responsibility. It is only in the fifth regnal year that the third daughter, Ankhesenpaaten, reaches an age that allows her to participate in the worship by rattling a sistrum beside her parents. Not until almost the end of the reign can the elder daughters make offerings: the older trio in fact comprise the acolytes in attendance on the royal pair who are the chief worshippers; and on many occasions they are reduced to a single attendant, the senior princess, Meritaten. Their duties are limited to playing the sistrum while the parents make the offerings. Only exceptionally, and then late in the reign, does the eldest assist at an offering of incense, handing a pair of braziers to her parents, while on another occasion the four eldest carry bouquets which their parents offer to the Aten. The children appear all together only in ceremonies which are more secular in character, *Fig. 27* such as the durbar of Year 12, or a presentation of awards at the Window of Appearance. The presence of the daughters in attendance on their parents cannot therefore be used as a means of fixing the date of a particular scene.

There is, moreover, another factor that argues that the birth of the children was earlier than the monuments suggest. It is now evident from the inscriptions that have come to light from the talatat found at Hermopolis that the three eldest daughters bore children before the end of their father's reign. We have already inferred that Meketaten must have died in childbirth before her mother, and therefore requires to be born as early as possible in her father's reign, by Year 3 at the latest. Yet she does not appear on the monuments at Amarna before Year 5, when her figure is squeezed into Stela K as an afterthought. The writer therefore regards it as necessary as a working hypothesis to assume that the three eldest daughters were all born by the third year after the advent of the king.

26 Copy in line of a fragmentary wall-painting in the King's House at Amarna.

The central area of Akhetaten, the 'Island Distinguished in Jubilees', was completed on its eastern side by the Mansion of the Aten and its associated mudbrick storehouses. A wadi separates this part of the town from the southern section which was largely residential, being occupied by the great mansions of the officials such as Ramose, Ranofer and Nakht. The western side *Pl. 22* of the Island, lying between the Sikket es Sultan and the river bank, was entirely taken up by the Great Official Palace stretching along the road in a frontage of 900 metres or more, and comprising gardens, residences, pillared halls, harim quarters, courts and workshops. A great deal of it lies under the modern cultivation and has never been excavated. In recent years it has become a dump for spoil from new irrigation schemes in the vicinity.

The Island also extended eastwards into the desert and included within its *Fig. 7* bounds the Records Office with the clerks' quarters housing the cuneiform *Pl. 23* correspondence with Asiatic rulers. Adjacent to this was the 'House of Life', a scriptorium where texts were compiled and inscriptions copied. Further east, on the verges of the open scrubland, were the police barracks and stables whence patrols could range over the military roads that encircled the site, and whose operations are depicted in the tomb of Mahu, the Chief-of-Police.

By the end of the eighth regnal year the Island was largely built, though not perhaps completely decorated, and was subject to changes of plan and minor schemes of rebuilding throughout the next decade or more. The town was occupied and functioning as the king's chief residence from this time onwards, attracting new artisans and a populace from afar, including foreigners from Asia and the Aegean together with their families. Coincident with this stage in

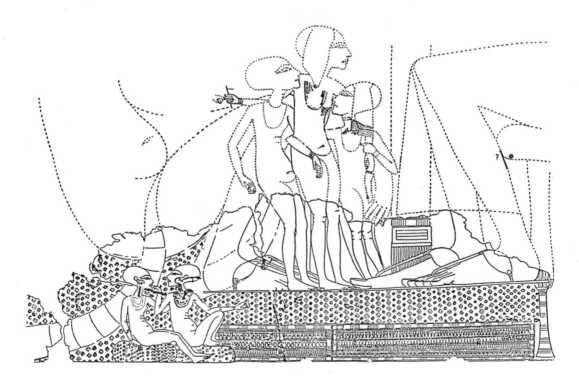

Fig. 3

Fig. 20

the life of Akhetaten, a new development had been reached in the king's religious ideas. The codicil appended to Stelae A and B, dated to the fifth month of Year 8, is the last occasion on which the name of the Aten is given in a form which had first appeared in the early months of the reign. The next dated document is the representation of the durbar in the tombs of Huya and Meryrē II, accompanied by a text dated to Year 12 in which the name of the Aten has been changed. It now reads, 'Rē lives, the Ruler of the Horizon, rejoicing in the Horizon in his aspect of Rē the Father who returns as the sun-god [the Aten].' Its exact translation, however, has been a matter of dispute among modern scholars. It is still contained within two double-bordered cartouches, like an exalted pharaoh; and one of its titles, 'Who is in Jubilee', has been changed to, 'Lord of Jubilees', suggesting that it had celebrated another official jubilee; but it has been purged of all references to other gods, such as the falcon of Herakhte and the feather of Shu (light).

At the same time as this doctrinal reform other expurgations took place. Thus the word *maet*, 'truth', for example, was now spelled phonetically and not by the glyph of a woman squatting with a feather upon her head, symbolizing the goddess Maet, the personification of the word. Similarly, *mut*, 'mother', was also spelled out in glyphs, and not by its homophone, the vulture (goddess) Mut. The word for 'god', in fact, was not used in the plural, though it was not at first altered in the texts to make it apply only in its singular form. The common title of the king, 'The Good God', was also avoided, and a new version, 'The Good Ruler', used in its stead. These changes were all in the direction of making the divinity of the Aten clear and unambiguous, and, above all, unique. These qualities became more significant as the reign progressed and ultimately resulted in that exclusiveness that brooked no rival to the regality and omnipotence of the Aten.

The exact moment between Years 8 and 12 when this change of name was effected is not recorded in any pronouncement that has survived, but it has been inferred from the phrase 'Ankh-rē' (Rē lives!), which may be an abbreviation of the later name of the Aten, and which is found particularly in the dockets of meat-jars at Amarna dated to Year 9. This would give a *terminus ad quem* for its introduction and hence is generally agreed to be the year when the name of the Aten was changed.

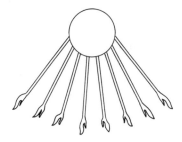

CHAPTER 24

The Last Years of Akhenaten

The most important event of Akhenaten's last years is the durbar of Year 12 when a large concourse of representatives from vassal states and the great powers in Asia, Africa and the Aegean came to Akhetaten bearing gifts for the *Fig. 27* pharaoh, and begging his blessing. As we have argued above, the occasion for this was Akhenaten's accession to sole rule on the death of Amenophis III. The preliminaries to this festivity occurred in Thebes where Akhenaten had gone earlier, probably to attend the burial rites for his father in the western branch of the Valley of the Kings and in the great funerary temple at Kom el Heitan on the western bank. It is likely that it was in the Malkata palace nearby that he received the Mitannian messengers, Pirrizi and Pupri, who brought a dispatch from their king Tushratta, complaining that wooden statues covered with gold leaf had been substituted for the solid gold statues that had been promised by his predecessor before he died. This deception caused a coolness between the two courts which apparently lasted for the remainder of the reign left to Tushratta.

A month after the receipt of the letter, however, the pharaoh was back in Akhetaten to receive delegates from foreign nations at the great presentation of gifts. We are dependent upon the damaged reliefs in the tombs of Huya and Meryrē II for the details. At this impressive ceremony the majestic 'lion furniture' was brought into use, the traditional carrying-chairs employed for the most solemn occasions, as at the kings' coronations and jubilees. In such litters, borne on the shoulders of stalwart bearers, the king and queen, accompanied by their retinue, were conveyed to the reviewing dais which had been set up in the desert to the east of the city. Here the royal pair are shown seated upon their gilded thrones, having laid aside their royal sceptres, and holding hands in a kind of domestic ease. The six daughters are ranged on both sides under the baldachin, the three eldest in one group, the remainder in another. Their poses with hands clasped, or playing with pet gazelles which the two youngest hold in their arms, are affectionate rather than formal.

Legates from the Hittite lands, Naharin, Cyprus(?), Syria and Palestine, together with Libya and Punt, parade before them, being introduced to the

27 The durbar of Year 12 at Akhetaten: copy in line of a relief in the tomb of Meryrē II at Amarna showing Akhenaten and Nefertiti enthroned beneath the state baldachin with their six

cf. Pl. 44   pharaoh and his family by high Egyptian functionaries. They proffer their gifts – ornate weapons, chariots, horses, copper ingots, exotic animals, lions, oryxes, antelopes, great bowls, vases and rhytons in gold and silver, ostrich feathers and eggs, incense and gums fashioned in the shape of pyramids and obelisks. Also included in this rich treasure are young slave-girls and a number of rebel malcontents in handcuffs, escorted by armed guards; and we are reminded that earlier Tushratta had sent to Amenophis III prisoners whom he had captured in a foray against the Hittites. On another occasion he sent thirty women.

    The African representatives make an equally resplendent appearance with gold in the form of dust in leather bags, or as massy rings sewn onto textiles, or trophies of barbaric workmanship; long-horned cattle accompany more exotic animals, hunting hounds and cheetahs held in leashes. Ebony is carried as logs

daughters beside them while the delegates from Nubia and Kush present their gifts, the
meritorious are decorated, and festal games are held.

or as finished furniture. More ostrich feathers and eggs appear, and resins and
gums in baskets; slave women march in groups, their children in panniers slung
on their backs, and other 'black ivory', shackled by slave-yokes, is hauled along
with them. Gold *shebu*-collars are ready on stands to be awarded to deserving
officials in the procession. For other entertainment in this pageant of empire,
festal games are arranged, wrestling, boxing and single-stick fencing, while the
groundlings applaud, and the police escort together with a troop of Bedouin
rangers are present to keep order.

This glittering and joyous occasion is the last glimpse we get of a happy and
united royal family seemingly at peace in an admiring world, worshipped by
their subjects at home and abroad. Dark days were ahead and a more sombre
sequel was to follow. The strings of captives from Asia were already portents of

the unrest that now became endemic in the Levant as war broke out between the Hittites and the Mitanni, with their vassal states in Syria getting drawn into the conflict. The fortunes of the main contestants ebbed and flowed; but eventually the Hittites prevailed and Egypt's ally was defeated, Tushratta murdered, and Naharin wiped from the map of Western Asia.

For a time Egypt herself had kept out of the major struggle, but had trouble from turbulent dynasts eager to exploit the general unrest to their own advantage. One by one she saw her lieges fall into the power of rival vassals, particularly into the rapacious hands of the Amurru in the coastal plain of Syria, under their energetic and unscrupulous king, Abdi-Ashirta. The Egyptian district commissioners must have done their best to support any local vassal who had shown himself loyal, but we lack their reports on the fluctuating situation, and cannot be sure whether the picture we receive from the Amarna Letters is not highly coloured in a particular aspect. The Egyptian garrisons at Sumura and Kumidu in this region of Amurru were called upon in times of crisis to intervene with local levies and come to the aid of beleaguered princes who were often threatened with revolt by their own subjects. An arch-schemer like Abdi-Ashirta was violently removed by a task-force when Egyptian patience had at last been exhausted: but his son Aziru proved an equally galling thorn in the flesh, and the governor in the key centre of Sumura was eventually forced to give in to his intrigues and return to Egypt. Other commissioners won temporary successes, but the tale is one of defeat and withdrawal as loyal vassals like Ribaddi of Byblos disappeared from the scene.

After the high compaigning days of Tuthmosis III and Amenophis II, the Egyptian armies had been recruited more from auxiliaries, Semitic spearmen, Nubian bowmen, Libyan slingers and Bedouin skirmishers. The Egyptian commissioners had to recruit such mercenaries, including roving bands of Apiru cut-throats, to support the loyalist vassals in keeping the pharaoh's peace. What the age demanded was the presence of the pharaoh as the all-powerful war-lord at the head of his troops with his chariots and archers, vanquishing the insolent and treacherous, and sustaining the morale of the loyal and resolute.

But the practice of the pharaohs of making triumphal promenades from time to time around their dominions, and settling the quarrels of the local dynasts, had apparently fallen into abeyance during the later reign of Amenophis III and that of his son. The army, which had been trained in the profession of arms by fighting in the field under the leadership of valiant pharaohs, had now become an instrument of centralized domestic policy, more concerned with labouring in quarries and vast building projects than combating in foreign theatres of war. The diminution in the role played by former temple staffs reduced also the collecting of taxes from tenants of temple estates, and prompted the use of a rapacious soldiery to gather what dues they could exact, thus creating abuses that later had to be suppressed with a heavy hand. An army demoralized by inaction and neglect of martial virtues was in no position to take the field even under a dynamic leader, and hence the reliance on mercenaries equally lacking in discipline, as for instance the unruly Nubian troops who broke into the palace of Abdi-Kheba, the prince of Jerusalem whom they were supposed to be protecting, and nearly murdered him. It is not surprising, therefore, to read in the Amarna Letters of defeats and withdrawals, not only in Syria, but further south in Central Palestine, where a serious threat developed through the ambitions of a guerilla chief, the Apiru Labaya of Shechem. He, however, met his end in a skirmish with loyalist forces; but his sons who succeeded him were no less factious. Towards the end of the reign, unrest in Gezer imperilled the whole Egyptian position in Central Palestine and it would seem that men and supplies were being marshalled for a more serious campaign, which may have been mounted in a later reign, for there is no indication that Akhenaten himself ever took the field in the manner of his forebears.

While the foreign situation was ominous in Asia, particularly in the face of impotence and supineness by the Egyptians, conditions at home were no less dismal. Plague was raging in the Near East. We hear from the king of Alashia that Nergal, the god of pestilence, was abroad in his land (Cyprus ?), reducing the production of copper ingots for the pharaoh. Plague is also recorded on the mainland at Byblos and Sumura. Later it spread from the Amqa region of Lebanon into the Hittite lands where it ended the life of Suppiluliumas. With the close connections between Egypt and the coastal region of the Levant, and with the coming and going of soldiers, captives, officials and traders, not to mention the importation of handmaidens, needlewomen, musicians and slaves directly into court circles, it would be surprising if the Egyptians could escape the scourge of epidemics. The 700 or more statues erected by Amenophis III of Sekhmet, the goddess of pestilence in Egypt, appears significant as a prophylactic measure to ward off disease from the nation, just as the Hittite king sought to deflect divine anger from his own people by offering up 'plague prayers' to the offended gods.

Perhaps the first notable death at this time was the demise of Akhenaten's *Fig. 5* second daughter Meketaten, whose burial is represented in chamber gamma of the Royal Tomb where she is seen as a corpse laid out upon a bed in a chamber of the palace. She is mourned by the whole court, prominent among whom are Akhenaten and Nefertiti, weeping and wailing and pouring dust on their heads. *Fig. 28* Meketaten, however, did not die of disease but in child-birth, as is evident by the presence of a nurse suckling an infant immediately outside the death-chamber, and attended by two fan-bearers to denote the high rank of the child.

The obliteration of the text on the wall at this point has deprived us of the name of the child, if it were ever inscribed; but it is doubtful if the babe survived long; certainly there is no other record of its existence.

The departure of Meketaten, however, may have been preceded by the death of Queen Tiye, since she cannot be recognized among the mourners and it would be natural to expect her to be present among them if she had been living at the time. She had evidently taken up residence at Amarna after the death of her husband, for not only had her steward Huya been awarded a tomb there, but her sunshade temple for her daily rejuvenation by means of the sun's rays had also been built for her by Akhenaten, probably in the Great Temple at *Fig. 29* Akhetaten. A relief in the tomb of Huya shows the king leading her by the hand into the chapel at her induction. Shortly afterwards, in Year 14, we receive the last mention of her affairs in jar dockets from Amarna. She died about that time, and was presumably buried in a tomb in the Royal Wadi at Akhetaten. *Pl. 55* For this the king provided the funerary furniture, including a gilded wooden shrine, similar to the four that nested around the sarcophagus of a pharaoh, together with alabaster shawabtis, of which an incomplete example was found in the Valley of the Kings by a member of the Napoleonic Expedition. It bore her title of Queen Mother as well as Chief Queen, and had apparently been inscribed for her posthumously; but there is little doubt that both it and the shrine had been brought to Thebes from Amarna. Thus passes from view one of the great queens of a dynasty of great queens, whose spiritual descendants, under the name of Candace, defied the might of Rome, and wrung from the Emperor an honourable peace.

28 *The Princess Meketaten, anointed and clothed, stands in a bower either as a statue or as a mummy, while her parents and sisters pour dust over their heads in a last farewell.*

29 *Akhenaten leading his mother Queen Tiye by the hand into her sunshade, followed by her retinue and that of her young daughter, Beketaten, who carries an offering of lettuce.*

About Year 14 also, that other great queen, Nefertiti, disappears from the scene. Jar dockets referring to her under the name of Neferneferuaten have not so far been found after Year 11: but this cannot have been her last year since she was present at the durbar of Year 12, and later at the funeral of her daughter Meketaten. She, too, was buried in a tomb in the Royal Wadi, for although nothing belonging to her funerary equipment has been officially excavated in that location, the lower part of an alabaster shawabti figure inscribed for her *Pl. 68* came into the art market at a time when a number of other fragmentary shawabti figures of Akhenaten were acquired from the same source.

With the deaths of Nefertiti and Tiye, attention shifts to another queen, Kiya; not because she usurps the position and duties of a great queen, but because to a large extent modern scholars have made her a focus of notoriety by resurrecting her personality from total obscurity. The name, Kiya, which like that of other harim ladies of the period is evidently a pet form, abbreviated from a longer or more formal name, has been considered as a contraction of a foreign version, probably a Mitannian name such as Gilukhipa or Tadukhipa, the princesses from Naharin who were married in turn to Amenophis III, and afterwards to Akhenaten. Gilukhipa has, however, been ruled out of consideration because, as she was married to Amenophis III in his tenth regnal year, she would have been too old to be nubile by the reign of Akhenaten. This alliance, however, is not impossible, taking into account a twelve years' co-regency between the two kings and a diplomatic marriage between Amenophis III and a royal child-bride. Nevertheless, Tadukhipa seems more probable if she is the wife in question.

But Kiya may not in point of fact have been of Mitannian origin; and the name could be capable of interpretation as derived from *Ky*, the Egyptian for 'monkey', a suitable pet-name for a 'jolie laide'. Whatever the meaning of her name may be, she was given the familiar title of 'The Favourite' (*ta-shepset*), with the epithet, 'the greatly beloved'. While the wife of a king, she was not described as an 'heiress', however, or a 'chief wife', and her name was not enclosed in a cartouche; nor in any representation of her is she seen to wear a uraeus. Her identification as, 'The Favourite from Naharin', is suggested from an inscription on a funerary cone of contemporary date belonging to a steward buried at Thebes called Bengay, a name with a distinctly foreign ring. The unusual titles and attributes of Kiya have close parallels to those of an Asiatic princess, 'the favourite', who appears in the role of 'femme fatale' in a near-contemporary novel, *The Tale of Two Brothers*. This analogy, which has been ingeniously developed by Lise Manniche, may have been inspired by the real-life example of Kiya. Foreign princesses who entered the harim of the pharaoh, however, generally passed their lives in complete obscurity so that, for instance, envoys from Babylon were unable to recognize the daughter of their king standing among the other wives of Amenophis III. But it might occasionally happen that one such queen would achieve legendary fame as a favourite, like the Hittite princess Maatneferurē, who was married to Ramesses II and also became a character in a later story (the Bentresh Stela).

It may well be, therefore, that such an exceptional beloved queen, if only a secondary queen, was granted the privilege of burial in or near the Royal Tomb. In the case of Kiya, enough of her funerary equipment has survived to show that it was exceptionally opulent and made before Year 9 of her husband's reign. Perhaps her burial was intruded in chamber alpha, but any evidence for such a deposit has been destroyed by the deplorable way the Royal Tomb was brought to light and plundered. Akhenaten, like any other oriental king of his day, had an extensive harim, as a relief in the tomb of Ay reveals. The preoccupation of the court artists with the exclusive image of Nefertiti and her daughters has given a monogamous character to the many scenes of domestic life in the royal family, which so impressed Petrie, among others. But secondary wives of Akhenaten have also left traces of their existence, such as a

Pls. 53, 57

certain 'royal ornament' Ipy, 'a true favourite' of the king. None, however, is so important as Kiya who, in addition to her splendid funerary furniture, had a sunshade temple in the *Maru*-aten, and chapels for her cult near the entrance to the Great Temple at Akhetaten. It may be that the exceptional privileges which she enjoyed were because, in addition to a daughter, she had borne the king a son or sons, a distinction which would have added immeasurably to her appeal in oriental eyes. Unfortunately, all her monuments are extensively damaged and any evidence in this respect is lacking.

Following the death of Nefertiti, probably early in Year 14, three years were still to run of Akhenaten's reign. Crammed into that period are a number of known events, but in what order they may have occurred is less certain since evidence from dated monuments is also lacking.

Even before Nefertiti's departure, the relations between Akhenaten and his eldest daughters had reached a sexual basis, as the death of Meketaten in childbirth demonstrates, not, be it mentioned, as a result of libidinous preference, but as a programme of accepted obligations among a divine circle. In what may seem a frantic insistence on incestuous *droits de seigneur*, Akhenaten, during the last three or four years of his reign, apparently became the father of at least two daughters by the princesses Meritaten and Ankhesenpaaten. These children were called by their mothers' names, with the addition of *ta-sherit* ('junior') in each case (see Chapter 20). The need of the pharaoh was for male issue to ensure that his divine line would be perpetuated. Each pharaoh in turn was described at his advent as 'the divine seed that came forth' from a particular deity, usually Atum or Amun, as ithyphallic gods. In the case of Akhenaten, his kinship with the one and only Aten made him the sire *par excellence* of the next generation of princes. In the event, however, there were disappointments in as much as the royal daughters produced only other daughters. A royal prince at this time is mentioned on the Hermopolite talatat, 'The King's son, of his loins, Tutankhuaten', but who his parents were is not known for certain and will be further discussed below.

The death of Meketaten, probably early in Year 14, gives some kind of indication when Meritaten and Ankhesenpaaten became pubescent. Another critical date in the period is the coronation of the prince Smenkhkarē as the co-regent of Akhenaten on reaching manhood. For reasons which will be considered in the next chapter, this event must have been in the fifteenth regnal year of Akhenaten. At the same time, as part of the coronation ceremonies, Smenkhkarē would have been married to the senior heiress Meritaten, who *Pl. 71* would then have taken the titles and ornaments of a chief queen. Akhenaten meanwhile made Ankhesenpaaten his next consort.

Between Years 14 and 15, Meritaten is referred to in letters to Akhenaten by such correspondents as Burnaburiash II of Babylon and Abi-milki of Tyre as 'your daughter Mayati'. Whether it is her or her sister Ankhesenpaaten who is also addressed as 'the mistress of your house' to whom Burnaburiash promises a present of lapis lazuli seal-rings in his last letter to Akhenaten, is unknown.

A number of heavily damaged reliefs from Hermopolis have been extensively restored by Hanke to show Kiya functioning in scenes from her chapels in the Great Temple of the Aten at Akhetaten, and the presence of the later name of the Aten reveals that these must be dated towards the end of the reign. The absence of Meketaten and Nefertiti from the scenes suggests that both may be dead, and therefore may narrow the date of the reliefs to Year 14 or later. Meritaten and Ankhesenpaaten, however, are shown as very much alive, wearing garments and coiffures of a mature style in place of their more infantile fashion of dress. The princesses prostrate themselves in a religious service at which their father officiates at an altar; and, as we have seen from the great stela from Heliopolis, the pose demonstrates the importance of the participants and the culminating stage they have reached in the worship. On a separate register Kiya, followed by an infant, presumably her daughter, also makes an offering. But despite the single ray of the Aten, which brings an *ankh* to her nostrils, and the fact that this is a major icon from her own chapel, her position seems merely incidental compared with the figures of the princesses who are drawn on the same base-line as their father, and immediately behind him, with Meritaten in advance of Kiya. In the writer's opinion, this indicates that the princesses are of a superior status to Kiya.

Like the reliefs from Hermopolis, fragments of monuments excavated by Woolley in the *Maru*-aten show that the sunshade temple there had also been taken from Kiya and bestowed upon Meritaten, the inscriptions being changed to apply to her and the features of the Favourite being recarved, and where necessary enlarged into 'the dropsical cranium' of the eldest princess. As it is most improbable that such an arrogation would happen while the Favourite was still alive, unless she had suffered deep disgrace, for which there is no evidence – her estate continued to send wine to Amarna as late as Year 16 without a change of name – we must presume that she died about this time and that her monuments were usurped by the senior princesses as a matter of urgency and economy before Meritaten became queen.

Putting all this data into order produces the following scenario for the last three years of Akhenaten's reign. Early in Year 14, on the death of the Chief Queen Nefertiti, Akhenaten advanced her eldest daughter to the position of his consort and the 'mistress of his house', by whom he was to father her daughter, Meritaten-ta-sherit. The death of Kiya, also about the same time, obliged him to bury her in the Royal Tomb, or in a tomb nearby, in the equipment he had provided for her. Her monuments, such as her sunshade temples and chapels at Akhetaten, were now redundant, and were hastily adapted for Meritaten because she was unlikely to want them for long, since she, as heiress, would shortly become queen when the young prince Smenkhkarē was crowned as co-regent on reaching manhood. This in fact happened soon afterwards, in Year 15, when Akhenaten took the next princess Ankhesenpaaten as his consort.

The crowning of Smenkhkarē, possibly in a hall at the southern end of the Great Official Palace in Year 15, brought a new actor on the scene whom it will be convenient to consider in the next chapter. Here it must suffice to record that he is a somewhat evanescent figure in the history of the last years of Akhenaten's reign: and it is hardly surprising that a scholar like J. R. Harris, for instance, should be disposed to dismiss him as a mere chimera. He did not rule long enough to exhibit a character that transpires through his monuments. These are, moreover, exceedingly scanty and mostly usurped by others. He was content to add the epithet, 'beloved by Akhenaten' (with various spellings) in both of his cartouches, a practice which renders him a mere shadow of his more dynamic partner. Nevertheless, a certain independence of thought must be accredited to him or his mentors in the policy which emerges in his funerary equipment, as will be mentioned later.

The storm-clouds at the end of Akhenaten's reign must have oppressed his last two years. The deaths of Tiye, Meketaten, Nefertiti, Kiya and Meritaten, besides Neferneferurē, and probably other younger daughters and granddaughters, seem hardly coincidental, but more like the visitation of the pestilence that was abroad in the Levant at this time. The measures that were open to mankind in the Late Bronze Age to deal with such a visitation were almost exclusively confined to magic incantation, like the plague prayers of the Hittites and the litany of Sekhmet of the Egyptians. In this connection we have to consider whether the anathema which was now pronounced against the gods of Thebes is at all relevant as an expiation. The outburst of destruction that now assailed the monuments of Amun and his consort Mut has an element of desperation in its thoroughness and ubiquity. The tallest obelisks and highest architraves at Thebes were scaled to hammer out the name and figure of Amun. His statues were smashed; even small scarabs that bore his name were defaced; and the Amun element in the nomen of Amenophis III was obliterated from intimate toilet vessels belonging to Queen Tiye. Such iconoclasm has been dated to various periods in the reign, such as the removal of the court to Akhetaten in Year 6, or the change in the name of the Aten in Year 9. The exceptional completeness, however, with which this policy was discharged, and its wide extent, disclose something more than official execration and suggest general panic. In the writer's view this destruction belongs to the last years of the reign when crises were mounting. The name of Amun, for instance, was excised from the nomen of Amenophis III on one of the doors of Tiye's gilded shrine made for her by Akhenaten. This object was disintegrating even before Daressy published it; and in the absence of other testimony we are now dependent upon Ayrton's copy made before its removal from Valley Tomb No. 55. It reveals that even when the shrine was made, probably not earlier than Year 12, the name of Amun could still be employed in an official inscription, but that by the time it was used in Tiye's burial in Year 14 it was interdicted.

The troubles that must have crowded fast upon the king in the last years of his life were not only domestic and mortal, but also political. Egyptian influence in Syria looked very near to complete collapse, and its hold further south in Central Palestine was also threatened. The ascendancy of the Aten had proved baleful for those realms on which it shone.

In the midst of these set-backs, Akhenaten died in circumstances that are wholly obscure. The Egyptians did not make a tragic or heroic event of the death of royalty: rather they hushed it up as the triumph of Evil over Righteousness. It was usually announced obliquely – the falcon had flown to his horizon, and the divine flesh was mingled with Him who had begot him. We have no official account of Akhenaten's end, but in his case it would have been only fitting if his apotheosis had been into the falcon of Rē-Herakhte.

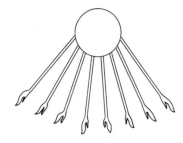

CHAPTER 25

The Amarna Aftermath

The death of Akhenaten, probably after the grape harvest in his seventeenth regnal year, brought his young co-regent to the throne in his stead. Hitherto we have called him Smenkhkarē for the sake of clarity, but as co-regent he had taken the nomen that Nefertiti had favoured as a name or title, though with a slightly different arrangement of the glyphs – Neferneferuaten. As prenomen he employed the name Ankhkheperurē, and to both cartouches, as we have indicated, he added an epithet having the meaning, 'beloved of Akhenaten' in various renderings. Later, however, he adopted the nomen of Smenkhkarē, which is less commonly found at Amarna, and dropped the epithet 'beloved of Akhenaten' from both names, as though he no longer claimed the sanction and authority of his senior partner. At his advent he was also nominated as the husband of 'the Chief Wife, his beloved, the Mistress of Upper and Lower Egypt, the Lady of the Two Lands, Meritaten'. This is the heiress by whom he *Pl. 71* obtained the throne in accordance with the now well-established tradition of the dynasty. A box found in the tomb of Tutankhamun, and a damaged box-lid from the same source, not only give the names of the same pair but also connect them with the titulary of Akhenaten. Another association of the co-regent with his consort is the sketch on a wall of the hall in the tomb of Meryrē II which shows the pair as a king and his queen with his name as Smenkhkarē-Djeserkheperu. There are also small items such as faience ring-bezels and furniture-knobs which have lent support to the conclusion that the epithet, 'beloved of Akhenaten' and the nomen 'Neferneferuaten' were abandoned on the death of Akhenaten, and a clean break in the titulary was made with his former associate. This also subsumes that Smenkhkarē and Meritaten outlived Akhenaten.

The parentage of the chief queen is well known. She was the daughter of Akhenaten and Nefertiti, as is so insistently mentioned on numerous inscriptions; but the parents of her husband are much less certain. In theory he should have been the son of his predecessor, but he never claims Akhenaten as his father, and the nearest relationship that he assumes is 'beloved' of him. Also, as we shall see, he was of such an age that he was born before Akhenaten came to the throne, which according to the normal pattern of royal inheritance in the dynasty would not have been legitimate, or physically probable. It will be convenient, therefore, to leave his parentage until later.

As the ruling king after the death of Akhenaten, it would have been Smenkhkarē's duty to officiate at the burial of his predecessor in the tomb he had prepared for himself. During the seventy days of his embalment, all preparations would require to be completed. The tomb in the Royal Wadi at Akhetaten was still unfinished and it was necessary to resort to improvisation to make it ready to receive its destined occupant. The pillared chamber beyond the well was converted from a corridor into a burial hall, and further constructional work on it terminated. The decoration of the walls would probably have been hastily completed in plastered relief, but until the proper publication of the tomb appears, we are without the means of forming an opinion. What has so far emerged is that the heavy equipment, such as the king's granite sarcophagus and lid and his alabaster Canopic chest, were in position. The latter bears no signs of staining by sacramental oils and resins; but as Geoffrey Martin points out, it has been so heavily restored in plaster that there is now no certain evidence to prove that the chest was never used. The tomb in its present vandalized and decrepit state, and in the signs of haste and careless workmanship in what survives of the relief decoration, gives an impression of a distinct decline from the standards of other royal tombs of the dynasty such as, for instance, the Theban tomb of Amenophis II. Yet one may hazard a guess that the furnishings were remarkably rich, setting a precedent for certain gold-covered grave goods which was to be followed by his immediate successors.

The last rites at the burial would be performed by Smenkhkarē as the dutiful successor, and probably before the tomb was closed additional burials, such as those of Nefertiti, Meketaten and other relatives, would have been taken from elsewhere in Akhetaten and installed in the Royal Tomb, if they had not already been deposited there. Afterwards the burial-chamber would be sealed off by a wall of limestone blocks cemented together, and the protective well at its entrance cut and decorated. Finally, the tomb would be sealed at its entrance and a guard mounted.

The burial of Akhenaten must have been followed shortly afterwards by the burial of Queen Meritaten, though this was probably at Thebes where her husband's tomb was being prepared. We hear nothing more of her, or of her daughter, Meritaten-ta-sherit, who probably succumbed to the general mortality in the royal family about the same time. At this point there is evidence that Smenkhkarē wedded the next heiress, Ankhesenpaaten, and made her queen in her sister's place. The marriage, however, could only have been of very short duration, because in the space of the same twelve months the king himself had died, and another had assumed his crown. His successor was the next senior prince, a young boy scarcely more than eight years old whom we have met on the fragment of talatat from Hermopolis as 'The King's son . . . Tutankhuaten'. Smenkhkarē had reigned for a brief three years, revealed on a graffito dated to that year which was scribbled on a wall in the tomb of Pairi at Thebes by a scribe of the divine offerings of Amun in the 'funerary temple of Ankhkheperurē'. A docket on a honey-jar found at Amarna, with the Year 1 written below a partly expunged Year 17, is against the view that he ruled longer than three years because another jar docket from the same site reads, 'Year 1, wine of the Estate of Smenkhkarē, deceased'. In both cases, Year 1 must refer to the first regnal year of Tutankhamun during which Akhenaten and Smenkhkarē must have followed each other to the grave, not to mention Queen Meritaten. The incidence of events in the last years of Akhenaten cannot leave room for the appointment of a co-regent before Year 15. Moreover, the body found in Valley Tomb No. 55, and generally identified as Smenkhkarē, has been estimated by Professor Harrison to have reached the age of twenty by the time of his death, which would mean that he had been made co-regent on reaching manhood, the usual pattern.

The new king is named on the lion throne of his coronation as Tutankhaten _Pl. 75_ as well as the definitive Tutankhamun, though it bears on its back-panel the radiant Aten-disk. How far it has been modified to combine the Amun element with an original Aten design cannot now be determined, but it illustrates the compromise that was already being made between the solar cult of Akhenaten and the old orthodox religion of Thebes, which had rendered the name of the queen on the back-panel as Ankhesen_amun_.

The parentage of the new boy-king, who adopted the prenomen Nebkheperurē, presents a problem. Even before his elevation to the throne, he is described as a 'king's son of his loins'. If he were such a son, so then must have been Smenkhkarē, who would otherwise never have succeeded in preference to a royal son, even if the latter were a mere child. The close physical resemblance between the distinctive platycephalic skulls of the two kings is repeated in the identity of their blood group, A2 and MN. They are now generally recognized as brothers, one born twelve years before the younger. The king who was their father cannot on this account be Akhenaten, since he was crowned some three years after Smenkhkarē was born, but must be Amenophis III, as Tutankhamun claimed on a statue he completed for the temple of Sulb. The mother of them both who, by virtue of their complete identity must have been the same woman, has been recognized as Queen Tiye by some scholars who point to the close resemblance of her facial features, as rendered in certain intimate statue-heads, to the portrait-mask of Tutankhamun. The lock of her hair, enclosed in a reliquary and deposited in his tomb as a memento, also suggests a close relationship between the two; but that they are mother and son has been firmly rejected by others on the grounds that she would have been too old to bear children by the time Tutankhamun was born, despite the presence of the young princess Beketaten in company with her during Tiye's last years. Until the body of Tiye has been identified beyond all doubt, and submitted to more stringent analyses, the matter will remain an enigma.

The marriage of Tutankhamun to Ankhesenamun was at the beginning of his full nine years' reign, which estimate is derived from the dockets written on wine-jars from his tomb. His first important decree was a proclamation, which has come to be known as the Restoration Stela, found near the Third Pylon at Karnak, together with fragmentary duplicates also from Karnak, all usurped by Haremhab. They purport to describe the situation that faced the king at his accession, with the temples from one end of the country to the other desecrated and fallen into neglect, and the land topsy-turvy through the indifference of the offended gods who had turned their backs upon Egypt because of what had been done. Foreign military expeditions failed; and the prayers of suppliants remained unanswered.

The story may be somewhat overdrawn, just as the oppressive conditions prevailing at the end of the Hyksos rule are exaggerated in the similar account by Hatshepsut: but there seems little doubt that the land was indeed troubled. In the world of the Late Bronze Age, the death of so many of their divine rulers within a short time of each other would have added considerably to the crisis of confidence brought about by defeats abroad and confusion at home. Motivation would have been lost, a blight would be thought to have settled on everything, and all enterprises great and small would seem ill-fated. The Egyptians, like other peoples of the ancient world, were directed largely by magic, by a faith in the supernatural that generally worked for a beneficent end by giving them a confidence and discipline which enabled the odds of adversity to be overcome. Often a hazardous enterprise, the outcome of which was uncertain, was crowned with success when an oracle of a god had instigated it and promised it good fortune. Similarly, in all the many little undertakings of daily life that had to be met with fortitude and patience, the will to endure and overcome set-backs was lacking when once the view took root that the gods were alienated and had withdrawn their support. Such a breakdown of morale seems to have been the chief legacy of Akhenaten's reign; and his successors had the task of getting Egypt back on the well-trodden paths that over the centuries had led to prosperity.

The restoration of confidence was the prime need for the young king to satisfy, as indeed it was for every pharaoh at his accession, when his reign was thought to inaugurate a new era of joy and success after an interlude of evil and death. The measures which Tutankhamun adopted, according to his great proclamation, were the typical Bronze Age solutions of propitiating the gods and securing their support. These included the fashioning of new statues and sanctuaries of the chief deities in gold and precious materials, the repair of shrines and the restoration of their sequestered treasure and revenues. New priesthoods were established to revive the lapsed services; and to these were nominated the sons and daughters of notables who had the respect of the local populace. The male and female servitors, temple singers, dancers and musicians were consecrated from the palace personnel; and their subsistence was charged to the king. Certainly a great deal of reconstruction and restoration of former temples was initiated during the reign of Tutankhamun, and the *Pl. 73* epithet that is applied to him on one of the seals of his tomb, 'who spent his life in making images of the gods', might well serve as his epitaph.

Since the king was a mere child when these decrees were promulgated, it is clear that the measures detailed in the stelae were mostly the work of his council, among whom the most prominent was the vizier and regent Ay, Akhenaten's father-in-law and Master of the Horse. The General Minnakht, probably a close relative of Ay, may have commanded the armies of Upper Egypt, while another general, Haremhab, whose previous career is obscure, was evidently in charge of the northern armies, and as such was responsible for the conduct of any warlike operations in Libya and in Asia. The Treasurer and Master of Works, Maya, was also an important official whose recently rediscovered tomb at Saqqara awaits investigation. The southern vizier, Pentu, had survived the reign of Akhenaten, whom he had served as Chief Physician, and had been granted a tomb at Amarna; but he was as ready as Ay to reverse the policy of his former royal master and return to orthodoxy.

These and other officials, such as Huy, the viceroy of Kush, were zealous in recommending a policy of reversion to the traditions of the dynasty which had served the country well in the past. The reins of government were picked up from the point where Amenophis III had dropped them. Work on the temples of Luxor and Sulb was resumed. The avenue of sphinxes from the Tenth Pylon to the Mut precinct at Ashru was continued by Tutankhamun and by subsequent kings. He also built a new temple of a very respectable size at Karnak, 'The Mansion of Nebkheperurē-in-Thebes', which was later demolished by Haremhab and incorporated in other structures. It is now being studied in its dismantled state by Dr Marianne Eaton-Krauss, to whom the writer is much indebted for her preliminary disclosures.

A decision must have been taken early to move the court from Akhetaten. The great palace complex founded by Tuthmosis I at Memphis was still flourishing, and the king is reported in his Restoration Stelae as residing there when he issued his edicts. Probably Akhenaten and Smenkhkarē had also occupied it earlier from time to time, for a quartzite statue-head of Nefertiti was excavated on its probable site in 1916. But it was now made the main residence in the north, and the adjacent necropolis of Saqqara was reopened for the building of the tombs of court grandees such as Haremhab and Maya. The removal of the court from Akhetaten to Memphis, accompanied by a large retinue of officials and chamberlains, would have been followed by the hejira of most of the professional classes with their valuables and house-fittings. Some activity was still carried on in the town, largely at the faience and glass works attached to the Great Palace. The tomb workmen, however, were evidently moved back to their old quarters in Thebes at the site of modern Deir el Medina. Any abandoned objects of the slightest use were doubtless purloined by the squatters who moved into their abandoned homes, and very few household goods have been excavated at Amarna, apart from those that had been hidden and forgotten. But other things of no intrinsic value were left *Pls. 16–19, 74* behind, notably the master portraits, model reliefs, plaster-casts and half-completed studies excavated in recent times in the ruins of sculptors' studios. These works represented defunct persons, particularly members of the royal family, whose portraits were no longer being carved. In the House of the Correspondence of Pharaoh, too, was a mass of cuneiform tablets, comprising dispatches from the great kings and vassal princes of Asia which had been received during the years since the founding of Akhetaten, and filed away in the archives. These clay tablets were also not removed, though there is some evidence that they had been concealed in a hole dug beneath the office floor. The early date of the move is suggested by the paucity of tablets addressed to Tutankhamun, only one being ascribed for certain to his reign. The presumption is that the clerks did not trouble to take away with them these cumbersome and fragile records since they would almost certainly have had copies of their contents written in Egyptian on easily portable papyrus.

The withdrawal of the garrison and most of the police force from the town would have invited the looting of the local cemeteries by lawless elements in the population. Those of the inhabitants who had died and been buried at Akhetaten during its short existence must have been removed to family burying grounds in other parts of the country, since no cemeteries, apart from a few poor inhumations of uncertain date, have been found at Amarna.

It is, however, probable that the burials in the Royal Wadi were not transferred at this time to the dynastic necropolis at Thebes. Unlike most of the private burials, these interments of the king and his relations had been made at his express wish and expense in accordance with his eschatological beliefs regarding the destiny of them all; and there would have been great reluctance on the part of his successors to countermand so early the arrangements that he had vowed to make. In our view, the chances are that the royal burials were not removed until later (see below). Perhaps the remoteness of the tombs in the high desert and periodic inspection by the police patrols may have been considered sufficient protection.

Meanwhile, in the sphere of foreign policy, some vigour was also injected into war-like operations, as had been promised to the Egyptian district commissioners at the advent of the king by Haremhab acting as his mouthpiece. The military crisis at Gezer which threatened the Egyptian position in Central Palestine had evidently been dispelled, and Palestine and Lebanon, so far as we can tell, were firmly held by loyal vassals supported by Egyptian garrisons. Haremhab in his tomb inscriptions speaks of himself as the guardian of the footsteps of the king 'on this day of smiting the Asiatics'. But the situation further north on the Syrian border was rather different. The Amurru had passed into Hittite vassalage, or were about to do so. Later in the reign an attempt was made to recover lost ground. The Hittite cuneiform records, on which we are almost exclusively dependent for an account of what happened at this time in the Syrian theatre of operations, reveal that they raided the Amqa in the Beqa Valley area of Lebanon which was a flagrant violation of Egyptian sovereignty and against their treaty obligations. As a riposte, Egyptian forces captured Kadesh on the Orontes and fomented the revolt of the Nukhash lands further south which were Hittite dependencies. Their triumph was short-lived, however, for the following year the Hittites drove the Egyptians out of Kadesh and recovered their lost territories, laying siege to Carchemish.

The Egyptians also mounted expeditions against Nubians and Kushites in the African theatre beyond the Second Cataract; but such campaigns were often little more than punitive police actions, or slave-raids conducted by the viceroy, though the king took the credit. Reliefs from the king's 'Mansion in Thebes', and the painted box from his tomb, both with their unusual and vivid detail, may indicate, however, that operations were on a larger scale than usual. It may be that it was in some such skirmish, or hunting accident, that the king met his end. The recent re-examination of his mummy has shown that he sustained a wound, probably by an arrow, which penetrated his skull in the region of his left ear. His hair had been shaved off his head, a prescribed preliminary to treatment for an injury to the skull, according to the Edwin Smith surgical papyrus. He lingered long enough to grow a short stubble before he died. His unexpected death, according to the Hittite account, caused consternation among the Egyptians; understandably so, since he left no heir and the glorious line of Amosis was extinct.

As we saw above, it was in this crisis for the Egyptian state that Queen Ankhesenamun wrote to Suppiluliumas asking him to send one of his many sons to Egypt so that she could marry him and make him the next pharaoh (see Chapter 19). This unprecedented request aroused the suspicions of the Hittite king, and he thought it prudent to dispatch a chamberlain to Memphis to find out at first hand what the situation was at the Egyptian court. By the time his envoy had returned, the hour for decision had passed; and although Prince Zennanza was duly sent, he was murdered on his way to Egypt; whereupon Suppiluliumas again attacked Amqa, drove the Egyptians from it and brought back prisoners who carried with them a plague that afflicted the Hittites for years afterwards.

Those who regard human history as the chronicle of a constant conspiracy between one individual or faction and another will see this whole episode as a prime example of duplicity and intrigue devised with Macchiavellian cunning. Those, on the other hand, who take the view that human error and bungling are more prevalent could just as well ascribe the killing of Zennanza to fortuitous circumstances, such as death at the hands of bandits who infested the border regions of Western Asia, as the Amarna Letters bear witness. At least, half a century later, when Ramesses II repeated Ankhesenamun's *détente*, but in reverse, he took the precaution of sending an army to escort his Hittite bride from her homeland to his.

In *c.* 1315 BC, however, time having run out for Queen Ankhesenamun, she was obliged to forego marriage to a prince with the blood of divine kings, and accept one of her own subjects. This was her grandfather Ay, who had only tenuous links with royalty, and secured the throne in the same way as had been promised to Prince Zennanza, by marriage with the royal heiress. We hear nothing more of her: the only testimony of her unhappy portion being the two stillborn children, almost certainly hers, who were entombed with their father Tutankhamun; and a blue glass finger-ring, now in the West Berlin Museum, with her name and Ay's engraved upon the bezel.

The sudden and unexpected death of Tutankhamun left his burial arrangements in disorder, and it doubtless fell to his successor Ay, with the Master of Works, Maya, as his adjutant, to complete all preparations and bury *Pl. 76* him with due rites among his ancestors. The tomb that was being leisurely prepared for him is believed to be No. 23 in the western branch of the Valley of the Kings. It is probable that it was started in the reign of Amenophis III for his eldest son Prince Tuthmosis; and then inherited in turn by Amenophis IV during his sojourn in Thebes, and by Smenkhkarē. But apparently it was found impossible to complete and furnish it in time for Tutankhamun's burial. *Pl. 75* Certain items were ready, such as the palace furniture which the king had used during his life-time and which was imbued with his own aura; or his clothing *Pl. 42* and accoutrements, jewels, sceptres, weapons, chariots and the like. The trough of his splendid quartzite sarcophagus was finished, but the lid, coved on its underside, was not ready and had to be replaced by a cracked granite slab which did not close properly over the projecting foot-piece of the outermost coffin. The many deaths among royalty in the recent past must have depleted considerably the supply of precious materials available to the craftsmen for making the exclusively funerary equipment that was still lacking.

In this predicament, Ay must have decided to complete the severance with the Amarna past by evacuating all the burials in the Royal Wadi, grouping them in one or two family tombs in the Theban necropoleis where they could be better protected. It was not unknown for the interment of a king to be made the occasion of a rearrangement of earlier burials, as occurred for unknown reasons in the case of Sethos II, for instance, in the Nineteenth Dynasty; and periodically with the plundered royal burials throughout the Twenty-First Dynasty. To receive the reburials from Amarna, small tombs were hastily excavated or improvised in the necropleis of Thebes; and as each of these was to contain several occupants, their funerary furniture would have to be reduced. This gave an opportunity to commandeer part of their equipment and alter it for Tutankhamun.

The moving spirit behind these redispositions was almost certainly Ay, not only as the pious successor of the late king, but also because it was his dead relatives that were the subject of concern. It was probably at this point rather than earlier in the reign that the Amarna royalty were reinterred at Thebes. The reburials were sealed with the cartouche of Tutankhamun, because this was still effective until his own entombment. Hence in a small quasi-private tomb in the Valley of the Kings, now designated as No. 55, Queen Tiye and two (?) of her sons, Akhenaten and Smenkhkarē, were reburied. In another, No. 62, a few yards away, Tutankhamun was buried in great splendour by Ay acting as the filial *setem*-priest at the last rites depicted on the north wall of the burial-chamber.

The two other kings, however, had been reinterred in much less opulent trappings. Though we lack any indication of the quality of Akhenaten's original burial, it was doubtless impressive, as the fragments of his smashed sarcophagus and Canopic chest bear witness. He was, however, reburied in Kiya's coffin with perfunctorily altered inscriptions and modifications that *Pl. 53* made it barely refer to a king instead of a secondary queen. It was accompanied by Kiya's Canopic jars, fitted with uraei, and with deletions in their *Pl. 57* inscriptions that made them also apply to him, though evidently the contents were not changed. What other grave goods were included in the deposit in Tomb No. 55 is unknown, apart from a set of 'magic bricks.' It may be that his burial had already been robbed or damaged at Amarna, a further incentive for removing his remains to Thebes. The sarcophagus, Canopic chest and some 200 stone shawabtis were left behind to be vandalized over suceeding years.

Other equipment not perhaps required for a devotee of the Aten cult, such as images of the gods in their black varnished shrines, may have been taken over by Smenkhkarē and remodelled for Tutankhamun; but the bulk of the latter's funerary furniture was requisitioned from that supplied for Smenkhkarē, who had probably been buried at Thebes, as the reference to his funerary temple there implies. This equipment included at least one shrine from around the sarcophagus, probably the second coffin, the entire Canopic outfit, except perhaps its enclosing tabernacle with its four guardian goddesses, and many smaller but precious objects. In addition, some items appear to be heirlooms, and others are gifts given by personal friends like Maya and Minnakht. Thus while Ay and Maya ensured that a rich and complete garniture would accompany the last of his line to the tomb, it is probable that the greatly reduced equipment for the two other kings in Tomb No. 55, while not matching the magnificence of the array in the adjacent tomb, was no mean affair, particularly as regards Queen Tiye, but since it was all subsequently removed or desecrated, we have no means of forming an opinion.

Pl. 54

While the kings and Tiye were transferred to the Valley of the Kings, it is tempting to suggest that in another part of the necropoleis, the burials of Nefertiti, her daughters, and perhaps granddaughters, were laid to rest in a second communal tomb, but no trace of them has yet come to light. What happened to Kiya and her children is equally obscure. Her opulent funerary equipment was adapted for her husband, but apparently not all of it. In the first two decades of this century an alabaster toilet vessel and a fragment of another, each bearing her name and titles, came into the art market and are now in New York and London; but from what sources has never been disclosed.

Fig. 19

King Ay ruled for a brief four or five years and continued the policies of his predecessor which he had doubtless persuaded him to adopt in the first place. The rehabilitation of Amun and the steady abandonment of the more extreme aspects of the Aten religion were quietly pursued. Ay continued the building projects at Karnak, adding his own names to them, without usurping his predecessor's work. He built his mortuary temple at Medinet Habu on the west of Thebes, at the southern end of a row of such structures, but it was subsequently taken over and extended by his successor. He finally finished Tomb No. 23 in the western branch of the Valley of the Kings as his own sepulchre. In the sarcophagus chamber is a wall-painting which is unique for a royal tomb, showing Ay with his wife engaged in the royal rite of spearing the hippopotamus and fowling in the marshes; but the queen who stands beside him in the hunting skiff is not Ankhesenamun, but that same Tey who in his Amarna tomb is described as Nefertiti's nurse and governess. The painting, however, has been damaged, and the names of the royal pair and their figures have been desecrated. The red granite sarcophagus, with the goddesses of the four cardinal points at the corners, similar in design to others of this period, has been smashed to pieces.

Pl. 4

If Ay had fathered any sons they died before the end of his reign; and with the royal line extinct, he presumably attempted to secure the succession to the throne of an able notability among his entourage. This was the General Haremhab who had played a key role in the rehabilitation of the land after the Amarna interlude, as the King's Commander-in-Chief. The coronation inscription on the back of a seated dyad of himself and his queen in the Turin Museum is the most complete account of his career, though the ornate style of the proclamation makes it a little ambiguous in places. It traces the steps in his progress to the throne, and indirectly implies that Ay accompanied him to Karnak to attend the Festival of Southern Opet, using the occasion to obtain the sanction of the oracle of Amun to Haremhab's induction as co-regent. The event was consummated by marriage with the next surviving heiress, in his case not Ankhesenamun, who was dead, but Mutnodjme, the sister of Nefertiti and a daughter of Ay. The fact that Haremhab considered himself in the main line of descent, and not as the founder of a new dynasty, is to be understood from the composition of his prenomen with the 'Kheperu-rē' element, which followed the tradition of most kings of the Eighteenth Dynasty, differing from the fashion set by the Ramessides of the next.

During the days of his initial ascendancy under Tutankhamun, he doubtless played an influential role in the return to orthodoxy. On the Turin statue he claims most of the reforms which Tutankhamun had announced on his Restoration Stelae a dozen years earlier, but his main statement of intent is contained in the greatly ruined stela which he erected at Karnak and is known in modern times as his Edict, apparently the inaugural decree of his reign, issued to 'seek the welfare of Egypt', by suppressing illegal acts.

It seems clear from this Edict that the authority of the pharaoh during the Amarna period had grown considerably, presumably at the expense of the religious foundations. Much of the administration had consequently fallen into the hands of court officials, notably in the army. The result had been widespread corruption, the oppression of free men by fraudulent tax-collectors, and arbitrary exactions and requisitions by an undisciplined soldiery in the name of the king. In his Edict, Haremhab quotes examples of such abuses and promises redress. The administration in fact reverted to an earlier code of behaviour, and the army was also organized on more effective lines with improved discipline. How far these reforms were initiated under Tutankhamun and Ay, or only by Haremhab on his assumption of supreme power, is doubtful; but his success in pursuing such a policy must have owed much to the tours of inspection which he claims to have made throughout the length and breadth of the land to ensure that his new measures were enacted with justice and vigour. His long reign of over a quarter of a century did much to re-establish the government of Egypt on sound and effective lines.

Haremhab's building programme at Thebes was at first restrained, perhaps because of the restorations that had to be made to temples all over the rest of the country; but from the middle of the reign a more ambitious scheme of works was inaugurated in the city of Amun. Plans were laid for the filling in of the basin before the Third Pylon and the building of an immense hypostyle hall in its place. A mighty gateway would be erected at its western end (the Second Pylon) and along the processional way to the southern entrance to the Great Temple of Amun, Pylons Nine and Ten were to be completed or rebuilt. This great project seems to have coincided with the death of Mutnodjme in his fifteenth or sixteenth regnal year, and her burial in the large and opulent tomb he had built for himself in the necropolis of Saqqara. Her departure from the scene must have cut the last links with the personalities of Amarna, and the king now seemed determined to obliterate all visible traces of the Aten religion and its memorials in Thebes.

There had already been a certain amount of random vandalism directed to Akhenaten's monuments at both Amarna and Karnak, probably as a result of personal hostility rather than through official policy, although Tutankhamun or his architects had re-employed some of the talatat from the constructions of Amenophis IV. Figures of Amarna royalty had been defaced in reliefs and statuary and their names expunged. Their memorials doubtless stood deserted and unprotected, inviting random demolition. A campaign was now initiated, presumably at a high level, for the total destruction of the recent past. The monuments of Tutankhamun and Ay were included in the execration, being neither finished off nor extended, but usurped, or destroyed, and their names excised and replaced by those of Haremhab. The temples which Akhenaten raised to the Aten at Karnak were dismantled and the spoil employed as fill and foundations for new constructions, or stored against future re-use. By the time the Ramessides had climbed into the saddle, virtually all visible traces of the Amarna reform and its instigator had ceased to exist.

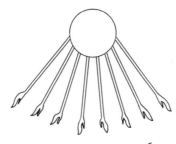

CHAPTER 26

'The Good Ruler Who Loves Mankind'

The personality of Akhenaten has continued to fascinate students of Egyptology, however much they may deny it, since the days of Petrie, who was the first to fall under his spell during the sondages he made at Tell el Amarna in 1891–2. Opinion has since varied from the enthusiastic, such as Weigall's encomium, 'For once we may look right into the mind of a king of Egypt and may see something of its working, and all that is there observed is worthy of admiration', to the less than enthusiastic – thus Professor Donald B. Redford, 'One of the most displeasing characteristics of the way of life Akhenaten held up as a model [is] refined sloth'. Comparisons have been drawn with other thinkers as diverse as Moses and the deranged Fatimid Caliph El Hakim.

The praise, as well as the blame, owes much to Akhenaten's practice of revealing himself rather freely to his intimates as compared with other kings. His family life with his chief queen, Nefertiti, and her daughters, has been disclosed with an intimacy and a humanity that is hardly found again anywhere *Pls. 15, 36, 58, 60* in antique art. If some observers have dismissed such scenes as effete, others have approved his taste for relaxed domesticity as significant. It is expressed not only in the scenes which he regarded as proper for the decoration of a tomb wall, but also in the surviving speeches with which he encouraged his followers. The psalm-like rhapsody on his god at the Foundation ceremony of Akhetaten reveal a religious fervour keen enough to inspire his wife with an equal devotion, and his intimates with their loyal acclaim.

The other compositions which we are pleased to think were from his pen, such as the Great Hymn to the Aten, have a lyrical ring about them which distinguishes them clearly from other pharaonic pronouncements. Even his sternest critics allow him unusual ability as a poet. Some of the religious ideas which he expresses are borrowed from earlier hymns, but are framed in a poetic form which seems inseparable from their sentiments and must have inspired his followers by their literary appeal. This may have animated their own imitations of his diction, if they were not indeed his own:

> Grant him, O Living Aten, whatever thy heart loves to the extent that there is sand on the shore, that fishes in the river have scales, and cattle, hair. Let

him reside here until the egret turns black and the crow turns white; until the hills rise up to depart, and water flows upstream, while I continue in the following of the Good God, until he ordains me the burial that he confers.

In his addresses to his courtiers his words are as stilted and banal as any pharaonic pronouncement, but praise and encouragement are more frequently heard at Akhetaten than elsewhere:

Lo, I appoint thee High Priest of the Aten to me in the temple of the Aten in Akhetaten, doing it for love of thee, saying: 'O, my servant who hearkenest to the Teaching, my heart is satisfied with every affair which thou performest. . .'

The royal gratitude is also as generous as the praise:

Let the Superintendent of the Treasury of Golden Rings, take the High Priest of the Aten in Akhetaten and put gold around his neck to the top of it, and gold around his ankles because of his obedience to the Teaching.

The contract between the king and his officials is mutual regard. The king rewards faithful service liberally; and the servant praises abundantly his lord's munificence:

Enter ye my tomb and see how great was that which was done for me. I was a servant of Wā'enrē the Ruler who lives by Truth. I followed him and he rose up early to reward me because I did his behests.

This has been rejected by modern critics as mere obsequiousness by place-seekers, but it is no more sycophantic than similar responses by courtiers of other kings during centuries of faithful service. When every king was hedged with divinity, his followers expressed their loyalty in a dutiful manner according to the conventions of their time. They bent low in the royal presence of Akhenaten, whereas the courtiers of the previous reign, though just as respectful, might have given a formal inclination of the head. But every pharaoh, as the vizier Rekhmirē proclaims, was a god by whom men lived, the mother and father of mankind, alone by himself, without a rival. This deference may seem hypocritical, and certainly is if we judge the occasion from a modern egalitarian standpoint of disillusion and scepticism. But the people of the Bronze Age held no such beliefs. The words came from the god incarnate and were therefore inspired. If he preached that the god, whose beautiful child he was, should be worshipped as a living, intangible being renewing himself in the dawn, and was not a stock or stone in the darkness of a sealed chamber, they had every incentive for believing him. His Teaching could only be proved wrong after his death when things might fall into a different perspective, and it could be seen that Falsehood had usurped the place of Truth and led all astray. A similar delusion has led modern totalitarian states into error, which has had to be corrected after the death of a charismatic leader whom Time has shown to be yet another false prophet.

Akhenaten has been condemned for presiding over 'an aggregation of voluptuaries bent on personal gratification and their opportunist following'. Unfortunately the Late Bronze Age neither inspired nor fostered an early Plutarch, still less a Suetonius, to give us a contemporary view of events and their impact on the rulers of their day. We have no means of deciding how far such modern disapproval is a prejudiced appraisal of an ancient oriental phantasmagoria. The king certainly did lounge in cushioned ease in scenes which seem more concerned with indolence than dignity. He did ride in a chariot rather than walk, an exercise adopted for representation by very few pharaohs at any period. But he could also be shown in the hunt, though such depictions are rare and fragmentary, and not a subject chosen for his followers to exhibit in their tomb reliefs.

On the other hand, Akhenaten has been castigated as a religious fanatic, an aberration in which he was faithfully followed by Nefertiti and some of his chief courtiers. A comparison with the unbalanced Fatimid Caliph El Hakim has been pungently drawn by Professor J. D. Ray in a recent critique. There was the same progression of Akhenaten from early revelation to a later austere creed, leading perhaps to the frenzied persecution of Amun, which bears the thumbprint of paranoiac fury. The temptation to overstep the limits, as indeed it was in the case of El Hakim, was greatly exacerbated in the case of a young ruler brought up in an atmosphere of adulation and autocracy in a luxurious milieu. One may not go quite so far, however, in speculating with Ray that 'the revulsion that seems to follow the Heretic's departure is hardly explicable as a mere reaction against a rather austere monotheism, and that "the Criminal of Akhetaten" must have been more than a misunderstood visionary'.

Whatever speculations the original and uncharacteristic reign of Akhenaten may arouse, we can only judge by what evidence his monuments have bequeathed us, tenuous as it may be. The expressions his artists recorded – when he groped for Nefertiti's supporting arm in his daughter's death-chamber, or registered grim distaste at the wringing of the neck of a sacrificial bird, or the affection between him and other members of his family, or the joy of his followers in his presence – all portray 'The Good Ruler who loves Mankind'. These and other touches strike a chord that is humane and sympathetic. The silence that immediately follows his end is the hush that falls

Fig. 5
Pl. 62
Pls. 15, 36
Fig. 2

on almost every pharaoh at death when once more Evil has triumphed over Righteousness. Later a delayed reaction may be a paean for the victory of Amun as much as an execration of Akhenaten:

Woe unto him who assaileth thee, O Amun! Thy City endures whereas he that assaileth thee is cast down.

In many respects, the rule of Akhenaten was an extension of his father's reign. The absolutism of the kings was the same: both married their daughters. The position of Tiye was as important and dominant as that of Nefertiti: both queens were incarnations of goddesses, Hathor or Tefnut. Where Akhenaten's creed differed from his father's was in the propagation of a monotheistic religion that excluded other gods. Akhenaten's preoccupation with the cult of Rē-Herakhte in his aspect of the light which came from the Aten diverted his attention and that of his officials from the minutiae of government which had been the chief concern of the Ahmosides from the beginning of the dynasty. Such a dereliction from statecraft to theology led to neglect, corruption and near-anarchy. Moreover, the wind of change was pestilential and resulted in the virtual extermination of the ruling family.

The eclipse of Akhenaten was complete. After the Amarna interlude, the life of Egypt resumed its flow through familiar channels. Yet perversely, the ideas to which Akhenaten had sacrificed so much did not wholly die with him. They continued to haunt the minds of others, and eventually prevailed as the ordinances for the conduct of Man *vis-à-vis* God in the decalogue that was part of another 'Teaching'.

Sources of Quotations

(For details of books see Select Bibliography)

Pages

15   Davies, N. de G. *The Rock Tombs of El-Amarna*, I, p. 2.

25   Davies, N. de G. *The Rock Tombs of El-Amarna*, IV, p 8.

47–50   Davies, N. de G. *The Rock Tombs of El-Amarna*, V, pls xxix–xxxii.

50–51   Davies, N. de G. *The Rock Tombs of El-Amarna*, V, pls xxvii–xxviii.

88   Legrain, G. 'Notes d'Inspection: 1. Les stéles d'Aménôthès IV à Zernik et à Gebel Silsileh'. *Ann. Serv. 3* (1902) p. 263–4.

111–2   Petrie, W. M. F. *Tell el-Amarna*, 13, §§ 93–5.

113   Breasted, J. H. *A History of the Ancient Egyptians*, pp. 264–5.

124–5   Knudtzon, J. A. et al., *Die El-Amarna Tafeln*, Nos 3, 7, 9–11, 19, 41, 44.

152   *The Tomb of Kheruef: Theban Tomb 192* (University of Chicago, Oriental Institute Publication, Vol. 102), p. 60.

169   Ray, J. D. Review of D. B. Redford's 'Akhenaten, the Heretic King' in *Göttinger Miszellen* 86 (1985), p. 83.

171   Gauthier, H. *La grande inscription dédicatoire d'Abydos*, 2, § 232ff.; 3, § 259ff.

172   Redford D. B. *History and Chronology of the Eighteenth Dynasty of Egypt*, p. 149.

178   Davies, N. de G. *The Rock Tombs of El-Amarna* III, pl. xiii.

180   Gardiner, A. H. 'A Pharaonic Encomium (II)', *JEA* 42 (1956) 8ff.

181   Knudtzon, J. A. et al., *Die El-Amarna Tafeln*, I, No. 27, pp. 229ff.

195   Davis, T. M. et al., *The Tomb of Queen Tiyi*, pp. 7–8.

200   Aldred, C. and Sandison, A. T. 'The Pharaoh Akhenaten: A Problem in Egyptology and Pathology'. *Bulletin of the History of Medicine*, 36 (1962), p. 303.

204   Hanke, R. *Amarna – Reliefs aus Hermopolis*, pp. 189–90; and Harris, J. R. 'Kiya', *Chron. d'Ég.*, 49 (1974), p. 27.

222   Davies, N. de G. *The Rock Tombs of El-Amarna*, III, pl. vi.

228   De Wit, C. *Le Rôle et le Sens du Lion dans l'Egypte ancienne*, p. 18.

240   Davies, N. de G. *The Rock Tombs of El-Amarna*, VI, pl. vi; pl. xxvi.

241–3   Davies, N. de G. *The Rock Tombs of El-Amarna*, VI, pl. xxvii.

247   Hanke, R. *Amarna – Reliefs aus Hermopolis*, pp. 171–4, 269.

247–8   Fairman, H. W. 'Once again the so-called Coffin of Akhenaten', *JEA* 47 (1961), p. 34.

303   Chapter heading: Davies, N. de G. *The Rock Tombs of El-Amarna*, I, p. 52, § 3.

303   Redford, D. B. *Akhenaten, the Heretic King*, p. 234.

303–4   Davies, N. de G. *The Rock Tombs of El-Amarna*, III pl. xxix, cols 8–14.

304   Davies, N. de G. *The Rock Tombs of El-Amarna*, I, pl. xxx, cols 1–3, left.

304   Davies, N. de G. *The Rock Tombs of El-Amarna*, I, pl. viii, cols 1–3.

304   Davies, N. de G. *The Rock Tombs of El-Amarna*, VI, pl. xix, W. wall, cols 4–6.

306   Erman, A. 'Zur Aegyptischer Religion' British Museum, Ostracon No. 29559: *ZÄS* xlii (1905), p. 106.

Select Bibliography

The entries under each chapter-heading are given in the order in which they are referred to in the text, with the following abbreviations:

Ann. Serv. Annales du Service des Antiquités de l'Égypte.
BIFAO Bulletin de l'Institut Français d'Archéologie Orientale.
BSFE Bulletin de la Société Française d'Égyptologie.
CAH Cambridge Ancient History, Revised Edition, Vol. II.
CCG Cairo Museum, Catalogue Général des Antiquités Égyptiennes.
Chron. d'Ég. Chronique d'Égypte.
Fouilles d'IFAO Fouilles d'Institut Français d'Archéologie Orientale.
JARCE Journal of the American Research Center in Egypt.
JEA Journal of Egyptian Archaeology.
JNES Journal of Near Eastern Studies.
LÄ Lexikon der Ägyptologie.
MDAIK Mitteilungen der Deutschen Archäologischen Instituts Abteilung Kairo.
Mém. Inst. fr. Caire Mémoires publiés par les membres de l'Institut français d'Archéologie orientale du Caire.
Mém. Miss. fr. Caire Mémoires publiés par les membres de la Mission archéologique française au Caire.
SAK Studien zur Altägyptischen Kultur.
ZÄS Zeitschrift für Ägyptische Sprache und Altertumskunde.

*Publications so marked have extensive bibliographies of their own.

1 The Discovery of Akhenaten
MARTIN G. T. *The 'Amarna Period and its Aftermath*: A Check-List of Publications. London 1987.
JAMES, T. G. H. (ed.) *Excavating in Egypt: The Egypt Exploration Society 1882–1982*. London 1982, ch. 5.
2 The Private Tombs of Amarna
BOURIANT, U. *Deux Jours de fouilles à Tell el-Amarna*, (*Mém. Miss. fr. Caire, 1*). Paris 1884.

DAVIES, N. DE G. *The Rock Tombs of El-Amarna*. 6 Vols. London 1903–8.
3 The Tombs in the Royal Wadi
BOURIANT, U. et al. *Monuments, pour servir à l'étude du culte d'Atonou en Egypte*. 1, Les tombes de Khouitatonou, (*Mém. Inst. fr. Caire, 8*). Cairo 1903.
*MARTIN G. T. *The Royal Tomb at Amarna*, 1 *The Objects*. London 1974.
MARTIN G. T. 'Expedition to the Royal Tomb of Akhenaten', *Illustrated London News*, No. 6998, Sept. 1981, 66–7.
EL-KHOULY, ALY, and MARTIN, G. T. *Excavations in the Royal Necropolis at El 'Amarna 1984*. Cairo 1985.
4 The Boundary Stelae
DAVIES, N. DE G. *The Rock Tombs of El-Amarna*, Pt V. London 1908.
MURNANE, W. J. and VAN SICLEN, C. C. American Research Center in Egypt, *News Letter No. 128*, Winter 1984. *The El-Amarna Boundary Stelae Project: A Preliminary Report*.
MURNANE, W. J. 'The El-Amarna Boundary Stelae Project', *University of Chicago, Oriental Institute, Annual Report 1983–4*, 13–16.
5 The Buried Evidence: the Early Finds
KNUDTZON, J. A. et al. *Die El-Amarna-Tafeln*. 2 Vols. Leipzig 1908–15.
PETRIE, W. M. F. *Tell el-Amarna*. London 1894.
SAMSON, J. *Amarna, City of Akhenaten and Nefertiti*. London 1972.
COONEY, J. D. and SIMPSON, W. K. 'An Architectural Fragment from Amarna', *Bulletin of the Brooklyn Museum* 12, 4 (1951), 1–12.
*HAYES, W. C. *The Scepter of Egypt*, Pt 2, 285–8, 295. New York 1959.
BORCHARDT, L. 'Ausgrabungen in Tell el Amarna', *Mitteilungen der Deutschen Orient-Gesellschaft*, 34, 46, 50, 52, 55. Berlin 1907–14.
6 The Buried Evidence: the Later Finds
PENDLEBURY, J. D. S. *Tell el-Amarna*. London 1935.
PEET, T. E., WOOLLEY, C. L. et al. *The City of Akhenaten Pt 1*. London 1923.
FRANKFORT, H., PENDLEBURY, J. D. S. et al. *The City of Akhenaten, Pt II*. London 1933.
PENDLEBURY, J. D. S. et al. *The City of*

Akhenaten, Pt III. 2 Vols. London 1951.

KEMP, B. J. *Amarna Reports I–III.* London 1983–6.

KEMP, B. J. 'The Window of Appearance at El-'Amarna and the Basic Structure of this City', *JEA* 62 (1976), 81 ff.

FRANKFORT, H. et al. *The Mural Painting of El-Amarneh.* London 1929.

—, *Preliminary Reports on the Excavations at Tell el-Amarnah, JEA* 12 (1926), 10–12; 13 (1927), 216–18; 15 (1929), 142–9; 18 (1932), 143–5.

7 **The Karnak Talatat**

SMITH, R. W. 'The Akhenaten Temple Project', *Expedition* (Bulletin of the University Museum of Pennsylvania) 10, No. 1 (1967), 24–52.

*SMITH, R. W., and REDFORD, D. B. *The Akhenaten Temple Project: Vol. 1, Initial Discoveries.* Warminster 1976.

DORESSE, M. 'Les Temples atoniens de la région thébaine', *Orientalia* 24 (1955), 113–35.

SAUNERON, S. and SAAD, R. M. 'Le Démontage et l'étude du IXᵉ pylône à Karnak', *Kemi* 19 (1969), 137–78.

COTTEVIELLE-GIRAUDET, R. *Rapport sur les fouilles de Medamud, 1932, (Fouilles d'IFAO* 13). Cairo 1936.

DESROCHES-NOBLECOURT, C. 'Un buste monumental d'Aménophis IV', *Revue du Louvre* 22 (1972), 239–50.

8 **The Other Monuments**

COONEY, J. D. *Amarna Reliefs from Hermopolis in American Collections.* Brooklyn Museum 1965.

ROEDER, G. *Amarna-Reliefs aus Hermopolis.* Hildesheim 1969.

HANKE, R. *Amarna-Reliefs aus Hermopolis: Neue Veroffentlichungen und Studien.* Hildesheim 1978.

HABACHI, LABIB. 'Akhenaten in Heliopolis', *Beiträge zur Ägyptischen Bauforschung und Altertumskunde,* Pt 12, *(Festschrift Ricke).* Cairo 1971.

LEGRAIN, G. 'Notes d'Inspection: 1. Les stèles d'Aménôthès IV à Zernik et à Gebel Silsileh', *Ann. Serv.* 3 (1902), 259 ff.

DAVIES, N. DE G. *The Tomb of the Vizier Ramose.* London 1941.

DAVIES, N. DE G. 'Akhenaten at Thebes', *JEA* 9 (1923), 132 ff.

HABACHI, LABIB. 'Varia from the Reign of King Akhenaten', *MDAIK* 20 (1965), 85–92.

FAY, B. Egyptian Museum, Berlin-Charlottenburg 1985. *Catalogue,* 78.

9 **Personalia**

SMITH, G. E. 'The Royal Mummies', *CCG 61051-100.* Cairo 1912.

*HARRIS, J. E. and WENTE, E. F. *An X-Ray Atlas of the Royal Mummies.* Chicago 1980.

QUIBELL, J. E. 'The Tomb of Yuaa and Thuiu', *CCG 51001-191.* Cairo 1908.

CONNOLLY, R. C. et al. 'An Analysis of the Inter-relationships between Pharaohs of the 18th Dynasty', *Journal of Museum of Applied Science: Center for Archaeology (Philadelphia),* Vol. 1, 178–181 (Mummification Supplement, 1980).

HARRIS, J. E. et al. 'Mummy of the "Elder Lady" in the Tomb of Amenhotep II', *Science* Vol. 200 (1978), 1149–51.

GERMER, R. 'Die Angebliche Mumie de Teje: Probleme Interdisziplinärer Arbeiten', *SAK* 11 (1984), 85–90.

MASTERS, P. and ZIMMERMAN, M. 'The Age of a Mummy', *Science* Vol. 201, (1978), 811.

CARTER, H. et al. *The Tomb of Tutankhamen, Vol. II.* London 1927, Appendix I.

LEEK, F. FILCE. *The Human Remains from the Tomb of Tutankhamun.* Oxford 1972.

10 **Interpretations**

PETRIE, W. M. F. *Tell el-Amarna.* London 1894.

BREASTED, J. H. *A History of the Ancient Egyptians.* London 1910, 264–5.

FREUD, S. *Moses and Monotheism* (trans. by K. Jones). London 1939.

REDFORD, D. B. *Akhenaten, the Heretic King.* Princeton 1984, 232–5.

11, 12 **Egypt in the Eighteenth Dynasty**

*JAMES, T. G. H. 'Egypt from the Expulsion of the Hyksos to Amenophis I', *CAH* II, ch. VIII. Cambridge 1965.

*HAYES, W. C. 'Egypt: Internal Affairs from Tuthmosis I to the Death of Amenophis III', *CAH* II, ch. IX, Pts 1, 2. Cambridge 1962.

LECLANT, J. (ed.) *L'Univers des Formes: le monde égyptien, les pharaons II, L'Empire des Conquérants.* Paris 1979.

13 The God's Wife and the Chief Queen

GITTON, M. *L'Épouse du dieu Ahmes Néfetary.* Besançon-Paris 1975.

GITTON, M. 'Le Rôle des femmes dans le clergé d'Amon à la 18e Dynastie', *BSFE* 75 (1976), 31 ff.

GITTON, M. *Les divines épouses de la 18e dynastie.* Besançon-Paris 1984.

ALDRED, C. 'Ahmose-Nofretari Again', *Artibus Aegypti* (Studia in honorem Bernard V. Bothmer). Bruxelles 1983, 7–12.

'Gottesgemahlin', *LÄ* II, 792–812.

BRUNNER, H. 'Die Geburt des Gottkönigs', *Ägyptologische Abhandlungen 10.* Weisbaden 1964.

14 The Reign of Tuthmosis IV

WENTE, E. F. and VAN SICLEN, C. C. 'A Chronology of the New Kingdom', *Studies in Honor of George R. Hughes.* The Oriental Institute, Chicago, Jan. 12, 1977, 229–230.

*HARRIS, J. E. and WENTE, E. F. *An X-Ray Atlas of the Royal Mummies.* Chicago 1980, 252–4.

15 The Reign of Amenophis III

HAYES, W. C. 'Inscriptions from the Palace of Amenhotep III', *JNES* 10 (1953), 35–36, 82–111, 156–83, 231–42.

HAYES, W. C. 'Egypt: Internal Affairs from Tuthmosis I to the Death of Amenophis III', *CAH* II, ch. IX, Pts 1, 2. Cambridge 1962.

PIANKOFF, A. and HORNUNG, E. 'Das Grab Amenophis' III in Westtal der Konige', *MDAIK* 17 (1961), 111–27.

DAVIES, N. DE G. *The Tomb of the Two Sculptors at Thebes.* New York 1927.

GERMOND, P. *Sekhmet et la protection du monde.* Geneva 1981.

YOYOTTE, J. 'Une Monumentale Litanie de Granite', *BSFE* No. 87–88 (1980), 46–75.

UNIVERSITY OF CHICAGO, Oriental Institute Publication Vol. 102, *The Tomb of Kheruef: Theban Tomb 192.* Chicago 1980.

16 The Question of a Co-Regency

SIMPSON, W. K. 'The Single-dated Monuments of Sesotris I: an Aspect of the Institution of Co-regency in the Twelfth Dynasty', *JNES* 15 (1956), 214–19.

HORNUNG, E. and STAEHELIN, E. Studien zum Sedfest, *Aegyptiaca Helvetica I.* Geneva 1974.

ALDRED, C. 'The Second Jubilee of Amenophis II', *ZÄS* 94 (1967), 1–6.

GARDINER, A. H. 'Regnal Years and the Civil Calendar in Pharaonic Egypt', *JEA* 31 (1945), 11 ff.

BREASTED, J. H. *Ancient Records of Egypt.* Vols 2 and 3. Chicago 1906.

REDFORD, D. B. *History and Chronology of the Eighteenth Dynasty of Egypt*, ch. 5 and 6. Toronto 1967.

KITCHEN, K. A. 'Further Notes on New Kingdom Chronology and History', *Chron. d'Ég.* 40 (1968), 313 ff.

CAMPBELL, E. F. *The Chronology of the Amarna Letters.* Baltimore 1964.

KITCHEN, K. A. 'Review of the foregoing', *JEA* 53 (1967) 178–82.

FAIRMAN, H. W. 'A Block of Amenophis IV from Athribis', *JEA* 46 (1960), 80 ff.

ALDRED, C. 'Two Theban Notables during the Later Reign of Amenophis III', *JNES* 18 (1959), 113 ff.

GARDINER, A. H. 'A Pharaonic Encomium (II)', *JEA* 42 (1956), 8 ff.

ALDRED, C. 'The Foreign Gifts Offered to Pharaoh', *JEA* 56 (1970), 105 ff.

MURNANE, W. J. 'On the Accession date of Akhenaten', *Studies in Honor of George R. Hughes.* The Oriental Institute, Chicago 1977, 163–7.

17 The Amarna Letters

Note: The abbreviation Kn. denotes the letters published by J. A. Knudtzon, below.

ALBRIGHT, W. F. 'The Amarna Letters from Palestine', *CAH* II, ch. XX, 98 ff. Cambridge 1975.

BEZOLD, C. and BUDGE, E. A. W. (eds.) *The Tell el-Amarna Tablets in the British Museum.* London 1892.

CAMPBELL, E. F. *The Chronology of the Amarna Letters.* Baltimore 1964.

KNUDTZON, J. A. et al. *Die El-Amarna-Tafeln.* 2 Vols. Leipzig 1908–15.

MERCER, S. A. B. *The Tell el Amarna Tablets.* Toronto 1939.

PRITCHARD, J. B. (ed.) *Ancient Near Eastern Texts Relating to the Old Testament.* 2nd edn. Princeton 1955.

18   Tomb No. 55 in the Valley of the Kings

DAVIS, T. M. et al. *The Tomb of Queen Tiyi.* London 1910.

AYRTON, E. R. 'The Tomb of Thyi', *Proceedings of the Society of Biblical Archaeology* 29 (1907), 85 f, 277 ff.

WEIGALL, A. E. 'The Mummy of Akhenaten', *JEA* 8 (1922) 193 ff.

SMITH, G. E. *The Royal Mummies (CCG 61051-100). Cat. No. 61075.* Cairo 1912.

ALDRED, C. and SANDISON, A. T. 'The Pharaoh Akhenaten: A Problem in Egyptology and Pathology', *Bulletin of the History of Medicine* 36 (1962), 203–316.

ENGELBACH, R. 'The So-called Coffin of Akhenaten', *Ann. Serv.* 31 (1931), 98 ff.

DARESSY, G. 'Le Cercueil de Khu-n-aten', *BIFAO* 12 (1916), 145 ff.

GARDINER, A. H. 'The So-called Tomb of Queen Tiye', *JEA* 43 (1957), 10 ff.

FAIRMAN, H. W. 'Once Again the So-called Coffin of Akhenaten', *JEA* 47 (1961), 25 ff.

ALDRED, C. and SANDISON, A. T. 'The Tomb of Akhenaten at Thebes', *JEA* 47 (1961), 41 ff.

HARRISON, R. G. 'An Anatomical Examination of the Pharaonic Remains Purported to be Akhenaten', *JEA* 52 (1966), 95 ff.

CONNOLLY, R. C. et al. 'An Analysis of the Inter-relationships between Pharaohs of the 18th Dynasty', *Journal of Museum of Applied Science: Center for Archaeology (Philadelphia)*, Vol. I, 178–181 (Mummification Supplement, 1980).

*REEVES, C. N. *Valley of the Kings. The Decline of a Royal Necropolis.* London (in press).

PEREPELKIN, G. *The Secret of the Gold Coffin.* Moscow 1978.

MARTIN, G. T. 'Notes on a Canopic Jar from Kings' Valley Tomb 55', *Mélanges Gamal Eddin Mokhtar*, 112 ff. Cairo 1985.

KRAUSS, R. 'Kija-ursprüngliche Besitzerin der Kanopen aus KV 55', *MDAIK* 42 (1986) [in press].

19   The Amarna Queens

DAVIS, T. M. et al. *The Tomb of Queen Tiyi*, xiii–xxi, London 1910.

ALDRED, C. 'The Royal Family at the End of the Eighteenth Dynasty', *CAH* II, Pt 2, ch. XIX, § VI, 77 ff. Cambridge 1975

NEWBERRY, P. E. 'King Ay, the Successor of Tut'ankhamūn', *JEA* 18 (1932), 50 ff.

SAUNERON, S. 'Quelques Monuments de Soumenou au Musée de Brooklyn', *Kemi* 18 (1969), 66 ff.

ALDRED, C. 'Two Monuments of the Reign of Haremhab', *JEA* 54 (1968), 103 ff.

HARI, R. 'La Reine d'Horemheb était-elle la soeur de Nefertiti?' *Chron. d'Ég.* 50 (1976), 39 ff.

LECLANT, J. 'Tefnout et les Divines Adoratrices thébaines', *MDAIK* II (1957), 166 ff.

LOEBEN, C. E. 'Eine Bestattung der grossen Königlichen Gemahlin Nofretete in Amarna', *MDAIK* 42 (1986), [in press].

GOETZE, A. 'The Struggle for the Dominion of Syria (1400–1300 BC)', *CAH* II, Pt 2, 1975, ch. XVII.

'Tefnut', *LÄ VI*, 298–9.

HELCK, W. 'Kiye', *MDAIK* 40 (1984), 159 ff.

SMITH, R. W. and REDFORD, D. B. *The Akhenaten Temple Project: Vol. I, Initial Discoveries*, 89–94. Warminster 1976.

REDFORD, D. B. *Akhenaten, the Heretic King*, 191. Princeton 1984.

REDFORD, D. B. *History and Chronology of the Eighteenth Dynasty of Egypt*, 173–4, 225. Toronto 1967.

HARRIS, J. R. 'Kiya', *Chron. d'Ég*, 49 (1974), 25 ff.

HARRIS, J. R. 'Nefernefruaten Regnans', *Acta Orientalia* 36 (1974), 11 ff.

HARRIS, J. R. 'Nefernefruaten', *Göttinger Miszellen* 1973, 15–17.

20   The Pathology

ALDRED, C. and SANDISON, A. T. 'The Pharaoh Akhenaten: A Problem in Egyptology and Pathology', *Bulletin of the History of Medicine* 36 (1962), 203–16.

HARRIS, J. R. 'Akhenaten or Nefertiti?', *Acta Orientalia* 38 (1977), 5 ff.

GHALIOUNGUI, P. 'A Medical Study of Akhenaten', *Ann. Serv.* 47 (1947), 29 ff.

DERRY, D. E. 'Note on the Skeleton hitherto believed to be that of King Akhenaten', *Ann. Serv.* 31 (1931) 119 ff.

HARRISON, R. G. 'An Anatomical Examination of the Pharaonic Remains Purported to be Akhenaten', *JEA* 52 (1966), 95 ff.

21   The Heresy

PIANKOFF, A. 'Les Compositions théologiques du nouvel empire égyptien', *BIFAO* 62 (1964), 121 ff.

PIANKOFF, A. 'Les Grandes Compositions Religieuses du Nouvel Empire, et la Réforme d'Amarna', *BIFAO* 62 (1964), 207 ff.

REDFORD, D. B. 'A Royal Speech from the Blocks of the Tenth Pylon', *Bulletin of Egyptological Seminar*, New York, 3 (1981), 87 ff.

DRIOTON, É. 'Trois Documents d'époque amarnienne', *Ann. Serv.* 43 (1943), 21–25, 25–43.

FAIRMAN, H. W. 'Once Again the So-called Coffin of Akhenaten', *JEA* 47 (1961), 34.

22   The Reign of Amenophis IV

REDFORD, D. B. 'Interim Report on the Excavations at East Karnak, 1977–78', *JARCE* 18 (1981), 11 ff.

REDFORD, D. B. *Akhenaten, the Heretic King*, 232–5. Princeton 1984.

*SMITH, R. W. and REDFORD, D. B. *The Akhenaten Temple Project: Vol. I, Initial Discoveries.* Warminster 1976.

*GOHARY, J. O. *Sed-Festival Scenes of Amenhotep IV on the Karnak Talatat.* Vols 1 and 2. (Thesis submitted for the degree of Ph.D., Liverpool University, 1976).

UNIVERSITY OF CHICAGO, Oriental Institute, Publication Vol. 102, *The Tomb of Kheruef: Theban Tomb 192.* Chicago 1980.

HORNUNG, E. and STAEHELIN, E. 'Studien zum Sedfest', *Aegyptiaca Helvetica I.* Geneva 1974.

GRIFFITH, F. W. 'The Jubilee of the Aten', *JEA* 5 (1918), 61 ff.

—, *JEA* 8 (1922), 199 ff.

23   The Reign of Akhenaten

HANKE, R. *Amarna-Reliefs aus Hermopolis: Neue Veröffentlichungen und Studien.* Hildesheim 1978.

ROEDER, G. *Amarna-Reliefs aus Hermopolis.* Hildesheim 1969.

GUNN, B. 'Notes on the Aten and his Names', *JEA* 9 (1923), 168 ff.

24   The Last Years of Akhenaten

ALDRED, C. 'The Foreign Gifts Offered to Pharaoh', *JEA* 56 (1970), 105 ff.

HARRIS, J. R. 'Kiya', *Chron. d'Ég.* 49 (1974), 25 ff.

MANNICHE, L. 'The Wife of Bata', *Göttinger Miszellen* 18 (1975), 33–35.

BOURIANT, U. *Deux Jours de fouilles à Tell el-Amarna (Mém. Miss. fr. Caire, 1)*, 286–94. Paris 1884.

HANKE, R. *Amarna-Reliefs aus Hermopolis: Neue Veröffentlichungen und Studien*, Abb. 25. Hildesheim 1978.

25   The Amarna Aftermath

HARRIS, J. R. 'Nefernefruaten Regnans', *Acta Orientalia* 36 (1974), 11 ff.

*ALDRED, C. 'The Immediate Successors of Akhenaten', *CAH* II, Pt 2, ch. XIX § IV, 63 ff.

KRAUSS, R. *Das Ende der Amarnazeit.* Hildesheim 1981.

KITCHEN, K. A. 'Review of the foregoing', *JEA* 71 (1985), *Supplement*, 43–4.

BENNETT, J. 'The Restoration Inscription of Tut'ankhamūn', *JEA* 25 (1939), 8 ff.

FAIRMAN, H. W. 'Tutankhamun and the End of the 18th Dynasty', *Antiquity* 46 (1972), 15–18.

HARRISON, R. G. and ABDALLA, A. B. 'The Remains of Tutankhamun', *Antiquity* 46 (1972), 8–14.

GARDINER, A. H. 'The Coronation of King Haremhab', *JEA* 39 (1953), 13 ff.

SCHADEN, O. J. 'Clearance of the tomb of King Ay (W. V. 23)', *JARCE* 21 (1984), 39–64.

MARTIN, G. T. 'Excavations at the Memphite Tomb of Horemheb. Preliminary Reports', 1976–79. *JEA* 62, 5 ff; 63, 13 ff; 64, 5 ff; 65, 13 ff.

26   'The Good Ruler Who Loves Mankind'

See entries under **Chapter 10** above.

REDFORD, D. B. 'The Monotheism of the Heretic Pharaoh', *Biblical Archaeology Review*, May–June 1987, 16–32.

RAY, J. D. Review article of REDFORD, D. B., *Akhenaten the Heretic King*, (*Göttinger Miszellen* 86 (1985), 81–83).

List of Illustrations

Line Drawings

(For details of books see Select Bibliography)

Monochrome Illustrations

AFTER PAGE 32

Index